remote control

a sensible approach to kids, TV, and the new electronic media

Leonard A. Jason, PhD
and
Libby Kennedy Hanaway

Professional Resource Press
Sarasota, Florida

Published by Professional Resource Press
(An imprint of Professional Resource Exchange, Inc.)
Post Office Box 15560
Sarasota, FL 34277-1560

Copyright © 1997 by Professional Resource Exchange, Inc.

All rights reserved

Printed in the United States of America

No part of this book may be reproduced, stored in a retrieval system, or transmitted, in any form or by any means, either electronic, mechanical, photocopying, microfilming, recording, or otherwise, without written permission from the publisher.

The copy editor for this book was David Anson, the managing editor was Debra Fink, the production coordinator was Laurie Girsch, and the cover was created by Carol Tornatore.

Library of Congress Cataloging-in-Publication Data

Jason, Leonard, date.
    Remote Control : a sensible approach to kids, TV, and the new electronic media / Leonard A. Jason and Libby Kennedy Hanaway.
       p. cm.
    Includes bibliographical references and index.
    ISBN: 1-56887-022-1 (alk. paper)
    1. Television and children. 2. Television and family.
3. Parenting. I. Hanaway, Libby Kennedy, date. II. Title.
HQ784.T4J37   1997
306.4'85'083--dc21   96-11472
                                                                                                               CIP

Dedication

For parents everywhere working hard to raise happy, healthy kids. Whether you're striving to help your kids cut back on TV or simply trying to get them to eat their peas, we salute you.

Acknowledgments

They say it takes a village to raise a child. Indeed, few good efforts are truly solitary ones, and *Remote Control* is no exception. The authors wish to express their grateful appreciation to a host of "villagers," beginning with the staff of Professional Resource Press. Thanks to PRP president Lawrence Ritt for believing in our message, to managing editor Debra Fink for helping to shape our message into a book, to copy editor David Anson for keeping us in grammatical order, and to production coordinator Laurie Girsch for her cheerful assistance. Thanks also to Rick Benzel for early encouragement, to Sharon Johnson for research on reduction techniques, and to all of the families who shared their stories of life in the TV trenches. We also thank the many DePaul University students who helped evaluate TV control devices, including Michele M. Klich, Patty Rooney-Rebeck, Gregory Sarlo, Cheryl Lonak, Michael McCanna, and Ester Brackshaw. We appreciate the help of Ron Black, Marty Durbin, and Walt Rucker for their ideas and technical support. The authors also wish to thank Jay and Lynn Jason and the Kennedy and Hanaway families for their patience and encouragement. Finally, special thanks to Rick Hanaway, whose support, humor, proofreading skills, and culinary abilities make him a village unto himself.

Table of Contents

Dedication	iii
Acknowledgments	v
Introduction	ix
A Diminishing Childhood	ix
Children and Television	xii
About This Book	xv
There Is Hope!	xvi

PART I — UNDERSTANDING TELEVISION

Chapter 1: The Myths and Messages of Television	3
Blood and Guts: Violence on Television	5
S-E-X	18
The World According to Hollywood: Stereotypes and Other Myths	25
The Advertising Engine	40
A Closer Look at Children's Television	49
Summary	59
Chapter 2: A Child's View of Television	61
A Special View of Television	62
A Child's Involvement With Television: Passive or Active?	64
A Child's Understanding of Television: Attention and Comprehension	69
A Child's View Beyond Television: Video and Computer Technology	84
Summary	91
Chapter 3: The Charm and Cost of Television	93
The Lure of the Small Screen	94
The Cost of Heavy Viewing	104
Summary	122

PART II — MANAGING TELEVISION

Chapter 4: A Parent's Role — 125
   Our Responsibility With Television — 126
   Getting Started: Understanding Your Child's
      Viewing Habits — 136
   The Rules of the Road — 141
   Summary — 145

Chapter 5: Options for Change — 147
   The Low-Tech Road: Family Rules — 150
   The High-Tech Road: Electronic Tools — 166
   The Middle Road: Behavior Modification — 179
   Summary — 186

Chapter 6: Family Life (With and Without Television) — 187
   With Television: Co-Viewing Strategies — 187
   Without Television: Alternative Activities — 200
   101 Fun and Simple Things To Do With Your Family — 213
   Summary — 218

Appendices — 219
   A: Sample Log of Activities — 221
      Log of Activities — 223
   B: Sample Contract — 225
      Contract — 226
   C: Contacting Networks — 227
   D: Suggested Reading — 229

End Notes — 235
   Introduction — 235
   Chapter 1 — 235
   Chapter 2 — 239
   Chapter 3 — 241
   Chapter 4 — 244
   Chapter 5 — 245
   Chapter 6 — 246

Indices — 249
   Subject Index — 251
   Author Index — 257
   Index of Television Programs — 261

Introduction

On the surface and at its core, *Remote Control* is a book about television. The word "television" flashes fast on every page, and by the time you reach the book's end you will have become a veritable expert on the topic. But in a broader and perhaps more significant sense, *Remote Control* is also a book about childhood, or the current decline thereof. Excessive or age-inappropriate exposure to television is just one of a great number of forces that today have altered the very fabric of childhood. Indeed, childhood has been stretched and frayed and faded to the point that we must sometimes squint to recognize it anymore. Fortunately, television's powerful influence on children is also one of the easiest factors in a child's life to negotiate or negate, giving us hope that at least part of that thin fabric can be mended.

A Diminishing Childhood

It hardly takes an expert to observe that the foundations of childhood are shifting right before our eyes. Surely this has been the complaint of each passing generation, but today it seems to occur with dizzying breadth and speed. We watch our children play, grow, fight, and love in a world that is considerably different from that which we remember. And we grieve for the childhood they cannot have.

When confronting the uncomfortable realities of today's childhood, it is always our first tendency to compare what *is* with what *was*. Collectively, we recall a childhood filled with firefly hunts and warm cookies baked by Mom, neighborhood games of Kick the Can, and family dinners at five o'clock. Life back then seemed safe, predictable, simple, and hopeful. Of course, nostalgia always has a way of smoothing out rough edges and unpleasant realities. For most of us, childhood was hardly the idyllic dream that thrives in protected memory.

The picture of family togetherness was likely blurred, and fireflies only came around a few nights of the year, anyway. Yet despite such allowances for reality, most children of yesterday are relieved that they are not children of today.

In the past decade or so, a convergence of forces both social and economic seems to have plucked the child right out of childhood. We now watch uneasily as our own children grow up in a world in which kids kill kids, kids give birth to kids, and kids run the household while Mom and/or Dad work. For children of low-income families, such realities quietly have been played out for several decades. Childhood for the poor, especially the urban poor, has never approached the milk, cookies, and Crayolas image that has long reigned in comfortable middle-class minds. It is instead a ragged mix of stray-bullet-drop drills at home and in school, drug dealers on the playground, and defiant gang colors parading in the streets. For most low-income kids, the idea of a safe, protected, and hopeful childhood is plainly unrealistic.

Today the comforting ideal of childhood is becoming a quaint notion, even for Middle America, as many of its most pressing childhood issues cannot be solved by surrounding a child with financial comfort and a tree-lined neighborhood. Little, for example, can protect a child from the painful remains of a crumbled family life. Divorce continues to split 1 of every 2 households in America, wreaking havoc with a child's tender sense of trust, loyalty, and security. Stepfamilies, for their part, often find it hard to achieve a harmonious blending, and divorced mothers who remain single face a difficult path in balancing the financial, emotional, and physical needs of their families. Nearly all single mothers work, as do increasing numbers of their married counterparts. Indeed, sober financial realities combined with expanded opportunities for working women have made the stay-at-home mom something of an oddity. As for fathers, the national workplace (strictly steered by conventional thinking) remains hostile to the idea of men as significant family caregivers, the result being families further stretched for time and energy. The essentials get covered, but not much else. At the end of a long workday, parents—male or female, single or married—must concentrate on a nonnegotiable sequence of events: helping with homework, preparing and eating dinner, running baths, fixing the next day's lunches, reading a quick bedtime story, and then enforcing the family's lights out policy. Exhausted parents, relieved just to find time to pay bills and do a load of laundry, discover that the heralded pursuit of quality time isn't as easy as it sounds.

In addition to family issues, there are mounting concerns about child safety. Fear of crime keeps kids limited to the house or the fenced-in backyard; children allowed to venture beyond those boundaries are now seen with colorful, kid-sized personal alarms hooked to their belt loops. Sensational media reports about child sex-abuse cases and child abductions have turned the person next door into a potential criminal and transformed chit-chat with friendly strangers into a definite "no-no." The growing shadow of AIDS, meanwhile, means that kids as young as 6 years old understand the benefits of condom use. Children themselves are even beginning to admit fear, much pertaining to the youth violence that flashes in and out of their small world. A bright fifth grader we know is reluctant to head to middle school next year, fearing not braces or algebra, but gang violence and guns.

Finally, certain parenting trends have altered the nature of childhood. Childhood, especially early childhood, was once considered a fairly carefree time in one's life—wake up, eat, play, eat, play, eat, play, and get tucked into bed again. Not so any longer. Particularly in upper-middle class families, children are called upon to join in their parents' competitive rat race. And so there is Mozart in the womb, violin lessons at age 2, French at age 3, and all sorts of motor coordination activities squeezed in between. Whether they fear diminishing economic opportunities for their kids or their own social rejection, high achieving parents often project competitive attitudes on kids who would actually prefer to play in the mud. The natural result of this imbalance is a population of high-strung children and worn out, stressed out parents.

A second major shift involves the level of world knowledge now held by young children. In our post-Watergate, hold-no-secrets era, children are privy to all of the habits and manners of the adult world. This is no accident. Most Americans now raising children spring from the famed Baby Boomer generation. Once the young leaders of the "free to be you and me" 1960s and 1970s, many have now become parents who earnestly desire a similar freedom and openness for their own children. In a grand spirit of liberty many parents let their kids determine their own bedtimes and curfews, write notes excusing their fit-as-a-fiddle children from school, wink at sexually active teens, and reveal the twists and turns of their middle-aged love lives to kids too young to have love lives of their own. While some may shudder at such candor and permissiveness, others see it simply as the sign of an understanding and sympathetic parent. In her article "Little Big People," Pulitzer Prize-winning journalist Lucinda Franks explains this uniquely Boomer philosophy on child rearing:

The parents of many of these children—those of us who began our families later in life—came of age in the Vietnam War years. Our ideas of child rearing were like our ideas about everything else: radically different from our parents, who thought a child was just a child, even when that child got old enough to march against wars and otherwise protest the way the elder generation ran the world. Those of us who were veterans of the '60s and '70s swore that we would treat our children with respect. We vowed that we would fold our own offspring into our daily lives, treating them like "little people," empowering them with the rights, the importance and the truth telling we had been denied. We wanted to create the children we yearned to be. And now, many years later, we are confronted with the results. Did it turn out the way we meant it to? Will our independent children thank us for making them the center of the universe, or have we robbed them of a childhood they never can regain?[1]

Children and Television

Right beside these social, safety, and parenting issues sits the television. Billed as a simple entertainment machine, it can just as surely pull kids from the moorings of childhood.

Television's culpability in this regard is easy to miss or ignore, for it has been heartily embraced as a natural and essential part of family life. With 98% of the homes in America owning at least one television set, watching television has become the foremost national pastime for Americans of all ages. Children seem particularly enchanted with the medium, with the average child tuning in 3 to 4 hours each day. Kids watch TV during breakfast, after school, before dinner, after dinner (sometimes during dinner), and, naturally, they beg to watch it past their bedtime. By the time the average child is 18 years old, the only activity he or she will have spent more time doing is sleeping. With great ease, television has become an ever-available companion for our youngest generation.

Of course, plain old television is simply the most basic starting point of today's entertainment spectrum. Our technological possibilities have exploded, and the fallout lines the walls and floors of our living rooms: behind the once-almighty TV set trails a twisting mass of plugs and cords powering the VCR, the cable box, the automatic video rewinder, the video game systems, and well-used joysticks. Nearby sits the remote control and teetering stacks of game cartridges and video tapes. Meanwhile, in the next room sits a little mouse, a ready guide to the home computer, the CD-ROM, and the uncharted waters of the Internet.

Though the salience of the electronic media in our age has important implications for both the young and the old, there are particularly significant consequences for children. Most compelling, perhaps, is the fact that all the secrets of adult life tumble freely and abundantly from the television set, and, more recently, the Internet. There was a time not too long ago when words and ideas inappropriate for children were either whispered in hushed tones or were locked safely away in a book, the ability to read being the only workable key. In contrast, media scholar Neil Postman dubs television the "total disclosure medium." In his 1982 book *The Disappearance of Childhood,* Postman writes

> Through the miracles of symbols and electricity our own children know everything everyone else knows—the good with the bad. Nothing is mysterious, nothing awesome, nothing is held back from public view. Indeed, it is a common enough observation, particularly favored by television executives when under attack, that whatever else may be said about television's impact on the young, today's children are better informed than any previous group of youngsters. The metaphor usually employed is that television is a window to the world. This observation is entirely correct, but why it should be taken as a sign of progress is a mystery. What does it mean that our children are better informed than ever before? That they know what the elders know? It means that they have become adults, or, at least, adult-like. It means—to use a metaphor of my own—that in having access to the previously hidden fruit of adult information, they are expelled from the garden of childhood.[2]

Exposed repeatedly to the violence, sex, stereotypes, and commercialism of adult content, children are confronted with messages that they cannot yet synthesize, much less understand. Still, they watch, listen, and absorb. As a result, we now have a generation that speaks a sophisticated adult language with no mental or emotional map to back it up. They are indeed "little people," tripping on the hems of their oversized dress-up clothes.

Equally disturbing is the simple fact that watching television replaces hours that might otherwise be spent doing regular, everyday kid-stuff: building forts and castles, reading books, and skinning knees — the mundane but essential acts of a healthy childhood. Because television appears to be a legitimate childhood activity, there is an easy tendency for kids to wile away the hours in front of the small screen. Watched in excess, though, television becomes more of an "inactivity" than an activity. The piano sits unplayed, the Legos gather dust, and the fort in the backyard is all but forgotten. Meanwhile, television drains away imagination and initiative as another generation of couch potatoes takes shape.

In excessive or age-inappropriate doses, television is a noisy, potentially damaging interference with the normal business of growing up. On the other hand, it would be both naïve and inaccurate to label television as the Biggest Bad Wolf of child life. Other influences may be more immediately and more deeply harmful. And unlike other painful aspects of childhood, television is not damaging in and of itself. Intrinsically, it is a neutral entity, and in fact it holds tremendous power for good. Certain programs can be wonderfully educational and entertaining, and television's very universality has made the world a familiar, if smaller, place. Moreover, though family traumas, illness, and other crises intrude on a child's life with great and often unpredictable force, television permits tremendous control. Those who feel captive to its power are forgetting that it is just a machine, after all. When turned off, the set is rendered virtually useless, a chunky piece of postmodern suburban furniture.

Turning it off, though, never seems as easy as flicking a switch. For many, it means a steady companion will disappear. Others find that their primary source of information and laughter will fade away. For children, the prospect of turning off the television is especially daunting either because it has become a firmly entrenched habit or because there is little else for them to do. One of these problems typically feeds the other, producing kids who spend hour upon hour gazing at a glowing screen. As parents, educators, and other concerned individuals, our common sense tells us that excessive television watching is not a good use of children's time. But parents are busier than ever, and the dual role of parent and worker brings enormous fatigue. Television, we must often admit, is an extremely effective baby-sitter, keeping the kids quiet and out of our hair for the moment. Moreover, any parent who suggests scaling back TV watching quickly earns the title of "The Meanest Mom/Dad Ever, Ever, EVER." A parent-child power struggle then ensues, culminating in an all-out family battle complete with angry yelling, long-term pouting, and steely-eyed stares. Sound familiar? Do not lose hope. This book just might be the help and motivation you need.

About This Book

Remote Control is for anyone concerned about raising and nurturing healthy, well-adjusted children. Television's central presence in the lives of American families ensures that this subject involves a great number of people. Parents, naturally, are most directly involved in this issue. Whether the concern is over the quantity or the quality of television, many moms and dads across the nation are stumped over how to tame the tube. On the front lines of those hard-fought television battles, parents are most in need of strategy and reinforcement. It is primarily for them and to them that this book has been written. We do hope, however, for readers beyond this one important category. While our use of the conversational "you" in this book generally assumes a parent audience, the message of *Remote Control* extends also to educators, mental health professionals, physicians, clergy members, grandparents, aunts, uncles, and anyone else who spends time with children and families. Together, through limiting the influence of television, we can work toward the restoration of childhood.

Depending on your needs and goals, *Remote Control* is at once an information source, a how-to manual, a pep talk, a scientific review, and an ode to common sense. In presenting complex and controversial information about children and television, we seek to strike a balance between current scientific research and age-old conventional wisdom. The result, we hope, is a practical and understandable book backed by thorough, balanced research. The first few chapters of *Remote Control* offer a broad overview of the current research on the subject of television and children. Chapter 1 looks at the content of today's television, from the sex and violence of adult programming to Big Bird's educational agenda. Chapter 2 examines the physiological and psychological aspects of children's television watching, focusing on the following issues: Whether children are active or passive viewers, the extent to which children comprehend television's content, and the special considerations involved in video game playing and computer use. Chapter 3 discusses two related issues: children's attraction to television; and the academic, physical, social, and emotional consequences that result from excessive viewing. In Chapters 4 and 5 we shift to offering practical advice on how to take control of the problem of excessive or inappropriate television in our families. A number of tested methods will be analyzed, complete with case studies and detailed instructions to help you achieve success in your own home. And finally, Chapter 6 will help families learn to enjoy themselves both with and without television. Television can be a legitimate and enjoyable family activity if approached from the right direction. To that end, we will offer a number of suggestions for choosing content and for making your family viewing fun and active. More importantly, though, the chapter also seeks to remind families that there is a world beyond TV. In this television age, it is easy to forget that there are plenty of simple, creative, and engaging activities that can entertain kids and grown-ups alike. We firmly believe that once children are reintroduced to the joys of discovery and imagination, the passive world of television will soon lose its appeal.

One final word of explanation: In this book our focus is television. We realize, however, that many kids lose hours each day to other electronic pursuits like video games, computer activities, and cruising around the Internet. Though we've concentrated our efforts on providing research about TV and strategies for television reduction, much of this information is broad and sensible enough to be helpful as your kids explore other media technologies. Keep in mind that the issues of inappropriate content and excessive devotion are no less compelling when they involve a computer screen instead of a TV screen. On the other hand, if the seemingly unmanageable range of children's electronic entertainment options is causing you heartburn, remember, too, that age-old assets like common sense, discipline, and responsibility will remain essential tools no matter how sophisticated our electronic entertainment systems grow.

There Is Hope!

If you have tried in the past to scale back your children's television viewing to no avail, we urge you to try again, choosing a method that will work best in your particular family situation. Do not give up! If you have never before attempted such a feat, you are in for a true adventure. No doubt there will be resistance and setbacks, but again, do not give up. A bit of work and patience on your part will bring about great dividends in the life of your child. By limiting excessive and age-inappropriate television, you will help put your children back into childhood, right where they belong.

remote control

a sensible approach to kids, TV, and the new electronic media

PART I

Understanding Television

1

The Myths and Messages of Television

Once upon a time, in days long ago, villagers would gather in the evening around the local storyteller. Sitting on the ground or perhaps a rugged bench, the young and the old would listen to tales of the past, thoughts of the future, and lessons for the day. The storyteller—a peasant with a gifted tongue, a village elder bent with years, or a traveling minstrel bearing tales and songs of lands far away—was a much-heralded figure in the community. Upon him was conferred a special power, for he was the essential link to both information and imagination.

Over time, our hamlets and villages grew to sprawling cities and suburbs, and while our thirst for stories remained, the voice of the storyteller changed. In the first shift, the bard gave way to the book. The printing press altered the story's basic form, shifting the public oral tradition to one that was primarily visual and private. Those with the ability could now read the tales of Homer, the teachings of religion, and the latest discoveries in science and exploration. The book held sway for nearly 500 years. Then, as the 20th century unfolded, the story passed rapidly from words on a page to a bold voice on the radio to the flickering light and crackly sound of talking moving pictures. Motion pictures seemed the peak of the storytelling tradition, but by the early 1930s the very public experience of motion pictures was further refined. The end product—the television—provided an experience that was much more personal and significantly more powerful.

Though books still line bookshelves, radios croon, and bards still roam the folk fair circuit, television is today our chief storyteller. It is one that boasts an astonishingly broad repertoire: dramas, comedies, news reports, weather reports, stock reports, movies, commercials, cartoons, infomercials, editorials, and all other varieties of news and stories. As for quality, the same broad range exists. Some of television's content is truly impressive, providing wide windows into worlds unknown. And some of television's content is truly terrible — windows that might better be left shut. The discerning adult learns which is which, and clicks the remote control accordingly.

Children, however, generally lack powers of discernment. Most kids' criteria for viewing a given show has little to do with quality or suitability and has everything to do with whether it is discussed in the lunch line. And unlike the communal days of the provincial storyteller, kids today are often on their own when it comes to seeing and hearing television's stories. What, then, are they watching? Some kids are perfectly content staying within the relatively safe bounds of children's programming. Kermit and friends have charmed preschoolers for decades, and today the options for children's television have never been more abundant. Most children, though, especially as they grow older, are not so easily satisfied. In an age where childhood is egged on at a furious pace, the majority of kids over the age of 7 or 8 yearn to be included — at least peripherally — in the adult world. Television offers a quick and ready passport. While some young viewers might find watching a major league baseball game to be "adult" enough, others stretch further, expertly responding to adult cues. Kids snicker and slap their knees at sex-oriented adult sitcoms and become downright giddy as the body count on a violent program keeps climbing.

This first chapter will explore the content of television, with an eye toward the child audience. As we'll see, TV does offer a number of engaging and innovative programs for kids and their families. Too often, though, the quality shows are crowded out by programming that caters to violence, sex, stereotyping, and commercialism. This uneasy mix makes putting a child in front of the TV set a dicey move because, as a storyteller, television lacks that sensible human gauge that indicates propriety for a given audience. Television reads its audience not in terms of mental and emotional readiness but in terms of economic utility. Because children tend to rate low on television's economic scale, adult messages creep in early, juxtaposing Mr. Rogers and Mr. T as models for adulthood. Lines of quality and suitability blur, creating for the child viewer an incoherent blend of Big Bird, guns, lust, commercialism, and bad jokes.

Blood and Guts: Violence on Television

It's a curious twist of logic. On the news, on the street, and at the funerals we abhor the pain and agony that violence brings. Yet on television and in the movies, we can't seem to get enough to satisfy our cravings. Leave it to the great psychological minds of the world to sort out this strange dichotomy; meanwhile, the television industry is getting rich off our secret penchant for blood and guts.

This appetite for televised violence — and Hollywood's eagerness to indulge it — has stirred up what is surely the most controversial television debate of all. It is hardly one that will be settled here, for it involves issues that are themselves impossible to settle: notions like freedom of speech, censorship, fear of crime and crime itself, divergent scientific views, divergent social views, governmental obligations, and the imprecise development of a child's brain, heart, mind, and conscience. Such complexity makes the going a bit bumpy. Still, there are some things that can be said with certainty.

To begin, it is an incontrovertible fact that a great many Americans are attracted to violence on television. And a great many of these Americans are children whose tender developmental stages make them most vulnerable to television's mean streak. It is a fascination that begins innocently enough. Toddlers giggle and grin as the hapless Wile E. Coyote gets steamrolled flat as a pancake by Road Runner at every turn. Never fear, for he is always back in full, furious form in the very next scene! A few years later they tune in to watch morphed teenagers and masked turtles, the adored vigilantes who karate chop and flip-flop their way to the moral high ground. Alas, the adoration is temporary, for growing children will self-consciously realize that these shows are made for kids. Never mind that the young viewers are still kids — peer pressure and simple curiosity propels them on. At the next level of television violence the gates of adult fare swing wide open: knife-wielding sadists in tacky horror films, fleeing crack sellers on *Cops*, fiery car explosions on *Walker, Texas Ranger*, and stretchers bearing bloody victims on the six o'clock news.

These are the scenes our children dutifully watch again and again and again. The litany of statistics is familiar, though still astonishing. A recent 5-year study by the American Psychological Association estimates that the average child has watched 100,000 acts of violence and 8,000 acts of murder by the time he or she leaves elementary school. By the end of high school, 200,000 acts of violence have flashed before most kids' eyes.[1]

To be sure, scenes of violence vary greatly, ranging from a cartoon coyote being blown to bits by Acme dynamite to the high psychological drama of a round of Russian roulette. Do both examples count as true TV violence? A team of researchers led by George Gerbner of the University of Pennsylvania subscribes to the following definition of violence: "The overt expression of physical force (with or without a weapon, against self or others) compelling action against one's will on pain of being hurt and/or killed or threatened to be so victimized as a part of the plot."[2] Importantly, their standard does not omit violence occurring in an accidental, natural, humorous, or fantasy context, landing the cartoon coyote and the Russian roulette in the very same category.

Using this broad definition, the research team conducted a nearly two-decade-long project analyzing the violence content of network television. Through the use of a "Violence Index," the researchers found that the frequency and patterns of violence remained remarkably stable over the past two decades. In the last year of the project, 1979, they found that 70% of all prime-time programs contained violence. Nearly 54% of all leading characters were involved in the violence — men, typically, as its perpetrators and women, particularly nonwhite and older women, as its most frequent victims. Shifting to children's weekend and daytime television, the team determined that over 90% of the programs contained violence, with nearly 75% of its leading characters inflicting or suffering it.[3] More recently, in 1992 the American Psychological Association reported that violent incidents occur 5 to 6 times an hour during prime-time television and 20 to 25 times an hour during children's Saturday-morning cartoons.[4] To be fair, the 1996-1997 network prime-time season has scaled back on violence, but for reasons likely more economic than altruistic. Guns have been temporarily set aside in favor of shows featuring hip, frisky young adults, a sign of the enduring and still profitable cloning power of *Friends* and *Seinfeld*. Aside from some obvious examples of both gratuitous and nongratuitous violent regular programming (*Walker, Texas Ranger; New York Undercover; The X-Files; NYPD Blue; Homicide; Nash Bridges; High Incident;* and *Profiler;* among others), the main network offenders now seem to be victim-oriented made-for-TV movies, edited films previously shown in theaters (*Under Siege* or *Home Alone,* for example), and commercials for current-release films. In discussing the results of a 1996 violence study, one UCLA researcher noted that the television commercial for the theater-release film *Assassins* had 24 scenes of violence in 30 seconds.[5]

With the exception of gradual shifts reflecting seasonal trends, the incidence of TV violence has remained fairly stable over the years. The nature of that violence, however, has not. Over the years it has become more mean, more realistic, more random, and more sophisticated. Early Westerns featuring dueling white and black hats seem refreshingly tame compared to today's fare. For example, the weaponry seen on TV is highly advanced and highly visible, with characters flashing pistols, Uzis, and M-60 machine guns with practiced regularity. Moreover, sexual, verbal, and psychological violence are now regular programming themes, offering rape, sexual assault, hostage situations, terrorist campaigns, and psycho-killers as familiar plot elements in many of today's action shows and movies. And finally, the hats have fallen off the good guys and bad guys, allowing their characters to take on more and more moral ambiguity. While real people have never been as flat and predictable as television often portrayed them, TV characters are now swinging to the other extreme. Perhaps spurred on a number of disillusioning news stories in recent years, television has responded with its own version of the human condition. There is now a plethora of "bad cops" roaming the TV streets, menacing both criminals and innocents alike. The thugs, on the other hand, have been infused with a strong measure of humanity and humor, further complicating questions of guilt and culpability. This shift in characterization is not a problem per se, for humans are complex creatures. Children, however, tend to see things in black and white, and those kids who routinely observe such heavily shaded characters may struggle with the issues of trust, integrity, and fear.

Advances in electronic technology have also changed the face of violence. Cable and video options, for example, permit a highly flexible viewing schedule. In TV's pre-cable days, the dedicated viewer had to fight off yawns and sleepy eyes to watch scary stuff on the late, late show. Concerned parents could in part monitor their children's violence intake by simply declaring an early bedtime. Today that approach is not nearly so effective as kids have 'round-the-clock, every-day-of-the-week access to gunshots and gore. This problem of access is exacerbated by the fact that cable programs and video movie selections enable children to see violence far more graphic than that allowed by network television. Whereas violence might once have been suggested by a menacing shadow, today it is shown in its full Technicolor glory. Blood squirts, eyeballs dangle, knives meet flesh, and skulls shatter in slow motion. The unspeakable stuff of nightmares is now played over and over again on the small screen.

Indeed, every raunchy slasher film ever created seems to find eternal life on a cable channel. These B-grade efforts only represent the extreme, however. The bulk of cable programming and video selections—from 24-hour cable news channels to the latest movie of the week—contains violence that is rarely so absurdly graphic, yet which may be equally or perhaps more disturbing. And as increasing numbers of both major and minor cable channels squeeze their way into the cable line-up (or video selections find their way onto store shelves), the access grows even greater. This abundance creates a unique opportunity for the determined young viewer. Armed with a TV schedule and nimble channel surfing ability, he or she can watch virtually nonstop violence for hours on end. In an instant, a child can flip from the silly, blood spurting antics of the evil doll Chucky to the haunting scenes of *The Deerhunter* to news clips of the world's latest terrorist act. One form of violence becomes indistinguishable from another, and the essential lessons of motive and consequence are lost in the tense anticipation of another round of bloodletting.

If cable and video movies have expanded the options for violent television, video and computer games offer an entirely new arena. Though there are many popular educational and sports-related games on the market, a tremendous number of video games are based on openly violent premises. The goal in most of the violent games is simple enough: obliterate one's enemy through whatever means necessary. In Sega's well-known Mortal Kombat, for example, Kano punches through his opponent Scorpian's chest and yanks out a still-beating heart. He then raises it in victory, with drops of bright red blood trailing to the ground. Among young boys, the Mortal Kombat series remains one of the hottest-selling video products the industry has ever seen. Newer game options prove that the industry will not be heading in a more gentle direction any time soon. The leading CD-ROM games, for example, boast names like Hellbender ("Shoot to Kill. Think to Win"); Pray for Death; Nihilist; Killing Time; Daggerfall ("Prepare to Experience Your New Obsession"); Necrodome; Ravage ("Life, Liberty, and an Ample Supply of Ammunition"), and Nuke It 1000. Subtlety is not a major selling point. Decorated with pictures of glinting knives, lightning bolts, and snarling mercenary types, the brightly packaged boxes are carefully designed to lure young purchasers. The box for Sega's Dynamite Duke video game, for example, promises that the lucky player will "Tear through six levels of violence! . . . Get up close and nasty with elbow bashes, kicks, uppercuts, and gunstock smashes. Your bionic punch is vicious!"

As with television, there is growing concern that the playing of violent video games can lead to aggressive or antisocial behavior. Yet an important distinction exists between the two mediums: Whereas viewing television is a fairly passive experience, playing video games is highly interactive. Players actually participate in, control, and even "commit" the violence themselves. The competitive quality of the games, meanwhile, ensures that they will be played repeatedly. Stripped of the immediate thrill and excitement, the image is disturbing.

The Public Responds

Children's exposure to televised and video violence has not gone by unchallenged. Perhaps more than any other feature of TV's content, violent images and storylines have fueled front-page headlines and politically savvy opposition. Over the past several decades, angry citizen and professional groups like Action for Children's Television (ACT), the National Council of Churches, the American Medical Association, the National Parent Teacher Association, and the American Psychological Association have become increasingly outspoken in their criticism. The topic has also become a staple on Capitol Hill. Congressional hearings on the subject are frequent, and a growing number of prominent lawmakers like Rep. Edward J. Markey (D-Massachusetts) and former Senator Paul Simon (D-Illinois) have placed TV violence near the top of their political agendas.

In 1993 political pressure against the violent content of television was so strong that the networks—ABC, NBC, CBS, and Fox, along with their affiliates—agreed to air warnings on shows that contain excessive violence. This was an unprecedented and much heralded move, though many in the antiviolence coalition complained that the warning labels were simply token gestures that had no teeth. To begin, they pointed out, the action erroneously assumes that most children watch television in a supervised environment in which a parent can flip the channel when such a warning appears. The measure also ignores a fundamental lesson in child psychology: Claim that it is bad for them, and kids will flock. Like the citizen groups, neither concerned legislators nor the current Attorney General seems fully satisfied with the label system, and in the background the threat of further governmental regulation looms large.

In fact, what was once just a low rumble has grown a full-fledged debate about the next step in limiting the violent images and storylines. The topic of the moment revolves around the much ballyhooed V-chip (violence chip), a device that for all its controversy is not yet a working reality. Discussed further in Chapter 4, the V-chip concept hinges on two major developments that have recently turned the entire industry on its ear: First, the television industry's promise that by early 1997 a voluntary ratings system for violence and other potentially objectionable material will be in place and, second, in accordance with the 1996 Telecommunications Act, television manufacturers' obligation to soon include in their TVs an electronic chip that will read the encoded ratings. The hoped-for result? Parents will gain some control in the TV wars, allowing them to program their television sets to only air those shows rated within their comfort zone. Though it may seem like a logical approach, the prospect of allowing the federal government wide authority in regulating TV violence raises a number of thorny issues, not the least of which is First Amendment protection under the Constitution. Many in the industry assert that within the bounds of current Federal Communications Commission (FCC) regulations, they are simply exercising free speech and creative liberty. In addition to claiming constitutional immunity, the networks, with plenty of advertising revenue behind them, argue that they are simply giving viewers what they want.

On the other hand, lawmakers must face an increasingly vocal constituency, one filled with parents weary from battling television's crude messages and images. Additionally, many government leaders find it hard to ignore the possibility that violent programs may breed a violent society. The current TV violence debate comes at a time when crime—especially youth crime—seems epidemic. According to a recent Justice Department survey, crime in America is now at its most violent point in 20 years. For youth, the picture is particularly grim. A few statistics tell the story:

- The rate of 15-year-old males arrested for murder increased 207% between 1985 and 1993.
- More than 2,900 children and youth between the ages of 10 and 19 were murdered with a firearm in 1993—an average of more than eight young people a day.
- Between 1984 and 1993, juvenile arrests for weapons violations increased 125%.
- Juveniles accounted for 19% of all violent crimes arrests in 1994.[6]

It would be naïve and misleading to directly associate this increase in juvenile crime with televised violence. At the very least, though, these figures point to the volatile climate in which the TV violence debate is being conducted. As for more direct examples, there have been a few very high-profile, copy-cat incidents that do seem to link televised violence with real-life, imitated violence. In 1977 a 15-year-old boy killed his elderly next door neighbor during a bungled burglary attempt, apparently as a conditioned response to what he repeatedly saw on shows like *Baretta, Kojak,* and *Starsky and Hutch.* The resulting trial was unprecedented in the fact that television was actually named as an "accessory to the crime." Similar cases have been documented: In 1974, a 9-year-old girl was attacked and raped on the beach by four teenagers in a near direct copy of a scene from the TV-aired movie *Born Innocent.* And in 1993 a 5-year-old boy set fire to his 2-year-old sister. The mother claims her son got the idea from watching MTV's tribute to teenage dysfunctionality, *Beavis and Butthead.* Though many claim such linkages are sensational and circumstantial, these and other incidents continue to fuel a national debate on the subject of violence on television.

Of course, it is hardly fair to tag TV as the primary source of youth recklessness and lawlessness. Child abuse and neglect, poverty, the dissolution of the family, and educational issues certainly play a more direct role in adversely influencing a child's life. As for the above copy-cat incidents, television has never been implicated on legal grounds for inciting viewers to violent action. According to the arguments, the cited shows and movies did not purposefully invite imitation. Children, so the argument goes, should simply "know better" than to follow in Kojak's foolish footsteps, and if they are too young to make such discernment, their parents should not let them watch such shows in the first place.

Fair enough. Yet television cannot altogether escape responsibility. The primary age group that is killing and being killed today are major consumers of a medium that very attractively packages violence as an effective solution for problem solving. When a character is insulted, his or her powerful right hook sends the offender sailing across the bar. With a POW! the problem is solved. Or when a character fears an ugly secret is headed for broad daylight, he or she chooses to "silence" a possible informant rather than come clean with the truth. With a BANG! the problem is solved. The issue of violent problem solving becomes particularly frustrating when TV heroes resort to violence to save the day. This common plot device has an unintentionally amusing twist on *The Mighty Morphin Power Rangers.* In a public service announcement that follows every show, the program's actors soberly advise kids not to use violence to solve their problems. Yet for the preceding 30 minutes the program has been showcasing witty, friendly, good-looking teenagers triumph on the side of good with one well-placed kick or the graceful swoop of a laser sword. Which approach to life's troubles does the young viewer choose? Which approach seems more fun?

Television has an amazing knack for glamorizing violence. It's violence with a wisecrack. It's violence with rock music in the background. It's violence with spectacular special effects. It's also often violence without consequence. Despite a steady stream of gunshots, grenades, kidnappings, and beatings, few viewers see grieving families, hospital bills, prison time, lasting physical pain, or psychological damage. Such omissions heartily feed the myth of youthful invincibility.

Violence Research

Public interest in the issue of televised violence has been paralleled by, if not exceeded by, scientific interest in the topic. In the past 30 years, well over a thousand studies investigating the role of televised violence have been published by the scientific community. The bulk of the research focuses on one compelling question: Is there a link between viewing violent behavior on television and the viewer's own subsequent aggressive behavior? From the start, efforts at testing this hypothesis have triggered a rigorous debate. Complete with political intrigue and factious in-fighting, the history of consensus-reaching in the field proves to be an engaging tale in itself.

Though studies on televised violence quietly dated back to as early as 1955, psychologist Albert Bandura brought the issue to the public's attention in the 1960s. In the 1963 *Look* magazine article "What TV Violence Can Do to Your Child," Bandura put into popular form the theories and hypotheses that he and his students had been testing for several years. Though the initial intent of Bandura's work was to validate his evolving social learning theory, along the way he implicated television as a source of teaching aggression.[7]

According to Bandura's social learning theory, children learn their personalities from experiences and interactions with culture, subculture, family, and peers. The process of *modeling*, in particular, plays a fundamental role in the child's social development. As a result, Bandura theorized, the best and most effective way to teach children new ways of acting is to show them the behavior you wish them to learn and display.

Though social learning experiments had been conducted with laboratory animals for years, Bandura set out to test the theory on humans. In a series of now-famous "Bobo" studies, Bandura and his students turned to the new and controversial medium of television, testing the correlation between a child's viewing novel aggressive behavior and the child's own subsequent aggressive actions. Though the experiments varied slightly in focus and execution, the primary premise was generally the same: In most tests, preschool-aged children watched a film projected on a simulated TV set in which an actor (or a "model") verbally and physically attacked a large inflated plastic clown. After viewing the film, the children were left to play with a similar Bobo doll and a variety of other toys for 10 minutes. Observers hidden behind a one-way mirror recorded any imitative aggressive actions. Over and over again, children viewing aggressive models were observed exhibiting similar aggressive behaviors.

Some of Bandura's specific experiments are noteworthy. In a 1965 study he examined the effect that perceived consequences would have on children's aggressive actions. In the experiment, some aggressive models were punished for their actions, others were rewarded, and still others had no consequences. Children viewing the rewarded and no-consequence models exhibited significant imitative aggression, a troublesome finding in view of TV's consequence-free world. Moreover, even those who viewed the punished model were able to replicate the aggressive action upon request, indicating that the actions — though perhaps not immediately imitated — still had been acquired or learned.[8] In another experiment, Bandura studied how viewing an aggressive cartoon cat on television, as opposed to a human model, might affect children. The results showed that children learned as readily from Herman the Cat as they did from a human adult model, implicating television's seemingly innocuous cartoon creatures as models for aggression.[9] While Bandura's early studies have been eyed critically for their low ecological validity (the viewing experience in the Bobo studies was hardly typical and the clown, after all, was not human), they provided an important window for further investigation and debate.

During this period of initial investigation, Bandura was joined by other researchers during this period, including Leonard Berkowitz, Percy Tannenbaum, Seymour Feshbach, Robert Singer, and Leonard Eron. Despite the extent of their early research, clear answers on the relationship between children and televised violence were not forthcoming. Nevertheless, members of the public and a few key lawmakers continued to voice skittish opinions about the powerful medium. By the end of the decade, televised violence had become a bona fide public issue. In 1971 the government responded in typical fashion: It commissioned a study.

The Surgeon General's Report and Beyond

Though the government held hearings on the topic of media violence in the 1950s and 1960s, this was the first instance in which it would sponsor and direct original research in the field. Prompted by a Senate request, the Department of Health, Education, and Welfare tapped the Surgeon General's office for the job. In turn, they appointed a 12-person committee of prominent researchers and television industry executives to conduct the research. Controversy rolled in swiftly, however, when it was revealed that certain researchers had been "blackballed" (including Bandura, Berkowitz, Tannenbaum, and others concerned about TV violence), resulting in a committee stacked in favor of the television industry. From the start, the Surgeon General's Scientific Advisory Committee on Television and Human Behavior was mired in controversy.

Under the auspices of the National Institute of Mental Health (NIMH), 23 individual projects were undertaken to study television and children's social behavior. The studies included investigations of the levels of TV's violent content, levels of viewing, perceived reality, possible effects of viewing violent content, long-term effects of exposure to violence, and children's response to commercials. By early 1972 the research was in. The result was the highly publicized *Report of the Surgeon General's Advisory Committee on Television and Behavior*, or, as it was known by its published title, *Television and Growing Up: The Impact of Televised Violence*. Most simply referred to it as "The Surgeon General's Report."

Those seeking a mandate on the issue were surely disappointed, as the final report was inconclusive. Though there was general agreement on the *pervasiveness* of televised violence, the *impact* of such violence on children was still vigorously debated. Some participants found strong correlation between viewing violence and subsequent aggression, while others determined that the impact of televised violence was only significant on those children already "predisposed" to behave more aggressively. Industry-backed committee members, meanwhile, were beside themselves to quell a public backlash. Adding to the chaos, the Surgeon General's office was under pressure to produce a unanimous report that would settle the score once and for all. After much hedging and waffling, the result was merely unanimous ambiguity. In its wishy-washy summary, the report stated that while a causal relationship *might* exist, "a good deal of research remains to be done before one can have confidence in these conclusions."[10] So much for a mandate.

Few appreciated the report's vague position. Hearings followed more hearings on the subject. The networks conducted their own research and, not surprisingly, televised violence was fully exonerated. At the same time, however, independent research continued to point in the opposite direction. Finally, in 1982 there was another opportunity for a definitive answer. Ten years after the publication of the Surgeon General's report, the NIMH conducted a follow-up study entitled *Television and Behavior: Ten Years of Scientific Progress and Implications for the Eighties.* Though the new report was primarily a review of previously published studies (many from the 1972 report were resurrected), televised violence was much more clearly implicated as a cause for aggressive behavior in children.

> Most of the researchers look at the totality of evidence and conclude . . . that the convergence of findings supports the conclusion of a causal relationship between televised violence and later aggressive behavior. The evidence is now drawn from a larger body of literature. Adherents to this convergence approach agree that the conclusions reached in the Surgeon General's program have been significantly strengthened by more recent research.[11]

Network executives could hardly have been pleased.

Since that last major report, much research continues to be conducted on this topic. Though an ironclad conclusion still has not been reached, most research continues to show a positive correlation between televised violence and aggressive behavior. In recent years the research has also branched off into related areas. The primary question has shifted from "*Is* there a correlation between aggression and televised violence?" to "In *which* children and under *what* circumstances is that correlation manifested?" Despite mounds of research that indicate that children are affected by violence, social scientists know that not all children are affected by all forms of TV violence in the same way. Age and developmental level, for example, can be important indicators. Very young children, for example, rarely understand the motives and consequences of violence, and, being wonderful imitators, they delight in replicating the exciting action. Children around the ages of 9 to 12 appear to be most sensitive to TV violence partly because that age range consumes such great quantities of television. As they mature, however, children in that age group begin to understand television better and view its violence as less realistic. They also tend to be more detached, tend to respond less emotionally, and are less frightened by the violence, all of which gradually serves to reduce their levels of aggression.[12] Gender differences also factor in, but not as strongly. Though many recent studies have found that both genders can be impacted, boys generally remain more susceptible to televised aggression than girls. Researcher Leonard Eron claims that vulnerability to TV violence begins by age 3 for both genders, but by age 8 girls have learned other behaviors, have developed other interests, and seem less affected by the violence.[13] In addition to age and gender, other variables like family background, personality characteristics, natural propensity for aggression, childhood disturbances, cognitive ability, and frequency of viewing impact levels of viewer aggression. The effects of *excessively* viewing violence are particularly salient and will be discussed in Chapter 3 (see p. 113).

Though individual viewer variables are important, researchers also consider the action on the screen. Certain forms and portrayals of violence elicit stronger and more predictable responses than others. Research points to four types of violence portrayals that are most likely to influence behavior:

1. *Social Approval.* When violence appears justified and it does not elicit critical comment, the viewer may perceive the violence as being more socially acceptable.
2. *Efficacy.* When portrayals imply that a particular kind of violent behavior is likely to result in a reward — either social, such as approval by others, or material, such as monetary gain — the viewer may assign more utility or worth to the act.
3. *Relevance.* When portrayals are perceived as real and appropriate to the circumstances, the viewer may attach more meaning to the act. (Importantly, this does not exclude cartoons as many young viewers perceive animated action as realistic. Also, given the rash of real-life crime series on the air, this aspect gains further significance.)
4. *Arousal.* The more exciting the action on the screen (fast pace and quick scene changes, for example) — with or without violence — the more aroused viewers become and thus more likely to behave aggressively.[14]

The Myths and Messages of Television   17

Importantly, each of these four factors also works in reverse; that is to say if the violence is punished or deemed socially unacceptable, the likelihood of viewer aggression decreases.

Though the relationship between televised violence and viewer aggression forms the heart of the violence debate, other important questions are now being considered. For example, could televised violence's most damaging effect be more subtle than mimicked kicks to the stomach and blows to the head? Indeed, TV violence's broader impact is likely to move most swiftly in the fuzzy realm of perception and attitudes. Psychologist and TV violence expert Edward Donnerstein explains it this way:

> The notion that I watched a lot of violence on TV and never killed anybody doesn't mean that there aren't any other effects. We don't say everybody is going to go out and commit a rape, but they certainly might have a different attitude about victims of rape, or about what rape is. They might be desensitized about violence and have a callous attitude toward victims of violence which, given the events of our time, we should be concerned about.[15]

This observation points to what we see as perhaps the most important and least considered aspect of the violence debate. It is easy to grow smug, certain that one's own children would never lose grip with reality and raise their fists or brandish a gun in imitation of their small screen heroes. It is considerably more difficult to be certain that repeated exposure to violence won't change their children's attitudes and beliefs, making them less compassionate and sensitive when life offers pain, suffering, and distress.

The issue of televised violence is not going to go away. Nor will it become any simpler in the face of rapidly developing technology. Barring a miraculous clean-up of the airwaves, it remains up to parents and other concerned individuals to start taking action. Though scientific debate represents an enormous contribution to the issue, don't underestimate the simple power of common sense. In assessing the impact of violent television on children, consider your own kids. How does TV violence appear to affect *them*? Do they act it out on the playground and at the dinner table? Do their attitudes towards violence concern you? Are they fearful or agitated after viewing TV violence? Conversely, do they appear numb to violent acts on TV? Finally, do you want your children—no matter how well adjusted they might seem—soaking up violent images hour after hour, day after day?

Though TV violence is a serious concern, parents need not go overboard and banish every aggressive scene from their living room. Violence is a part of life, plain and simple. It can be effectively addressed on television, and with care, maturity, and involvement on your part, your kids might learn its true lessons. In the absence of such efforts, though, television—with its typically flippant handling of the incidence of violence, the consequences of violence, and the value of human life—will have the last word.

S-E-X

Historically speaking, TV turned to violence long before it turned to sex. While blood and guts made for entertaining fare from the start, producers were far more skittish about pressing one of America's greatest taboos. In television's early days, the very existence of sex was denied as actors cautiously maneuvered around the word "pregnant," and married couples like Rob and Laura Petrie cheerfully said goodnight from their separate twin beds. Censors for *The Ed Sullivan Show* even outlawed sex *appeal*, ensuring that Elvis' swinging pelvis would not corrupt the moral sensibilities of viewers. Hollywood was slow to let sex out of its tantalizing box, perhaps realizing that once it hit the small screen, television would never be the same. And that is precisely what happened. In a relatively short period of time, the once chaste television has today become a major purveyor of sexual mores.

The turning point came in the 1970s. The outrageously liberated *Love, American Style* was perhaps the boldest sign that the sexual revolution had finally reached Hollywood. Thereafter, it didn't take long to recognize the power of sex to draw an audience. In a study of sex on television, a team of researchers analyzed prime-time television for its sexual content in 1975, 1977, and 1978. Within these years, the frequency of hugging and kissing increased substantially, while the frequency of sexually suggestive remarks and innuendoes skyrocketed, posting a nearly tenfold increase.[16] This trend heralded TV's "jiggle" years, with such shows as *Charlie's Angels* and *Three's Company* winning the ratings game. Ironically, this increase in sexual themes and references was a direct result of the public's criticism of excessive violence. Packed with gun-slinging macho men, the 1976 television season had been the most violent to date; the resulting public backlash sent producers scrambling to find an alternate source of public titillation. Sex was their answer. And based on the ratings for the jiggly 1977 season, it was right on the money.

Those early seasons used sex strictly as a gag line. Less-than-subtle double entendres and sophomoric innuendo made up the bulk of the dialogue, aided always by a hearty laugh track. The first show to cross the public's fuzzy moral line was the situation comedy *Soap*, introduced in 1977 amid much controversy. Not only were most of the jokes explicitly sexual in nature, but the program was the first that dared to include an openly homosexual character. Some viewers applauded the show's frank acknowledgment of sexuality, while others saw in it the seeds of America's moral collapse. Regardless of public opinion, the sex-oriented sitcom was here to stay.

Throughout the 1980s, the small screen continued to heat up. In another content analysis, this time conducted in 1989, researchers examined 10 popular shows and tallied physical, verbal, and implied acts or references to sex. Among their findings: "touching behaviors," including kissing, hugging, and other affectionate touching, occurred at a rate of 24.5 acts per hour; sexual "suggestions and innuendo" were presented at a rate of 16.5 times per hour; sexual intercourse was suggested 2.5 times per hour; and "discouraged sexual practices" such as sadomasochism and exhibitionism were suggested at a rate of 6.2 times per hour.[17] Another study in the 1980s indicated that the most frequent forms of sexual activity in prime-time programs included sexual suggestiveness, erotic touching, and intercourse.[18] Today in the 1990s we have all this and more. *Seinfeld* hosts a no-masturbation contest, Roseanne is kissed by Mariel Hemingway in a lesbian bar, and Drew Barrymore wishes David Letterman a happy birthday by baring her breasts on national TV. And then there's the standard stuff: On network television men and women are in bed together on a daily and nightly basis, no wedding ring required. Daytime soap operas have long been notorious for their bed hopping escapades, yet even on prime-time television, 8 out of 10 sexually active characters are unmarried.[19] Premarital, extramarital, and gay sex is now the standard. As for married couples on TV, it seems their sex drive was left at the altar as few are portrayed enjoying a healthy, happy, monogamous sex life. In addition to frequently implying intercourse, TV movies and drama series now explore formerly taboo topics like rape, incest, and sexual abuse on a regular basis. Meanwhile, sitcoms, many airing during the traditional "family hour" at 7 p.m. Central Time, are loaded with sophomoric references to sexual encounters (fulfilling and unfulfilling), masturbation, oral sex, homosexuality, and the human anatomy; breasts, it seems, have practically been given character status. Perhaps the lowest form of sexually charged television is the TV talk show. The still proliferating format snags huge ratings shares with topics like "I'm Having an Affair With My Best Friend's Father" or "My Daughter's a Stripper, and I'm Proud of It" or "One-Night Stand Reunions." Guided by pandering hosts and whooping, hollering studio audiences, guests proudly and defiantly display their utter lack of commitment, self-esteem, and common sense. Sex in its myriad of implicit and explicit forms is now a staple of television.

Why such a surge in provocative TV? You could say that network television has been chasing a faster rabbit as it presses the limits on sexual acceptability. For nearly two decades, cable television has been offering viewers programming practically without limits. Cable television faces significantly less regulation than network TV, allowing unedited feature films and made-for-cable movies to compete against comparatively tame network fare for the same audience. The explosion in cable TV subscribers alone illustrates the medium's drawing power, and its success comes at a distinct cost to network television. In response, network TV often strives to become more cable-like. This shift in corporate vision was considered a significant reason for ABC's 1993 decision to air the controversial series *NYPD Blue,* the first program in network history to permit extensive profanity and nudity on prime-time television. *NYPD Blue* is hardly the only show heading in this direction, however. In an obvious effort to remain sexy, discussions of orgasm, impotence, and sexual satisfaction are all now routine elements of many prime-time conversations. Couples roll passionately under rumpled sheets, occasionally providing a momentary glimpse of a bare buttock or two. Of course, the networks continue to rely on traditional visual titillation, as well. Trim bodies still bound across the screen in skimpy clothes and swimsuits. Though the tactic sounds a bit retro, it still appears to work. *Baywatch*—a program filled to the gills with tan, fit, beautiful bodies—is currently the most watched program in the world. Why would the networks change a winning formula?

In addition to the usual exploitation of sexual themes on adult network fare, programs that target teens and preteens now explore the topic with surprising frequency. Though the networks often claim to be reflecting a more sexually active young viewership, it always seems that a popular young character is contemplating "going all the way" either in November, February, or May, the traditional ratings sweeps months. For the most part, weekly comedy or drama series that depict sexually active teens tread very lightly. Most programs try to make a big point of having the characters discuss using protection, and few — with the exceptions of *Party of Five* and *Beverly Hills 90210* — show teens actually in bed with each other. Notably, both of these programs try to show the "flip side" of sexual activity. Perhaps as penance for a host of sexual transgressions, the soap opera-esque *90210* offers some strategic concessions. Stylish Donna long remained a virgin, and the program frequently depicted her wrestling with sexual pressure. Moreover, when the actress who portrayed the mature, studious, but unwed Andrea became pregnant in real life a few years ago, the show's producers made an important choice. Rather than hide her behind pillows, countertops, and baggy clothes, they moved forward with a pregnancy storyline. *Party of Five* has perhaps more realistically dealt with teenage sex. While the program has momentarily shown teens together in bed, most of the related screen time depicts the agonizing fallout of becoming sexually active at a young age, including unplanned pregnancy, the painful debate about abortion, and feelings of confusion, embarrassment, and fear. While such truth-in-advertising efforts are welcome signs, they may not be enough to sway a hormone-addled teenage audience. Like the friendly but hypocritical advice that follows episodes of *The Mighty Morphin Power Rangers,* these messages are a weak match for television's persistent habit of showing fashionable young people together in bed.

If network television seems to be now pushing the boundaries of what is sexually acceptable on TV, cable television has broken clear through the fence, offering a virtual free-for-all of sexual standards, practices, and mores. Though the Playboy Channel and its gaggle of imitators might first spring to mind as examples of risqué television, there are other more accessible, "respectable" stations that offer lots of passion, panting, cleavage, and skin. Many feature films on cable and in videos contain nudity and scenes of sexual intercourse, and for an adult audience this isn't necessarily problematic. The issue gets trickier when children and youth join what should be a mature viewing audience.

Many kids will occasionally sneak a peek at questionable programs out of sheer curiosity — it's the modern, prepubescent equivalent of passing around a dirty novel filled with bad words and compromising situations. This secretive act is a normal rite of passage for many preteen inquiring minds. A major difference is that children today — many far too young to have any sense of understanding—are being openly invited to view the sexual side of the adult world. Clever marketing departments capitalize on kids' natural curiosities by deliberately pulling them in a more sexually explicit direction. "Sex sells," goes the famous advertising maxim.

No organization better understands this profitable truth than MTV. A potent arbiter of youth values and culture, MTV made its name by revolutionizing the experience of music. Along the way, the music channel has also served to shape many young viewers' impressions of men, women, sex, and power. Of course, music has been exploring the mysteries of love and lust for centuries; the presence of sexual themes in music should come as no surprise. The important distinction with music videos is that word and melody are matched with powerful, carefully orchestrated visual images. Videos are now a key tool in marketing music, with artists and the recording industry spending huge sums of money in an attempt to "tell the story" of a given song. According to conventional record industry wisdom, the more perplexing the video, the better; it's art, after all. But despite the enormous effort at creativity and artistic expression, there is a surprising lack of originality in terms of content matter. The reliance on explicit sexual themes is altogether predictable, yet still obviously profitable. Even extreme images now fail to shock. Crotch-grabbing, cross-dressing, leather-whipping singers are old news, though their potential influence on impressionable young viewers remains strong. Perhaps most disturbing is the unmistakable link between sex and violence in many music videos. A University of Georgia study that examined the content of three music video programs and stations found violence occurring in 56.6% of the videos. Of these violent videos, a full 81% also depicted forms of sexual intimacy.[20]

Video games, computer software, and web sites on the Internet further forge the relationship between sex and violence. In "Night Trap," another Sega offering, men in dark masks terrorize five beautiful young women. In one scene, three men burst into the bedroom of a young woman dressed only in a skimpy negligee. Unless the player makes the right moves, the men drag her off and plunge an electric drill into her neck, then hang her on a meat hook. Yes, this is a game.

Sex Education

Most adults—regardless of whether they approve of TV's sexual mores—are emotionally and psychologically equipped to handle the provocative content. But what about television's youngest audience? It would seem that continued lessons in exploitative sex, promiscuity, the objectification of women, and the dominance of men might easily distort the emotional, social, and physical development of young viewers. Scientific research cannot readily answer this question as the sensitive nature of the topic poses difficulties in researching children's perceptions of sex on TV. Consequently, much of the research regarding children and the sexual content of television has been gathered from adults and adolescents. Still, the findings are instructive.

First, numerous studies have established that most parents think there is too much sex on television. In one study, respondents were asked to rate the age-appropriateness of several specific sexual acts and themes.[21] Several hundred adults watched a sample of 15 prime-time shows and indicated the degree to which they thought that 13 kinds of sexual content—ranging from childbirth and marital sex to prostitution, rape, and child molestation—were suitable for an adult, a teenage, and a child audience respectively. While all 13 of the topics were considered suitable for an adult audience, many (including extramarital sex, prostitution, striptease, rape, and child molestation) were considered inappropriate for teenagers, and nearly all were deemed unsuitable for children by a majority of the respondents. The researchers went on to ask the parents what they thought the likely consequences would be of children watching sexual content on TV. Forty-eight percent of the respondents thought the children would "ask questions they were too young to understand," 41% said they would be "confused or upset," 41% said they would "use language that is unacceptable to the parents," and 35% said they would "tolerate behaviors or lifestyles that are unacceptable to the parents." However, 45% felt the children would "initiate useful discussions with their parents," and 19% believed that they would "learn something positive." Despite parental complaints about the increasing shamelessness of television, it is interesting to note that many worldly observers find that the treatment of sex on American television still seems puritanical compared to its TV exposure in Europe and South America (where TV violence is the bigger concern); the fact that many cultures don't bat an eye at watching naked game show contestants at 4 in the afternoon, however, tends to offer little comfort to those parents who want their children to gain emotional maturity before hearing about and seeing the sexual aspect of adult life.

If parents are frequently leery about television's recent sexual revolution, the young viewers themselves tend to be downright blasé about it. In 1986, 1,000 teenagers were asked about TV's role as a sex educator. Entertainment television ranked fourth (behind friends, parents, and courses at school) as a source of sex information. More poignant, perhaps, was the fact that over half believed that topics such as pregnancy, the personal consequences of sex, and the likelihood of contracting a sexually transmitted disease were presented on television in a realistic manner.[22] In an age when the rate of teenage pregnancies stands at over 300,000 per year and the threat of AIDS and other sexually transmitted diseases (STDs) looms large and real, such naïve acceptance of television's version of sexual reality can be tragic. With a few notable exceptions, television still largely fails to address the touchy issues of teen pregnancy and the incidence of STDs, including AIDS, among teenagers. On the contrary, at a time when young people are being urged to restrain from sex for their own personal safety, television continues to emphasize sex's glamour, while ignoring its unglamorous consequences. In a 1988 content analysis study, out of a total of 722 sexual incidents coded, researchers found only 13.5 references to pregnancy prevention and 18 references to STD prevention, 13 of which dealt with AIDS.[23] A study by the Planned Parenthood Federation of America similarly found references to sex education, STDs, and birth control to be extremely rare: a mere 0.07% of all sexual incidents in their program pool.[24]

There's no doubt that television is a salient arbiter of sex education. Some young viewers might learn that sex appears to be a quick route to intimacy and popularity. Others will determine that their beleaguered sex education teachers are overreacting—not *that* many sexually active girls *really* become pregnant. Still others will learn that sex can be an easy tool for power. On the other hand, given sensitive treatment on television, young people could learn some significantly more realistic and positive lessons about sex. They might learn, for example, the true risks and responsibilities of becoming sexually active, or about the fact that sex (in the proper context) need not be exploitative or manipulative, or, finally, that less physical (and perhaps more enduring) paths to intimacy exist. Clearly sex will continue to play a leading role on television in the years to come. Less certain is the nature of that role and the lessons our children will learn from it.

The World According to Hollywood: Stereotypes and Other Myths

If television offers windows into the world, it would seem that many are lopsided, shabbily constructed, and dim with haze. Through the small screen we see a world in which insults are funny, gunshots don't kill, and problems last no longer than 30 minutes. It's also a world that routinely buries physical and demographic truths. Men, especially white, good-looking, youthful men, abound. They are almost always in great shape (rarely a potbelly in sight) and have an amazing knack for success—in work, in play, and in love and lust. Women make fewer TV appearances, but maximize their screen time by being thin, beautiful, cheerful, and clever. Cute and precocious kids are plentiful, but as soon as they hit those cranky teenage years they disappear into adolescent obscurity; if lucky, they might resurface when they are twenty or thirtysomething. The elderly, meanwhile, have been quietly carted off to the old folks' home, not a wrinkle too soon. And finally there are TV's ethnic and racial minorities, who invariably can be found wearing their blue-collar uniforms to their blue-collar jobs in their blue-collar neighborhoods. Welcome to the world of creative TV.

It is no surprise that television perpetuates the myth of stereotype. In one-half hour it is hard to communicate the essence of a person's being or the subtle, quirky idiosyncrasies and habits that make real people real. For the sake of both expediency and ratings, producers want characters with whom their viewers can quickly identify. In order to be as broad and inclusionary as possible, real and compelling personalities are reduced to their lowest common denominator. Hence, we have the Nerdy Genius, the Streetwise Black Punk, the Kooky Old Lady, the Sexy Blonde Bombshell, and the Hunky Hero. These stock characters are flimsy, hollow things that defy gravity in their staying power.

Stereotypes are harmful and limiting wherever they appear, but their prevalence on television is particularly dangerous for children who, in their relative inexperience, are still feeling their way through a world filled with people of different shapes, colors, ages, and abilities. Through subtle acts of omission and misrepresentation, television plugs into children's love of categorization by offering a simple hierarchy of who is important and who is not. In addition to learning about others, kids are also on the lookout for clues about themselves—how they should act, what they should look like, and what they should be doing with their time. If most of their early lessons come from television, their perspectives and expectations will be shaped in very limited ways.

Minorities

Of all of television's stereotypes, none are more pernicious or pervasive as those defined by race and ethnicity. According to the historic laws of television, Brits are snobs, Italians are Mafiosi, Native Americans are blood-thirsty, Jews are cheap, Eastern Europeans are subversive, African-Americans are subservient, Hispanics are poor, and nearly all Asians are masters of Kung Fu. Real and significant contributions and gains by minorities continue to be discounted or ignored on television, and TV's reflection of their place in the nation's population is a slim shadow of their actual numbers. In recent years the roles for racial and ethnic minorities have expanded in depth and breadth significantly, but old habits are hard to break, and the improvement of minority treatment has been slow and scattered at best.

In its earliest years, television offered a neatly pressed, whitewashed world in which nearly all characters, both major and minor, were Caucasian. This initial, elite view was surely considered logical by the TV industry, for the great majority of television buyers were white and the still-enforced Jim Crow laws labeled African-Americans as subcitizens. For years a white hierarchy remained firmly in place, interrupted only rarely by the likes of the handsome Cuban bandmaster Ricky Ricardo ("Oh, Looooocy") and the dumb and happy antics of *Amos 'n' Andy*. Minorities were thus included, but only, it seemed, for their childish, slapstick entertainment value. The Civil Rights movement of the 1960s worked to eliminate the most blatant of stereotyping and omission of nonwhites, and as a result minorities on TV (mostly blacks) did increase slightly in number. As one of the boldest signals of change, in 1971 CBS allowed Norman Lear to introduce *All in the Family* to the American viewing public. Each week Archie, Edith, Mike, and Gloria flirted dangerously close to the heart of what roiled under the surface of American race relations. In an unintended twist of irony, the loudmouth bigot Archie Bunker provided fodder and reinforcement for a great many real-life bigots who failed to recognize Lear's subtle satire.

Though minority treatment has improved dramatically since television's early days, there is still room for progress. Researcher George Gerbner has tracked minority treatment on television since the late 1960s; in his most recent study he continues to find that minority representation is lacking. In a 1994 analysis of 19,642 speaking parts in

1,371 television programs on prime-time programming (situation comedies, dramas, and movies), whites comprise a full 86.8% of the TV population.[25] Of the characters, nonwhites were more frequently depicted as killers, in comic roles, as very poor, as service workers, and associated with criminal activity. Lest it appear that such stereotypes are confined to adult programming, one revealing study found that most of the "bad guys" on children's cartoons are portrayed with foreign accents.[26]

Of minorities on television today, blacks have achieved the greatest success. If shows like *What's Happenin'* and *Diff'rent Strokes* represented low points for African-American treatment on television, the widely watched 1977 epic *Roots* indicated the hopeful possibilities. In addition to being a vivid educational vehicle, *Roots* offered a full cast of black actors roles beyond that of court jester. Though *Roots* did not spark an overnight reformation in black treatment on TV, since its original airing the quantity and quality of black roles has steadily improved. Today the black presence on television now roughly reflects the actual population percentage of African-Americans in the United States. Moreover, several predominantly black shows (*The Cosby Show, A Different World, The Fresh Prince of Bel-Air, In Living Color*) have enjoyed huge success with both white and minority audiences. Yet even the most successful of these shows fall into a disturbing pattern: For the most part, such all-black shows are comedies, indicating a reluctance on the part of network producers to ascribe to blacks the range of emotions and human experience so readily given to white characters. According to a recent American Psychological Association report, the formulation of all-black casts also reinforces notions of segregation,[27] a theory that merits increasing consideration as new, specialized network and cable outlets develop. Most current programming featuring black casts, for example (including *The Parent 'Hood, In The House, Moesha,* and *Martin*), now appears on the newest "mini-networks," UPN and WB. Though this trend provides black actors and audiences with considerably heightened visibility, some see it as a sign of the "ghettotization" of black programming. Critics claim the traditional, more well-financed networks may feel less compelled to create vehicles for minority actors and minority audiences if the mini-networks are already doing so. Moreover, many white viewers, comfortable with the predominantly white programming on the major networks, may feel little reason to "visit" the minority-based programming on UPN and WB, further segregating black and white programming and audiences. As a final concern, though black cast members are now often included as part of otherwise all-white ensembles on traditional network programs, it is rare that they are given much power in relationship with whites (*Homicide: Life on the Street,* a critically praised show not appropriate for children, is one of the few exceptions). Such patterns signal a hesitation to upset Hollywood's social order.

Despite these concerns, blacks still fare far better than other minorities, both in treatment and representation. In a TV world where a mere 12% of characters are nonwhite, and of that 12% a full 79% are black, it does not take a statistician to determine that roles for other minorities are rare.[28] Hispanics, though the fastest growing segment of the U.S. population, have practically no role models on standard network television. While there are many successful independent Hispanic stations broadcasting their own soap operas, news programs, dramas, and kids' shows in Spanish, on network TV individual nonstereotyped Hispanics are hard to find. When they do appear, they are often cast as being lazy, poor, and criminal-minded. Their visibility and characterization may soon improve, however. Hispanic and Latino organizations have lately been asserting their voices in protest; in one of the most visible efforts, in 1995 the National Hispanic Media Coalition called for a boycott of ABC programming as a protest against the lack of Hispanics on television. Though all the networks can be considered negligent in this regard, ABC became the specific target when network president Robert Iger reneged on an apparent promise to heighten visibility of Latinos by fall 1994. Time will tell if this increased public pressure is a successful tact. In addition to African-Americans and Hispanics, Asians are another group that has been both disregarded and degraded by television. Largely due to propaganda efforts issued throughout American history, the traditional TV images of Asians were generally either of evil, subversive, untrustworthy "yellows" or passive, respectful foreigners who "know their place" in white society. More recently, their most visible roles seem to be ultra-brainy whiz-kids and sinister corporate raiders. In one brief bright spot, in its 1993-1994 season ABC aired a sitcom with a full Asian-American cast: *All-American Girl* depicted the life of Margaret Cho, a young adult in perpetual conflict between the customs of American life and the traditional expectations of her Korean family. Though it played primarily as lightweight comedy filled with the expected ethnic jokes, its very presence on network television was a promising sign. Its subsequent cancellation a year later was, on the other hand, a more typical sign. Native Americans, for their part, are still looking for a respectable vehicle. Long tagged with the stereotype as uncivilized scalpers and unscrupulous warriors, bands of warpainted, spear-wielding Indians were cast as frequent foils to the white hero's noble designs. The old cowboys and Indians routine has since faded into political incorrectness, and now television (with the standout exception of the now-defunct *Northern Exposure*) hardly acknowledges the Native American population at all. Finally, regardless of the ethnic or racial group, minority women suffer double injustice. Few make it to television in the first place, and those who do are rarely seen outside domestic or clerical roles. In personality and temperament, most are seen as helpless victims and servile workers, humble and without power.

The marginal, stereotypical depiction of minorities cannot simply be dismissed as one of television's annoying habits; it is one that is accompanied by subtle danger and consequence. For people who normally have little daily contact with people outside their own racial or ethnic group, television's distorted picture provides ready fuel for prejudice and ignorance-based fear. An illustrative 1975 study focused on this topic. Working to determine how television might influence the racial attitudes of a group of white and black children, researcher Sherryl Graves selected eight cartoons that showed both positive and negative portrayals of blacks. The positive portrayals showed blacks as competent, hard-working, and trustworthy, while the negative ones showed them as inept, destructive, lazy, and powerless. Graves found that there was a positive attitude change for the black children who viewed either portrayal and for the white children who saw a positive portrayal. However, after viewing *only one* negative portrayal of blacks, white children posted a clearly negative attitude change.[29] In addition to demonstrating the dramatic change in white attitudes, this research also indicated that minorities are apt to prefer any portrayal—even those that are negative—over invisibility.

Gender

On television, stereotypes are assigned not just by race or ethnicity, but also by gender. Sex-role stereotypes abound on the small screen, carefully defining what it means to be a man or a woman. To be a man on television is a fortunate fate, one that guarantees high exposure and plenty of action. In a 1987 prime-time analysis, males comprised 71% of the samples, women 29%. In weekend daytime—slots loaded with sporting events and home improvement programs—the male figure jumped to 77%, females only 23%.[30] Children's programming is even more lopsided. During Saturday morning children's programming, girls and women make up less than one-fourth of the casting, animated or otherwise.[31] Media critic Jerome Weeks describes children's programming as a "brightly colored sea of male hormones with the rare tiny island of pink froufrou set aside for little girls to play dress-up."[32] This gender imbalance reaches all the way to the hallowed halls of PBS where even the ever-sensitive *Sesame Street* has but one or two regular girl muppets. Snuggled among the boys—Ernie, Bert, Kermit, Oscar, Cookie Monster, Big Bird, Snuffleupagus, the Count, and Elmo—is the sweet little waif Prairie Dawn; in Weeks' words, she is a "pathetic simp."

Such is the lot of the TV female. Despite the increasing awareness of women's contributions, opportunities, and rights that has occurred in the real world, television continues to characterize girls and women in ways that are traditional and limiting. On children's television, for example, boys do most of the adventuring, the discovering, the planning, and the plotting. Girls, on the other hand, function primarily as cheery, ponytailed sidekicks or needy damsels in distress. Adult programming also needs some updating. Though a number of adult shows have thankfully broken through many of the old gender-based barriers, plenty of traditional female stereotypes still exist in prime-time programming. Men are typically the rational heroes of television, women the grateful, blushing victims. Studies indicate that while men are more often portrayed as knowledgeable, aggressive, rugged, and independent, women are typically seen as timid, emotional, and submissive.[33] Moreover, men are most often depicted as holding high prestige and traditionally masculine jobs such as lawyers, doctors, and police, while TV women are usually seen in the nurturing context of romantic interests, home, and family. On the other hand, when women *are* invested with intelligence and power, it is frequently of the catty, scheming, *Melrose Place* variety.

In her thoughtful book *Reviving Ophelia: Saving the Selves of Adolescent Girls,* well-known author and therapist Mary Pipher relates how girls in her practice see women portrayed on television:

> Cayenne noticed that television almost never features old, heavy, or unattractive women. She also notices that on TV even if a woman is a doctor or a scholar, she looks like a *Playboy* bunny. Another noticed that women are often victims of violence. Lots of plots have to do with women being raped, beaten, chased or terrorized by men. . . .
>
> She noticed that male voices carry more authority in commercials. Men are the doctors and scientists who give

product endorsements. She observed that women's bodies sell products that have nothing to do with women — tires, tractors, liquor and guns.

Another client hated the Old Milwaukee beer ads that featured the Swedish Bikini Team in which a group of bikini-clad women parachute onto a beach to fulfill the sexual fantasies of beer-drinking men. She said, "Women are portrayed as expensive toys, as the ultimate recreation."[34]

Indeed, of all of television's traditional roles for women, none is more stubborn and enduring than the gorgeous, sexy, buxom bimbo. Fifteen years ago, such a role was considered by many to be "cute"; today it is simply an insulting anachronism. Yet the persona persists, and nowhere more explicitly than on the cable music channels. Women who appear in many of these productions seem to excel only in grinding their hips and pouting their lips — anything more cerebral, forget it. Network television has its share of "window dressing," as well — lovely women who exist not to propel the plot but merely to decorate it. Testament to TV's fascination with beautiful, desirable women are the age statistics for characters on prime-time shows. It is no secret that women on television are typically younger than men. One study shows that 16- to 29-year-old women are the most heavily represented age group of their sex[35]; on the other hand, a mere 15% of middle-age characters are female.[36] The beauty myths reach all the way down to the youngest viewing set. TV ads for Barbie showcase a doll with a gravity-defying figure, enchanting blue eyes, and flowing, shimmering blond locks; that she represents pure physiological fantasy surely escapes most of her young devotees. Even a show as charming and harmless as *The Muppets* actively perpetuates TV's version of femininity. Young girls are steered toward the inimitable Miss Piggy, the pink, perky swine who gained muppet fame as a beauty and fashion queen. To her credit, Miss Piggy also emphasizes that "big" can be beautiful, attempting to liberate women of all ages from the tyranny of weight control.

In addition to defining how women should look, television also defines what they should do. For years we watched as women named June and Carol stayed (with smiles) in the kitchen as husbands named Ward and Mike made their way in the white-collared business world. Women were queens of their homes, men kings of the world. Prompted largely by the growing women's movement, the 1970s ushered in some positive change for women on TV with programs like *The Mary Tyler Moore Show* and *Rhoda*. Unfortunately, the career success that Mary

Richards found at WJM-TV was not shared by many of her fellow women on television—most who were allowed into the sacred halls of TV's working world remained employed as secretaries, nurses, teachers, and other traditionally female professions. Ironically, when the networks finally looked up and saw the changing demographics of working women, they let the pendulum swing too far in the other direction. In 1985, 56% of women were actually in the workforce, though television had a full 75% heading out the door for their job.[37] Additionally, far more of them were in professional positions than actually occurs in real life. Though these are exaggerations in a generally more positive direction, they illustrate that television is still unfamiliar with the real lives of women.

Though TV's sex-role stereotypes seem most damaging to women, in fact they can limit *both* men and women (and boys and girls) in how they approach decision-making and goal-setting, in how they pursue relationships, and in how they value themselves. Boys and men are told day after day, night after night that they should be macho, aggressive, and impervious to deep emotion. Girls and women are told that they should be beautiful, deferential, and ruled by emotion. Such persistent messages are potent influencing agents for developing attitudes and beliefs. T. S. Williams' famous study of three Canadian towns illustrates television's power to sway beliefs. At the beginning of her study, Williams found that girls in Notel (town without television) and Unitel (town with very limited television) had weaker gender-typed views than girls in Multitel (town with greater television availability). Two years after the introduction of television into Notel and an increase in availability in Unitel, the girls in Notel had become significantly more sex-typed, and the views of the girls from both Notel and Unitel were now similar to the girls in Multitel. Similar results were recorded for the boys in these towns.[38] Another well-known study examined the effects of stereotyped portrayals on self-concepts. In an experimental study involving high school girls aged 16 to 18, one group of girls was exposed to a heavy dose of beauty commercials (ads for health products emphasizing the desirability of sex appeal, beauty, and youth), while a control group viewed nonbeauty related ads (ads for dog food, soy sauce, and the like). Those in the beauty-ad group were significantly more likely than the control group to believe that being beautiful is an important characteristic and is necessary to attract men.[39]

Sex-role stereotypes greatly influence the fragile concept of what it means to be male or female. Fortunately, the outlook is brightening. Despite continued lapses in judgment, Hollywood appears to be earnestly working to reduce traditional stereotyping of both men and women and boys and girls. In part, this is due to increasing numbers of women occupying powerful, behind-the-scenes positions in the television industry, particularly children's television. For example, Geraldine Laybourne, former president of Nickelodeon/Nick at Nite and current president of Disney/ABC Cable Networks, has taken a public stand on presenting real girls on TV — spirited, athletic, opinionated, talented, ordinary-looking girls — in an effort to reach a previously neglected and misrepresented audience. She notes, "We cringe when we hear about cultures suffocating baby girls, but we do not help when we export programming that reinforces that boys are better, even if it's in subtle ways. Let's not be guilty of suffocating little girls' spirits."[40] Positive shows like *The Secret World of Alex Mack, Allegra's Window,* and *Clarissa Explains It All* are a step in the right direction. Today there are also a number of adult programs like *Grace Under Fire, Ellen, Murphy Brown,* and *Cybill* that feature strong women in fairly realistic settings, as well as shows like *Dave's World, Home Improvement,* and *Mad About You* that show men to be warm, involved fathers and husbands. Yet these more genuine characterizations remain the odd exception. Moreover, they exist primarily in sitcoms, a genre that tends to draw a predominantly female audience as opposed to action-adventure programs that attract male viewers. Thus, the shows most watched by males are the ones most likely to still depict females in traditional or limiting roles. It seems that bad habits like squeezing svelte young girls into short, tight skirts and keeping working women at the secretary's post are hard to break; for now television remains a club that caters primarily to boys and men.

Age

Women and minorities are not alone in being negatively stereotyped or underrepresented on television. Television also stereotypes by age. Older individuals, for example, are nearly invisible on TV. The one stand-out exception, *Murder, She Wrote*, now shares the canceled fate of *Matlock, In the Heat of the Night,* and *The Golden Girls* — all shows featuring classy casts of older actors with long, impressive résumés. With the loss of Angela Lansbury's adventurous character J. B. Fletcher, the appearances of competent older individuals on TV are even more scarce. One study showed that while people over the age of 65 represented 11% of the actual U.S. population, they were found to be only 2.3% of the dramatic population. The sample also revealed that when they *were* portrayed, two-thirds of older women and one-third of older men were depicted as silly, eccentric, or lacking common sense.[41] Rather than highlight the quiet wisdom and experience of older individuals, television often emphasizes traits like stubbornness, frailty, deafness, and senility for comic effect. Surely as the affluent Baby Boomer population ages, Hollywood will follow suit and find respectable vehicles for older actors and actresses. Meanwhile, healthy folks with wrinkles and gray hair appear to have been neatly banished from the small screen.

There are also disparities on the other end of the age spectrum. Though children under the age of 10 constitute 15% of the population, only 2% of prime-time TV characters and 3.6% of weekend daytime characters are so young.[42] Though in recent years television has experienced its own baby boom of sorts (*Full House; Step by Step; Family Matters; The Nanny; Sister, Sister; Boy Meets World*), these shows all belong to the lightweight domain of cute comedy. Moreover, the kids on these programs hardly ever approximate our own children at home. Always nattily dressed in the latest fashions, TV's children never seem to get dirty and sticky and pouty like the kids we know. And unlike our own lovable but flighty kids, TV children have infinite common sense and wisdom, often serving as a show's voice of reason.

Teenagers also have a difficult time finding realistic counterparts on television. At an age in which identity issues are at their most painful and confusing point, teenagers have few places on television to seek assurance. The fast jokes of *Blossom* and the *Fresh Prince of Bel-Air* often neglected the true heartache of those years. The impossibly hip *Beverly Hills 90210* is simply a young, rich soap opera. And the absurd superficiality of *Saved by the Bell* and *California Dreams* fools no one over the age of 10. The only current program that realistically deals with the issues of growing up is *Party of Five*, a Fox show about five siblings who live on their own after the deaths of their parents. Recent episodes have dealt with subjects ranging from teen suicide to body development (or the lack thereof) to the stresses of applying to college. The only other program that successfully captured the true complexity of teenage life — *My So-Called Life* — met the common fate of unprofitable television. (*The Wonder Years* was also terrific, but, alas, little Kevin Arnold grew up.) With sensitivity and a true knack for dialogue, *My So-Called Life* explored the issues of friendship, loyalty, family, sexuality, peer pressure, and school pressure through the wary eyes of high schooler Angela Chase. Though the show was a tremendous critical success, it hovered near the bottom of the ratings. When *My So-Called Life* continued to post weak numbers, ABC ignored a prime opportunity to finally put viewers ahead of the balance sheet.

Despite much public hand wringing, the network's position was clear: In the end, quality is a weak match for profitability.

It is a dreary irony that television's most frequent viewers are women, blacks, the poor, the elderly, and children,[43] as these are precisely the populations most plagued by television's stereotypes. That they must continue watching thin parodies of themselves is regrettable. One of the primary reasons for the neglect and stereotyping of these groups is Hollywood's perception that their buying power is limited. Without the dollars to fuel the advertisement engine of Hollywood, the industry is hardly going to extend themselves to accommodate these seemingly "marginal" groups. This is an unfortunate economic rule. Yet suspend reality for a moment and imagine what television *could* offer: In a utopian world with all advertising dollars being equal we might finally discover TV casts that include Streetwise Old Ladies, Blonde Geniuses, and Nerdy Black Heroes. Now *that* would defy gravity.

Other Myths and Misrepresentations

Stereotypes based on race, ethnicity, gender, and age form only part of TV's credibility problem. Particularly in the areas of family, work, and health, television often stretches the truth to accommodate perceived audience demands and, perhaps understandably, to make life more manageable for screenwriters and set designers. Exaggerations and simplifications sound like potential problems, but is truth or realism on fictional television programs absolutely necessary? Except for the case of news programming, viewers rarely come to television in an effort to see blunt reality. Instead, after a hard day at work or school, most viewers look for a little lighthearted escape. Glittery shows like *Dallas* and *Dynasty* drew millions of viewers in the 1980s because they represented something far beyond the monotonous norm. Who cared that perfectly coiffed Krystal and Alexis never wore the same thing twice? This was entertainment! Though television's entertainment function exempts it from having to faithfully reflect every hard truth of life, the myths of television — of which there are many — do pose some problems. First, many of television's creative liberties demean the truth, making violence, for example, seem like it is free of consequence, physical or otherwise. Second, television's myths often prompt viewers to expect the real world to mirror the one they see on television. This is an easy tendency for viewers of all ages, but children are at a special risk, having been weaned in their formative years on programs that feature laugh tracks and easy answers. Like the rest of us, they may face great disappointment when their own lives don't turn out the way they do on TV.

The treatment of families on television offers a case in point for television's reliance on myths and misrepresentations. The inherent drama of family life provides plenty of natural material for producers and writers. And because we can all relate to the experience of family, it is a genre that attracts a great number of viewers. It's a tricky subject, though, to capture in all its subtle shadings. The family is a complex social system, and because television cannot or will not get bogged down in the tangles of complexity, it tends to specialize in the extremes. Thus, we see TV families that are either picture-perfect or wildly dysfunctional. Whether it's the sunny surrealism of the Cleavers and the Bradys or the bawdy satire of the Bundys, television is hard pressed to show viewers a family they can truly recognize. Today's line-up of *Roseanne* (pre-lottery win), *Home Improvement*, and *Grace Under Fire*, does come closer to reality than most programming of the past, but these shows are the exceptions, not the rule. For starters, in its quest to entertain, Hollywood often fails to show the true complexities of child-parent relationships. On TV, parents remain ever open to the wisdom of their kids, and are considerably more lenient, patient, and understanding than most of us in real life. As for the kids on TV, even in critically praised shows like *Roseanne* and *Home Improvement*, the steady stream of smart-alecky remarks would earn most real-life kids a stint in time-out. Hollywood also struggles to present couples in healthy, loving marriages. Few good models exist. As media critic Jeff Greenfield notes, "Marriage on television today is a cross between a bad joke, a bad dream, and a nostalgia trip. Finding a contemporarily, happily married couple on television is like finding an empty taxi in midtown Manhattan at 5 p.m.—possible, but not very likely."[44] Tim and Jill of *Home Improvement* (appropriate for kids), Hilton and Ruth from *Cosby* (appropriate for older kids), and Paul and Jamie of *Mad About You* (not intended for kids) are among the few strong, committed, and *real* couples on television today. Few other programs capture the essential ingredients for a successful marriage—communication, compromise, forgiveness, physical affection, and humor; instead most shows either depict married couples as blandly happy or at each other's throats, divorce papers in hand. Not surprisingly, this latter scenario provides infinitely more punchlines and laughs. Moreover, it has become a springboard into a whole new subgroup of family shows.

The incidence of single parenthood via divorce (or occasionally widowhood) is one of the few areas in which television attempts to mirror family reality, though again the networks have gone overboard. Cashing in on emerging demographics, an inordinate number of family comedies now feature kids living with only one of their natural parents. The arrangement varies from Dad raising the kids (*Full House, Blossom, Me and the Boys, The Nanny*) to the more traditional (and more realistic) version of Mom taking charge (*Grace Under Fire, Murphy Brown*) to stepparents joining in (*Step by Step*). The up side of this trend is that it teaches young viewers that families come in all shapes and sizes. The drawback, however, is that most of these shows are wholly unrealistic in terms of the stresses of stepparenting and the demands of single parenting. Rarely do we see the financial worries, child care dilemmas, loneliness, and overwhelming fatigue that plague real-life single parents. Owing to television's tremendous power to influence, this simplified, optimistic view of single parenthood is a cause for concern in many circles—so much so that Murphy Brown's fictional choice of single motherhood was boosted to the level of national dialogue. To be fair, the majority of the single parent shows are comedies; as such, they do not claim to be the final voice on family life. Still, it would be refreshing to see more realism in an area that affects in complex ways ever increasing numbers of families.

Despite the shortfalls of the preceding programs, at the very least they show parents who clearly love their kids. The presence of loving, involved parents is a significant departure from many children's cartoons in which the pint-sized characters dash from one adventure to another like a merry band of orphans. Parents rarely fit into the picture, and most of the grown-ups that do appear are cast as evil nemeses or faceless killjoys. Many adult ensemble shows, especially those that revolve around the workplace, do no better in depicting individuals whose lives are integrated with those of their families. Coworkers often form a sort of 9-to-5 pseudo-family complete with nurturing mother and father figures, as well as the whole range of spoiled to responsible children. *ER* is one of the few current programs that find balance between work and family, depicting between hospital scenes the difficulty of balancing work and marriage, the embarrassment of wayward siblings, the loneliness of being single, and the troubling responsibility of caring for a sick, elderly parent.

Like the previous family-oriented shows, work-based programs form another popular television genre. Over the years we have spied on workplaces ranging from *Lou Grant* to *The Love Boat* to *Murphy Brown,* wondering perhaps why our own jobs never seem quite as fun. Despite their natural humor and drama, programs that revolve around the workplace often come up short on the reality scale. First, work on TV rarely seems as arduous or pedestrian as it often is in real life. The long-running series *LA Law* probably did more to attract students to law schools than any glossy brochure or earnest Career Day speaker ever could. And why not? The profession seemed to hold the promise of fresh fruit during morning briefings, gorgeous and witty coworkers, amusing depositions, impeccable wardrobes, and the chance to deliver stirring arguments before an oak-paneled court. While highly entertaining, the show did not deliver a realistic view of being an attorney—a job normally filled with hours of solitary writing and research, interminable negotiations, and few fireworks in the courtroom. Another problem with work on television is that it is generally confined to a few high-profile, thrill-a-minute professions. On TV there is an overabundance of police officers, detectives, doctors, and lawyers—a proportion that is completely out of line with a real world filled with factory workers, teachers, bookkeepers, office managers, and contractors. *Roc,* a since-departed series on Fox, was a terrific exception to this rule; it featured the title character as a streets and sanitation worker who went about his job responsibly and unaffectedly. In addition to overrepresenting certain professions, television boasts virtually no unemployment. While there are plenty of dramatic "You're fired!" scenes, later no one needs to line up for unemployment checks or pounds the pavement in search of another job. As for the less sensational instances of corporate downsizing and lay-offs, it appears they just don't occur in Hollywood.

If work on television doesn't always resemble the work we do in real life, at least it is acknowledged on many shows. In programs that take place in homes or other nonwork settings, the concept of work or employment is often ignored altogether. Few at-home characters discuss their work, mention the need to pay bills, or talk about financial matters in any way. It is as if all of television's middle- to upper middle-class lifestyles are subsidized by some invisible, generous hand. We rarely see the tough choices real people have to make regarding jobs, savings, insurance, education, and housing. Instead, beautiful homes and wardrobes seem to naturally fall their way, making those of us who use coupons, scrimp and save for a starter home, and buy our clothing at off-price retailers feel a bit like losers. We also rarely see evidence of the intangible benefits of hard work and discipline. In skipping over the need to work—and also the pleasure of work—television misses important opportunities to show the great personal satisfaction it can bring. This omission leaves many children believing that work is something to be endured and minimized, and that work's intrinsic value is fully subordinate to the kind of lifestyle it will buy.

Finally, in addition to slighting the realities of family and work, television also distorts issues related to health and physical well-being. Television is populated with thin, tan, fit individuals who rarely become seriously ill or injured. The most obvious complaint is that real people rarely look as stunning as those who appear on TV. It can be downright depressing to watch such relentless physical beauty until one realizes actors and actresses can combine their own good genes with implants, cosmetic surgery, flattering lighting, wardrobe consultants, and bellowing personal trainers—options not readily available or accessible to the general public. Another quibble involves the fact that TV characters' personal habits never seem to get them in trouble. Never mind that people who are as thin as those on TV often have eating disorders and that the deep tans of many light-skinned actors make them ripe candidates for skin cancer. TV characters seem impervious to the maladies that befall their real-life counterparts. For example, in many drama programs, when crises erupt (and they do with alarming frequency), fashionable characters are often seen dashing to the liquor cabinet to blunt the force of their problems. Alcohol flows bountifully on television, but few characters are depicted as struggling with alcoholism. Moreover, despite the frisky bed hopping that occurs on TV, few characters contract AIDS and other sexually transmitted diseases or find themselves facing an unplanned pregnancy.

Except for the world of soap operas in which 1 out of every 3 characters seems to be either blind, paralyzed, or suffering from amnesia, few TV characters are afflicted with any serious illness or medical problem (this in spite of the extreme levels of violence on television). One study indicated that physical injury afflicts about 8% of male characters and 7% of female characters despite the fact that 49% of TV men and 31% of TV women suffer some form of violence.[45] Those few main characters who have injuries serious enough to warrant a hospital visit nearly always make full, miraculous recoveries (except when their contracts are due to expire, in which case teary funeral scenes can be played out). The imbalance between violence and its logical consequences grows even greater when all the extras who suffer violence are considered. Wild chase scenes follow vehicles as they sideswipe and crash into nearby cars and pedestrians, but viewers never see the fallout. The action swiftly moves forward to the next scene, though in real life such an incident would leave a choppy wake of hospitalizations, insurance headaches, car repair nightmares, lawsuits, and possible deaths. Conveniently, these messy details are left out of the picture.

Perhaps in a real world filled with obesity, cancer, broken families, unemployment, alcoholism, AIDS, physical disabilities, mental illness, and gunshot wounds that kill, it is a relief to sit back and watch a semiperfect world in action. Nowhere along the way did dramatic television promise viewers logic and authenticity. And as long as viewers approach television with this caveat in mind, TV's tendency to stretch reality should not be belabored. But remembering Hollywood's fiction is easier said than done. The easy perfection of life on the small screen can be rather disillusioning to those of us with bulging waistlines, piles of bills, and children with the stomach flu. Why doesn't anyone on TV ever need to scrub the bathtub or undergo root canals? Though television's skewed reality can be annoying to adult viewers, it is especially hard on children, who with their limited world experience don't yet know that certain problems can't be solved in 30 minutes or less. Children's programming is also more cavalier in its depiction of logical consequences. Despite the repeated Bings! Bangs! and Pows!, who ever needs medical attention? Misrepresentations of physical and emotional truths may set some children up for a fall when the real world creeps in. There is shock for the child who sends his or her best friend to the emergency room after imitating a swift move from *The Mighty Morphin Power Rangers*. There is impatience and disillusionment for the kids whose minimum wage jobs seem to be getting them no closer to the high life. And there is heartache when the girl finally gives herself to her boyfriend, only to find that back-seat sex isn't as splendid as it seems on TV.

Unless they are told otherwise, children are apt to trust television as a guide for their lives. To safeguard against disillusionment and disappointment, be sure your own kids can tell the difference between the world according to Hollywood and the real world that awaits.

The Advertising Engine

Though many of us complain and object about the extraordinary level of violence, sex, and stereotyping on TV, why has there been so little change in programming? The fact is that not enough of us are complaining or objecting. If there were a dramatic, overnight change in the tastes of the viewing public, if millions of us suddenly voiced to Hollywood our opinion that *Hamlet* and oil painting shows were the cat's meow, television would undoubtedly scramble to satisfy our new desires. This giddy shift would occur because television has a higher call to answer: corporate sponsorship. And the primary concern of corporate sponsors is gaining a large viewing audience. Whether this feat is achieved by the likes of Shakespeare or Schwartzenegger is truly beside the point.

Television, like the rest of us, has an agenda. Network producers are not scrounging for storylines simply to satisfy a creative urge or to bring to the public a unique brand of enlightenment. While those elements may be part of the process, the fundamental motivation is much more basic. Simply put, the bottom line for the television industry is *the* bottom line. That is to say, money. Earnings. Profits. All of which are achieved through high ratings, which in turn secure lucrative sponsorships.

Television is a business after all. And while we tend to admire those businesses that are profitable, such respect is a bit more problematic when it comes to television. Somewhere along the line, people began expecting noble and edifying things from TV; as if by virtue of its tremendous power to inform and influence, television "owed" quality programming to its audience. While this is a good and optimistic hope, reality does not bear it out. For in order to achieve profitability—the lifeblood of any corporation—television generally sets aside good intentions and high ideals and focuses instead on capturing the biggest and broadest audience possible. Explains one TV advertiser

> Before anyone judges television, he or she must first understand that decisions in the television industry are economic decisions. The television business works on three simple principles: keep the audience up, the business costs down, and the regulators out. The reformers forget that television's first mission is not to inform, educate, or enlighten. It isn't even to entertain. Its first mission is to entice viewers to watch the commercials. If commercial television cannot move goods, it cannot be in business.[46]

There's no way around it: Commercials are a fundamental element of for-profit television. They provide the fuel and finances for elaborate sets, salaries for talent, crew, and administration, time in the editing booth, and every other aspect of television production. In turn, clever programming delivers to advertisers an affluent, ready-to-spend audience. Like the best of all symbiotic relationships, advertisers and program producers need each other to survive.

Both parties also need to maximize their limited opportunities. Television programs must often forgo subtlety and depth in order to squeeze their story into a 30- or 60-minute format. In a fight for the heavily prized audience share, networks and cable stations instead concentrate on delivering what they believe their viewers most want. This explains why television very frequently seems like an abundant smorgasbord of violence, sex, and stereotyping, for these are all features that have been successful in snagging and retaining large audiences. Despite their reliance on formula television, though, producers know that it's a fickle game, one that puts them at the mercy of ever shifting ratings shares.

If television producers must run to keep pace with changing audience tastes and whims, advertisers face an even greater challenge. While television programs ask only that viewers give up their time, commercials ask that viewers give up something much more dear: their money. In 30 seconds or less, advertisers must position themselves as friendly enlighteners, convincing the viewing audience of its absolute need to purchase *this* brand of orange juice, *that* kind of toothpaste, and the *latest* version of new and improved lemon-scented liquid laundry detergent; without them, they seem to whisper, you risk becoming a consumer misfit. To state their brief but hopefully lucrative case, advertisers rely on the tried and true strategies of humor, drama, sex appeal, guilt, excitement, prestige, celebrity, clarity, simplicity, and snazzy special effects. These are the essential advertising tools that keep television up and running.

Despite efforts at making creative, compelling TV ads (and despite the genuine effectiveness of many ads), commercials remain merely a tolerated, if not outrightly scorned part of the viewing experience. For many viewers, ads represent annoying, relentless cycles of interruption. Flashing onto the screen at the average rate of fifteen 30-second spots per half hour of television, TV ads simply become choppy punctuation between programs: a signal to reach for the remote control or make a quick trip to the fridge. With the possible exception of the commercials that debut on Super Bowl Sunday, TV ads generally are endured or avoided, but rarely enjoyed. Or are they? Ask a child and you'll probably hear a different perspective. In fact, for most children commercials represent half of the fun of television.

Advertisers know a good situation when they see one. On Saturday mornings and weekday afternoons, when kids across the nation are piled in front of the TV set, sponsors have a captive and often captivated audience. To the delight of many young viewers, colorful ads for cereals, snack foods, fast foods, toys, and clothing parade across the screen at a rate of 20 to 30 per hour. If the average viewing time is 4 to 5 hours a day, that works out to about 130 commercials daily; in 1 week the total climbs to 900, or 7.5 hours of pure commercials.[47]

To sell their wares, advertisers of children's products borrow many of the techniques and tactics used in full-length children's programs. Mini-dramas are played out in exciting but predictable form: Will the brave Crest team beat the Cavity Creeps in a fight for the dental health of Toothopolis? You bet they will, and with gleaming smiles to show for it. Short morality plays pitting Good (the advertised product) versus Evil (nonuse of the product or the use of other products) are common, with an occasional Pow! or Wham! to prove the advertised product's mettle. As for the products themselves, they invariably seem bright, exciting, engaging, yummy, and ever fun. The thrill of the product is typically reflected in the faces and actions of the commercials' young stars, who, coincidentally, nearly always appear in pairs or in groups. Indeed, acquisition of children's TV-advertised products seems to virtually guarantee popularity, if not life-long happiness.

Like ads for adults, children's ads are based on the powers of subtle manipulation. Children's ads, however, take the concept one step further: At its core, the concept of children's advertising hinges not only on manipulating kids, but also on kids' ability to manipulate their parents. Though children may not have a great deal of buying power of their own, they often accompany their mom or dad to the grocery store and the mall, whispering in their ears, tugging on their sleeves, and crying at the check-out counter. Banking on the tenacity of children and the weariness of parents (both good bets), advertisers funnel upwards of $40,000 to $60,000 per ad in the most popular Saturday morning shows. Their gambles seem to pay off. For example, one study indicated that as many as 87% of mothers surveyed indicated that they yielded to their children's cereal requests.[48] The clout of children is further revealed in a study that examined the economic impact of children's influence on household purchases. In 1992, researcher James McNeal analyzed 62 product categories ranging from athletic shoes to yogurt. Based on findings from surveys, sales figures, and market reports, McNeal estimated that children influenced a total of $131.77 billion dollars in annual sales. According to his specific findings, kids influenced $22.75 billion in fast food sales, $13.98 billion in soda sales, and $9.38 billion in toy sales. Though these industries appeared to be the big winners, even in smaller markets children's influence can be powerful. Fruit snacks represent a comparatively small $0.30 billion market; yet within that market, children influenced $0.24 billion of the spending.[49]

The rise of weekly allowances for children has also become a boon for advertisers and product manufacturers. Though parents make most family purchases, children today find that even a few wrinkled dollars and some loose coins gives them a measure of financial freedom. And when all those coins and dollars are added together, their impact in the marketplace is substantial. By the late 1980s, youth spending accounted for up to $6 billion of purchasing power in the United States. An analysis in 1989 found that kids under age 12 shelled out $2.07 billion on snacks, $1.87 billion on toys, $0.690 billion on clothes, $0.606 billion on movies and sports, and $0.486 billion on video games.[50] Children's television advertisements lead the way in convincing kids—and by extension, their parents—to part with their money.

TV's apparent impact on purchasing decisions is a marketer's dream come true—and every parent's nightmare. Each Christmas season, bleary-eyed parents line up outside stores like Toys "R" Us and Walmart in the wee hours of the chilly morning, convinced that they must get their hands on the limited supply of the year's hottest toy. To fail in this venture might mean risking their child's future happiness, social standing, and mental well-being—or so it seems at the time. Though the holiday season sparks a particularly manic form of consumerism, parents hear the plea for *this* toy or *that* cereal all year long. The urgency with which their children *must have* the product would be amusing were it not also so annoying. Commercial pitches permeate kids' lives. In response, they bring in Power Ranger lunch boxes for show and tell. They roam the house singing catchy jingles and songs from popular ads. They even put characters from the commercials themselves on their wish-lists. (Remember those wrinkly California raisins?) Reinforcing advertising's influence is the quiet, powerful force of peer pressure. The acquisition of TV-advertised products can very quickly create a kid-sized consumer caste system—if you have the hottest toy, you are in; if not, you might be out.

Many observers find it disheartening to see children's culture be so roundly shaped by the great minds of Madison Avenue (ironically, few adults see themselves as being manipulated by TV ads). But listening to a child whine about *having* to have the latest toy or doll is hardly the worst of it. Though most children's commercials seem to be just momentary annoyances, some are openly irresponsible and potentially harmful. For instance, commercials, perhaps to an even greater extent than their regular programming counterparts, are filled with gender, racial, and ethnic stereotypes.

The first rule of commercial casting seems to require the use of boys whenever possible. If advertisers are promoting a gender-neutral product like bubble gum or board games, chances are high that although girls might be present, an engaging white boy will lead the action. In a print ad promoting its services, one advertising agency spelled out this advice for winning television commercials for children: "If there is only one main character, make it a boy since boys will be accepted by both genders, but girls will only be accepted by girls."[51] Many other agencies apparently subscribe to this very same advice, for the legend of male superiority is repeated in 30-second snippets all day long. In ads for gender-specific products like action figures and dolls, the traditional roles ascribed to boys and girls are further defined. Production values aid in the distinction. Boy-directed commercials typically have more variation in scene changes and cuts, as well as more sound effects and loud music. In contrast, ads that target girls use more fades, background music, and other "soft and gentle" features.[52]

The distinctions, however, go far beyond these subtle cues. Indeed, when watching such ads, it appears that the two genders inhabit entirely different planets. The boys seen in boy-directed ads are usually sprawled on the grass or living room floor, rolling right along with their crashing, flipping, jumping, demolishing, and destroying trucks and Transformers. The boy actors are frequently aggressive and always action-oriented, accompanying their play with deeply growled "Vrroooms" and heroic cries of "Take that, you slimebucket!" In contrast to their down-in-the-dirt brothers, girls exist in a world of bright pink civility. In frilly bedrooms they quietly "ooh" and "ahh" over Barbie's sparkly glamour and Sleeping Baby's sweet gurgling sounds. Ellen Seiter, author of *Sold Separately: Children and Parents in Consumer Culture,* sees the difference this way: "Boys *become* their toys in play; girls take care of their toys."[53]

Children's commercials also do a disservice to members of racial and ethnic minorities. From the start, the problem has centered less around traditional stereotyping and more around the fundamental issue of nonrepresentation. In television's early days—the heyday of McCarthyism—there was no room or reason to cast a child who looked anything less than all-American (meaning, with some irony, kids who reflected the physical attributes of northern Europeans). The specifications for the ideal commercial child were thus determined and held firm for decades: blonde hair, blue eyes, rosy cheeks, deep dimples, and neatly pressed, coordinating clothes. Such characteristics seemed to represent wholesomeness, "Americanness," affluence, happiness, good breeding, and success—all seemingly desirable qualities. Clever advertising subtly suggested that purchase of the products such children were vending would in turn confer these sought-after traits on the consumer. In contrast, what could a dark-eyed child offer? Aside from these subtle psychological tricks, such predictable casting also made sense in a more direct way. These model children perfectly mirrored the toys they were representing—blonde, rosy-cheeked girls playing with blonde, rosy-cheeked dolls. With this ideal held up as the standard for American beauty, no wonder Barbie became a fixture in every little girl's heart and home.

It is not surprising that such a firmly rooted casting tradition took hold in the field of television advertising. Then as it is now, advertising is an industry based on the cautious art of packaging and presentation. At a time when African-Americans, Native Americans, and other minorities were still fighting for basic civil rights, advertisers hardly viewed minority children as suitable for persuading mostly white viewers to part with their hard-earned dollars. Even in the 1970s and 1980s when minority opportunity and presence expanded, the idea of changing a successful formula—however functionally outmoded and morally weak—was hard to embrace. Only in recent years have children's commercials begun to reflect the true spectrum of American children. Spurred on by the rise of political correctness and the recognition of expanding minority markets, black, Asian, Hispanic, Native American, and physically disabled kids now regularly pop up on the screen. Yet despite increased representation, there remains a hitch. In discussing the presence of black children in ads, Seiter explains

> Advertisers are interested in attracting the Black market if they can do so without offending the white one. The solution to the problem of including children of color without alienating white parents has been to express the dominance of white children nonverbally. Typically, ads reveal an implicit hierarchy of race relations. Anglos are the stars, African American children the bit players.[54]

Seiter further asserts that when black children do appear more centrally in ads, it is often in commercials that feature sport or music themes—the two traditional arenas in which white America is comfortable in seeing blacks succeed. Rarely, for example, are minority kids cast in the popular role of child genius or brainy nerd. The implicit message is that minority representation is now OK, but only on limited, carefully circumscribed terms. Perhaps just as minority representation finally increased in commercials, so too will the weight and nature of minority children's roles. Such changes come slowly, though, and while we wait, an enormous population of minority children continues to be ignored in the marketplace.

In addition to the dangers of stereotyping, there is concern over the extent of psychological manipulation to which some advertisements engage. Nintendo, for example, recently found itself in the middle of a heated controversy over its methods of persuasion. In a pending television advertisement filled with quick edits and flashing slogans, Nintendo encourages viewers to express their lurking hostility toward their parents and the world at large. Among their tidbits of advice: crank up the volume and "hock a loogie at life." Bob Garfield, a columnist for *Advertising Age,* blasts Nintendo's blatant exploitation of teenage angst and confusion:

> Pour gasoline on the fire of teenage anger. Encourage kids to be rude. Ridicule authority figures, parental and otherwise, as out-of-it decorum-obsessed dweebs. Assist young people in their often perilous search for identity by suggesting they embrace the most garish kind of self-centered nihilism. . . . What greater service can an advertiser perform, against the backdrop of teen suicide, for example, than to trumpet the meaninglessness of human existence? Bravo.[55]

Nintendo's ad is an extreme example, but many commercials follow a more benign version of the very same formula. In the world of children's television commercials, parents, teachers, and other grown-ups are often depicted as bufoonish, rigid, nerdy, and hopelessly uncool. In response, kids—both on the screen and at home in their living rooms—form a sort of wise, knowing community who must cope with the bothersome shortcomings of adult life. To the delight of young viewers, the common world order is turned upside down. As one researcher writes, "Adult order is manipulated so that what adults esteem is made to appear ridiculous; what adults despise is invested with prestige."[56] Junk food reigns and broccoli is forever banished from the land. Such an approach cleverly endows children with power—a heady sensation for a relatively powerless population. It's a smart tactic, and based on young viewers' giggles and smirks it seems to work. Few children will realize that their feelings of powerlessness and alienation are being co-opted to sell them a sugar-coated cereal.

Ironically, just as they seem to enjoy the on-air ridiculing of adults, many kids—especially older ones—are also intrigued by ads that target adults. Prompted by curiosity and perceived sophistication, a gap-toothed fourth grader may already have decided that it is preferable to drive a Mercedes over a Ford and that drinking Miller Lite appears more fun than drinking Budweiser. From adult ads young viewers learn that a pill takes away headaches and other pains, and that, given the right mouthwash, lasting love can be theirs. They see famous sports figures endorse alcohol and now-slim TV stars moonlight for weight loss systems. All of the cares and desires of the adult world become an open story during commercial breaks. Children, being children, are only too eager to peek in.

The pleasure children take in the commercial world is paralleled by the frustration it provides to concerned grown-ups. Aside from the specific issues described earlier, many parents and media watchdog groups are simply fed up with commercial television's quest to forever remind children of their wants, needs, and desires in the marketplace. Moreover, critics of children's commercials frequently argue that it is unfair to advertise to children, a population limited both in its discernment and buying power. Fortunately, some of the most blatant advertising gimmicks have been eliminated in the past few decades, largely through the work of the citizens' group Action for Children's Television (ACT). In the late 1960s, ACT petitioned both the Federal Communications Commission (FCC) and the Federal Trade Commission (FTC) to curb the "anything goes" mentality of ad-makers. ACT and other supporting groups eventually won the voluntary withdrawal of commercials for children's vitamins, the prohibition of host selling on children's programs, and a reduction in the maximum advertising time on weekend children's programming. Moreover, the National Association of Broadcasters and other industry organizations now routinely police themselves through a voluntary code. Guidelines have been established concerning the frequency and spacing of commercials, restricted product categories (no alcohol, for example), unacceptable advertising techniques, and presentation of product claims and premium offers. Despite these safeguards and the ACT victories, parents— many aggravated by repeated commercial-sparked family battles—continue to view kids' advertisements through weary eyes.

Unlike the issues involving violence, sex, and stereotyping, it is difficult to develop cogent arguments against television ads, in particular those that despite their irksome qualities are essentially fair. For one thing, commercials are the foundation upon which network children's television has been built; without the advertising revenue, children's network programming would all but disappear. Moreover, it is hard to escape the fact that America is a consumer-driven society. The range, depth, and availability of consumer goods in this country is astounding, and many consider access to these goods nearly a constitutional right. For all their annoying qualities, commercials do help keep the economy rolling along. Perhaps the problems adults have with children's commercials stem primarily from a convenient double standard. For adults to covet consumer products is an understood and generally accepted part of our culture; for children to madly desire them seems to be quite another. Yet television's insistent sales pitches fuel this very urge in all of us, spreading the message of commercialism and materialism to even the youngest in our world.

The core of our discomfort may be this: The freedom from the trappings of adulthood—material, emotional, or otherwise—is what we most admire in children. Television ads work against this natural instinct, convincing children that paper, crayons, and imagination are no match for the latest Sega Genesis cartridge.

A Closer Look at Children's Television

While a great number of children tune into adult or general programming, deep down they are probably much more interested in what has been created expressly for them. Childhood is a supremely egocentric period of life, and more than anything, kids want to find out about themselves. Television is extremely adept at plugging in to this need. As adults who occasionally tune into "kidvid," we know that shrewd program marketing and development hardly guarantees quality. In fact, many of the shows children adore are the very programs parents and critics cannot stomach, but arguing aesthetics with an enchanted 4-year-old is usually a lost cause. Regardless of perceived quality, the efforts of children's producers often pay off, and many shows develop intensely loyal followings. Young viewers forever laugh at, point at, imitate, and emulate the images and characters they see on the screen.

Children's television has a range of goals and messages. Some programs will have children believe that they all can be learners—and good ones at that. Other shows might convince them that vigilante crime-fighting is an ace idea. Still others quietly suggest that in order to be "in" you must have in your toy chest the XYZ toy based on the wildly popular XYZ show. Such disparate messages spring from disparate sources: Traditional network television and its bounty of advertisements; cable television and *its* bounty of advertisements; and public television, with relatively few advertisements. Each has its share of dedicated viewers, with many crossover viewers between them. And each sends out its own unique message to children.

Commercial television—which includes both network and cable programs —is the most pervasive of children's television entertainment. In order to better understand children's commercial television of today, it might be helpful to examine its evolution through the years.

A Short History of Children's Commercial Television

For one brief moment, children's television was golden.

The decade of the 1950s unfolded just as the incredible new television machine began mesmerizing a nation. Listening to radio shows seemed a primitive form of entertainment compared to the TV set, which blended sight and sound to produce a nearly magical experience right in one's own living room. Television was an instant hit among the middle-class masses, though the relatively steep price of a set kept the buying market small. As an inducement for young, growing, and eager-to-spend families, the nascent TV industry hit upon a capital idea: *create quality programming* to stimulate demand for TV sets. In particular, this would mean producing programs that would appeal not just to Mom and Dad, but to the little ones, too. The Baby Boomers—in diapers, in the womb, or perhaps still just twinkles in their parents' eyes—were already cultivating their prodigious marketing potential.

As a purchasing incentive, in 1950 NBC delighted both children and adults with high-quality prime-time shows like *Howdy Doody* and *Kukla, Fran, and Ollie*. This positive trend continued in 1951 when the four networks (ABC, NBC, CBS, and the now defunct DuMont) were offering over 27 hours of children's programming weekly, primarily at the hours when children would likely be watching—weekday evenings between 6 and 8 p.m.[57] It would seem that children were the apple of the networks' eye.

Targeting the child and family market was a viable and successful strategy, but not an enduring one. The tactic seemed to work too well for its own good. In a few short years the television set market had been saturated; suddenly there was no need to court youngsters and the image of family togetherness. Moreover, the age of network sponsorship had arrived, and children—with no perceived buying power at the time—did little to whet advertisers' appetites. On the other hand, dollar signs sprang up before their eyes when they considered the lucrative adult market, and the coveted prime-time slots were quickly filled for their viewing pleasure. Kids' programs were now low on the priority list and were relegated to the unused attic of network programming—early weekday mornings and afternoons.

Largely sparked by renewed sponsor interest, there was a brief resurgence in children's programming when ABC's wildly popular *Disneyland* (later known as *The Mickey Mouse Club*) hit the airwaves at 5 p.m. daily in 1955. Not to be outdone, this success prompted rival networks to quickly produce their own late afternoon kid shows including *Captain Kangaroo* and *Ding Dong School*. The advertising potential of such shows was great, and in 1956 the networks were offering up to 37 hours of children's television weekly, though nearly all took place during morning and afternoon time periods.[58] In terms of quality programs for kids, it was a banner year that would never be repeated.

The demographic truths of television had been learned in short order. The prime-time adult market corralled far more viewers than any other slot; this is where the fickle advertisers wanted to concentrate their money and creative energy. In response, the networks dumped the now undesirable 4 to 7 p.m. slots—the prime children's viewing hours. The "classics" of children's television—*The Mickey Mouse Club, Howdy Doody,* and *Kukla, Fran, and Ollie*—were now considered network television history.

Children's programming was not abandoned entirely, however. The networks left the afternoon slots in the hands of the local affiliate stations, who in turn made the proverbial lemonade out of lemons. Two powerful trends worked in their favor. The first came in the form of an ambitious pair of animators, William Hanna and Joseph Barbera, who together helped introduce the idea of economical animation. At the same time, advertisers were finding that local spot-buying was an extremely efficient way to advertise children's products like toys, especially when a popular local figure, or host, was used both to introduce the program and to sell the advertisers' products. The child market officially had been discovered. Advertising and animation forged a partnership when in 1958 Hanna-Barbera sold the rights to their first made-for-TV series to Kellogg. Meanwhile, by 1965 children's programming had found a third and very profitable home on Saturday mornings, a previously unmined time slot. There seemed to be winners all around, except, perhaps for the children themselves.

While members of the industry were obsessing about ad revenue, ratings, and enviable time slots, practically no one was discussing the ethereal and seemingly irrelevant issue of quality. In a few short years, network children's television had become a mecca for all that was violent, stereotypical, and exploitative. By 1961 both Congress and the FCC were calling the industry to task. Senate hearings on TV violence were orchestrated while the FCC chairman Newton Minow very publicly denounced TV as "a vast wasteland."[59] Though token efforts at improvement were made, no real or lasting progress was seen. In response to the industry-wide business-as-usual attitude, the advocacy group Action for Children's Television (ACT) was organized in Boston in 1968 for the express purpose of cleaning up children's programming. Its continued pressure on the FCC resulted in a landmark 1974 FCC ruling to the television industry: "Start regulating yourselves or we will do it for you." The impressive bark proved to have little bite. Though the combined work of ACT and the FCC eliminated some of the most outrageous transgressions of children's television (host selling, vitamin sales, extreme violence, and reduction in weekend morning advertising time), children's commercial television remained a thin, but effective vehicle for sales.

Despite renewed effort in 1990 that crafted and passed the Children's Television Act legislating higher quality and expanded air time for children's television, not a great deal has changed since the mid-1970s as far as children's network programming is concerned. Today the offerings for edifying children's television remain limited. They are first limited in a literal sense. While kid's programming previously had the advantage of being viewed on weekday mornings and afternoons as well as Saturday mornings, today the options are generally confined to a further-reduced Saturday morning schedule. In the late 1970s advertisers discovered the profitable "housewife" market and began peddling laundry detergent, pain reliever, and feminine products on weekday afternoons; as a result, soap operas and tabloid talk shows now reign. Meanwhile, morning kidvid has been bumped for more news programs. Indeed, it seemed the end of an era when CBS replaced the beloved *Captain Kangaroo* with an expanded version of the *CBS Morning News*. Though the Children's Television Act of 1990 stipulated that more air time be given to educational programs, 2 years later a media watchdog group discovered many stations throughout the country were airing their so-called "educational" shows after 10 p.m., long after children have been sent to bed. The upstart, youth-oriented Fox and WB are now alone among the networks in their active daytime courting of the child audience. As for the traditional "family hour," nearly every network has whittled it away to practically nothing. The weekday 7 p.m. time slot that once featured programs like *The Cosby Show* and *Family Ties* now offers shows populated with hip, urban, sexually active twenty and thirtysomethings. This shift can be explained almost entirely in terms of marketing and economics. The demise of ABC's *Full House* offers a case in point. For the 1994-1995 season, the family-friendly *Full House* aired opposite *Wings,* an NBC adult comedy series that manages to pack sexual innuendo into nearly every joke. Though the shows ranked closely in overall household ratings (*Full House* placed 24th and *Wings* placed 30th), among the coveted 18- to 49-year-old audience *Wings* was in 24th place and *Full House* was a weak 57th.[60] For the 1995-1996 season, *Full House* and its follow-up act *Me and the Boys* were canceled, replaced by sure-fire ratings winner *Roseanne* and a new adult-oriented comedy *Hudson Street.* Hollywood executives often gloss over this economic angle, defending such changes by reverently discussing virtues like "honesty," and "maturity." Says one CBS producer:

> The biggest problem in Hollywood is that we can be very removed. I've got a lot of family in Minnesota, in Florida, Chicago, throughout the country. And when I go out there, I try to assess what life is really like. Life is tougher, and kids grow up faster. And I'm afraid if we don't do shows that are real, then people find that it's just a bunch of pap that they can't relate to.[61]

Film critic Michael Medved disagrees:

> This is a very varied country. And not all young people are hip, sophisticated, jaded punks, thank God. There are far more youths involved in church and synagogue groups than in any gay or lesbian or sexual freedom organization. The idea of the "family hour" was that you show some re-

straint because you're dealing with a big national medium that goes into everyone's home. So you don't aim programming at the most experienced or "worldly" of kids.[62]

In addition to being confined by the clock, network children's television also remains limited in content, again largely due to the emphasis on ad revenue. Racial, ethnic, and gender-based stereotypes and omissions still run rampant. Traits like sassiness, physical strength, and macho bravery are celebrated while prosocial and intelligence values are often ignored. Boys remain the chief audience targets, violence the chief bait. *TV Guide* describes the recent crop of action cartoons:

> Psychological nuances seem to be the very last thing on the minds behind Fox's *X-Men*, CBS's *WILDC.A.T.S.* and *Skeletal Warriors*, and the syndicated *Marvel Action Hour*. Look at these shows and you come away with a buzzing head and a general impression of bad animation and menacing, interchangeable, steroid-pumped characters, zooming around futuristic cityscapes on rocket sleds, duking it out in martial-arts combat, and zapping each other with ray guns.[63]

It would be unfair and inaccurate to label all network efforts as mindless garbage. Some of television's finest moments have come from the networks. While most fall into the "family viewing" category, there are a number of shows and TV movies from the past and present that could positively influence the lives of children from all backgrounds. Among the standouts are *Roots, Little House on the Prairie, The Waltons, Brooklyn Bridge, Life Goes On, I'll Fly Away, The Wonder Years, Christy, My So-Called Life, Party of Five, Home Improvement, Gulliver's Travels,* and any number of the Hallmark Hall of Fame TV movies (for example, *O Pioneer, Sarah Plain and Tall,* and *The Piano Lesson).* These programs— some ratings successes and some not—thoughtfully show life in all of its rich, painful, and joyful forms. A few shows created expressly for children, including *Brand Spanking New Doug* (ABC), *Cro* (ABC), *Reboot* (ABC), *Name Your Adventure* (NBC), *Beakman's World* (CBS), *Bill Nye the Science Guy* (syndicated), *Steven Spielberg Presents Animaniacs* (Kids WB!), and *Bobby's World* (Fox), also land on critics' praise lists. The occasional after school specials that ABC and CBS air (*ABC After School Specials* and *CBS School Break Specials*) also offer poignant and compelling programs that speak to children and adolescents about the real issues in their lives. Finally, there has been an encouraging trend in opening "adult" topics up to children in the form of news specials. ABC's Peter Jennings has been particularly adept at letting the wise voices of children be heard on issues ranging from racism to the environment. He treats young people with respect and intelligence, a novel concept in the world of network children's programming.

No discussion of commercial television would be complete without a few words about cable TV. In many ways, cable TV is like network TV exploded into millions of tiny pieces. Like its network counterpart, cable TV relies heavily on advertising revenue, similarly making it a buyers' (make that "advertisers' ") market. Not only are traditional commercials aired, but cable also specializes in the now omnipresent infomercial, those 30-minute ads complete with a recognizable cast (actors and actresses lately down on their luck), a vexing problem (knives that just won't cut), and a climactic solution (cutlery that is "revolutionary!" and "one-of-a-kind!" but "not available in stores!"). In addition to experiencing the pleasures of so-called paid programming, subscribers to cable TV pay each month for their choice of stations, a major contrast to traditional network television. Perhaps a more significant difference is that cable TV works through wires not airwaves, and therefore is not limited to the networks' few available frequencies. As a result, it offers an unbelievable spectrum of channels and programs ranging from the venerable HBO to local stations featuring fly fishing and lessons in needlework. There seems to be something for everyone, children included.

Entire cable stations like the Disney Channel, the Family Channel, Nickelodeon, and the Cartoon Network are now devoted to children's and family programming 'round the clock. Many of these channels trace their short history to days when their line-ups primarily featured old programs still living in syndication, encouraging a whole new generation to make acquaintance with the likes of *Flipper* and *Lassie*. Now most make their mark by being the primary repository of original, often quite innovative programming including animated shows, quiz shows, game shows, educational shows, and movies. In theory such expanded offerings may or may not translate into improved programming, but the early signs are promising. Child-oriented cable channels are gaining in popularity not only by offering a full daily line-up of kid shows, but more importantly by paying attention to quality and innovation. Some programs are truly worth checking out. *Eureeka's Castle* (Nickelodeon), *Clarissa Explains It All* (Nickelodeon), *Rugrats* (Nickelodeon), *Allegra's Window* (Nickelodeon), *Madeline* (the Family Channel), *Gullah Gullah Island*

(Nickelodeon), *The Secret World of Alex Mack* (Nickelodeon), *Avonlea* (The Disney Channel), *Big Bag* (the Cartoon Network), and *Blue's Clues* (Nickelodeon) are all frequently cited for their quality and prosocial messages.

The success of child-oriented cable channels could teach the broadcast networks a lesson or two about kids' programming. Indeed, their formula seems to work as youngsters are now flocking in droves to the higher numbers on the channel spectrum. In the summer of 1996, for example, Nickelodeon attracted more children to its Saturday morning line-up than any of the broadcast networks did, even though Nickelodeon is available in only about 70% of American homes. Moreover, beginning in the fall 1996-1997 season, Nickelodeon took a stand to recapture the "family hour," offering kid-friendly shows at 7 p.m. Central Time every night. As reported early in the season, for the first 2 weeks, at least, those shows drew more children under the age of 12 than any broadcast network's seven o'clock show four nights a week.[64]

The traditional networks tend to view this development with a combination of resentment and resignation. They argue that it is impossible to compete with channels that offer 'round-the-clock kids' programming. Not only does this nonstop scheduling mean that kids can fall into the easy habit of immediately flipping on Nickelodeon or the Cartoon Network and know that a show created expressly for them will appear, but it also allows for nonstop promotion of their shows. The networks claim they cannot compete in either of these arenas. True enough, but they also continue to shoot themselves in the foot by offering a great deal of lame or inappropriate programming as competition. Soon, however, they will be forced to up the ante. In 1996 the federal government issued a call for Round Two in the children's educational television skirmish. The previously mentioned Children's Television Act of 1990 requested that broadcast stations increase quality and air time for children's television. It was not a true mandate, however, and, as noted, few stations took steps to voluntarily comply. In the fall of 1996 the Federal Communications Commission (FCC) went back to the drawing board and negotiated a stricter deal with the television industry. This time around, the FCC is *requiring* stations to air 3 hours of educational programming a week. In an effort to close sneaky loopholes, they also are tightening the definitions for educational programming and requiring that the shows be broadcast between 7 a.m. and 10 p.m. Central Time.

Though not every show on the child-oriented cable channels is top-notch in quality, positive programming efforts in recent years have challenged the conventional "poor me" network stance of throwing up its hands in a show of exasperated defeat, claiming that commercial television for children cannot be entertaining, edifying, and profitable at the same time. Indeed, it can. Keep an eye on the broadcast networks to see if, in working to fulfill the government's new mandate, they can eventually strike a similarly winning combination.

Public Television and Its Vision for Children

If network television exists primarily to serve advertisers, and cable television exists only for those who pay for it, public television is an oasis of quality television free for the viewing. For the uninitiated, public television (PTV) seems to offer only obscure documentaries on African beetles and travelogues to places they'd rather not go. For those who know better, however, public television offers intelligent, thoughtful, and entertaining fare for its viewers. And among the greatest beneficiaries of PTV's vision are children.

Public television is the uncontested home of quality children's broadcasting. The primary mission of PTV is to serve the viewer's interest, and its philosophy is reflected in its programming. As a result, parents normally leery of television's negative impact feel little guilt when their children watch the "good," "safe," and "educational" shows on their local public station. Over the years, PTV has built a great reserve of trust among parents, educators, and mental health professionals by offering timeless classics like *Sesame Street, Mr. Rogers' Neighborhood, Lamb Chop's Play-Along, Reading Rainbow,* and *Where in the World Is Carmen Sandiego?* These shows expand children's minds and imaginations with grace, humor, and gentleness.

Not only do such programs often represent a child's first immersion in "language studies," but many also serve as a child's most expansive window to the world beyond their neighborhood. Wonderful discoveries can be made right in their own living room. Suburban and rural kids see the frenetic pace of city streets, while urban kids watch, perhaps for the first and only time, a cow being milked. Moreover, many children's programs, either explicitly or implicitly, teach fundamental prosocial values like sharing, helping, tolerance, and racial and cultural diversity. For all of the nauseating sweetness of *Barney & Friends,* delirious parents can hardly disparage the simple, affirming messages that Barney sends to young children.

Public television's positive influence on children might best be seen in the case of *Sesame Street,* a show that now reaches nearly 6 million children between 2 and 5 years. Conceived in 1968 by the Children's Television Workshop (CTW), the goals of *Sesame Street* were purely educational. At the time, the deficiencies of America's educational system were being hotly debated in the public arena; at the same time, Lyndon Johnson's Great Society was recognizing the enormous educational disadvantages wrought by poverty. *Sesame Street* set out to address these two related problems by providing a sturdy bridge for low-income kids as they prepared to enter school. Edward L. Palmer, a founding member of CTW, explains the vision:

> A children's television series, broadcast nationwide, could reach children not privileged to be sparked to learning through other experiences. It had to appeal to all children, or it would not survive. But for children of low-income circumstances, it would be special—it would provide a conceptually and verbally rich learning experience, and important early exposure to school-related skills, all of which, we know, are less available to them in their homes than to their middle-class peers in theirs.[65]

Thus *Sesame Street* was born, and it has charmed children of all incomes and backgrounds for now over 25 years. *Sesame Street,* though, is just one of many public television offerings for children. Different shows are valuable for different goals. For example, *The Puzzle Place* emphasizes cultural diversity, *Katie and Orbie* removes the fear and dread of first-time experiences, and *Mr. Rogers' Neighborhood* offers gentle lessons on what the real world is all about. Though preschoolers represent PBS's most dedicated audience, there are a number of terrific shows targeted at kids as they grow older. *Reading Rainbow* introduces children to the world of literature, *Wishbone* the dog leads kids through the classics, *Where in the World Is Carmen Sandiego?* teaches geography in game show format, *Ghostwriter* hooks readers and spellers with clever mystery clues, and *The Magic School Bus* follows Ms. Fizzle, her class, and their big yellow bus as they embark on wild rides through the world of science.

Optimists will argue that for all of television's negative influencing power, such programs demonstrate that the medium can also work to society's benefit if the positive elements are harnessed. This is fortunate. Less fortunate is the fact that the onus of reaching television's potential is too often laid exclusively at the feet of public television, which itself comes with a few built-in limitations. Most important is the issue of limited funding. While grants and public funds have never flowed abundantly, today they are more scarce than ever. Operating on shoestring budgets, the expansion of children's broadcasting on PTV is held in check; as a result, it relies heavily on the use of reruns. In fact, the last 8 years of CTW's *The Electric Company* was entirely based on reruns. The financial situation looks to become even more strained in the future. At the time of this book's printing, the Corporation for Public Broadcasting was at the top of a list of federal government budget cuts. Though such a symbolically lamentable act will probably not lead to the full demise of PBS, it will severely limit its ability to reach children and adults alike with the best that television has to offer.

The other problem with public television involves the very quality we laud. In their search for decent programs, parents are frequently encouraged to turn on PBS for the young viewers in their household. This sound advice can backfire, though, when the consistently high caliber of its programming deludes even the most well-meaning parent into thinking that his or her child's intellectual and sensory needs are being wholly met through television. Quality aside, television should never—and can never—be substituted for real-world experience.

Summary

In 1994 the FCC debate over the lack of educational programming for children began anew. The deliberations came to an amusing head when certain broadcasters—in all sincerity—offered *The Jetsons, Donahue,* and *The Flintstones* as examples of educational shows. Though television executives were making a clumsy effort to demonstrate their FCC compliance, along the way they did make one valid, important, and unintended point: *All* television is educational. From lessons on the alphabet to views of the seamy, steamy side of life, children quietly watch and learn. Unfortunately, the great bulk of programming is seeped in stereotyping, violence, sex, and commercialism, and children who frequently tune in to such messages can be expected to master their lessons. On the other hand, television also offers some (but not enough) quality programming for children and families that packs positive messages and fun challenges for learning. No doubt, children can learn these lessons as well. What lessons are your children learning from television? What do you want them to be learning?

Typical parents rue television's flaws and applaud its achievements, all the while wondering how their children are being influenced by its content. By and large, scientific study shows television to be a powerful influence on children, capable of shaping both attitudes and actions. But how do children actually process TV? Do they really understand all that they watch? For some answers, turn to Chapter 2.

• 2 •
A Child's View of Television

A child's mind is a befuddling, charming, often exasperating puzzle. Rarely do the pieces fit together as we expect, or perhaps even as we hope. Accustomed to adult ways and habits, we grown-ups frequently expect children to act just like us. We then are thrown for a loop when our child, lacking any sense of decorum or propriety, suddenly throws a full-scale fit in the cereal aisle. The child thinks not of our embarrassment or the law of limited resources, but only of his or her immediate and desperate need of Fruity Pebbles. If only children could understand life from our perspective! On the other hand, that same child sees the world and its inhabitants with amazing clarity and openness, unencumbered by the prejudices and fears that cloud our more mature views. If only we could understand life from a child's perspective!

Indeed, the mind (and heart) of a child is fundamentally different from the mind of an adult. Though for centuries children were seen as merely smaller and slightly less capable versions of adults, over time we have learned that they form a unique population. In contrast to adults, children think more concretely, express themselves more fully, hope more wildly, and find joy more readily. Children simply view life from a different set of eyes.

A child's eyes are different in both a literal and figurative sense. From a physical standpoint, their lack of height keeps their eyes low, making everything loom tall and large, slightly askew, and frequently scary. On the other hand, being close to the ground allows them to spy wonderful things like ladybugs and lost coins, treasures that "taller" eyes easily miss. A child's special view offers more than a physical distinction, however. It is his or her "inner" eye—that mysterious connection between the brain, the heart, and the imagination—that truly makes the view unique. Through this eye, ordinary things take on extraordinary meanings. While we see our homely family dog, they see a wise and loyal friend. While we see a serving of spinach, they see torture on a plate. And while we see fluffy clouds, they see art spreading across the sky.

A Special View of Television

Of course, children also see and understand television differently.

At first glance, this fact may not seem particularly obvious. After all, in watching the same program, are we all not seeing the same sights and hearing the same sounds? On the surface, television appears to be a communal experience, providing binding conversation on the playground, at the office, in the car, and at the dinner table. There is in fact a peculiar sense of community and kinship when a group of people—either together in a room or scattered throughout the country—tune into the same program. But in watching the same show, does everyone—child and adult—see exactly the same thing?

Though it may seem that the whole gang is gathered 'round watching the same program together, each viewer, regardless of age, sees and remembers something slightly different depending on his or her experiences, knowledge, mood, level of attention, and a number of other variables. Think of Super Bowl Sunday, typically one of the most-watched TV events of the year. Every January people across the nation gather for an evening of nachos, pretzels, popcorn, and football. Yet, at the very same Super Bowl party, with all eyes turned toward the TV set, different people will see different things. One ardent football fan might intently watch the moves of a particular player, while another carefully studies a team's strategy, yelling at the screen when things do not go according to plan. Those not closely familiar with the rules of the game might just loosely follow their team of choice, cheering on cue when their team scores a touchdown. And then there is the group who simply tunes in for the creative commercials. Though at the end of the game everyone might accurately report the final score, getting there was a unique experience for each person involved.

If adults who watch the same program have different experiences, imagine what happens when children tune in. With children, the variations in what is seen, perceived, and remembered about a particular television program are far more pronounced. Though two adults in a room will generally agree on a program's theme and plot line, the toddler watching alongside will probably "see" something different altogether. For example, whereas Mom and Dad recall watching a funny sitcom about family life, their 3-year-old child talks only of the canine star of a dog food commercial that happened to look like the family's own furry friend. So much for communal experiences.

When it comes to watching television, children form their own special audience. In her 1986 book *Children and Television: A Special Medium for a Special Audience,* communications and education scholar Aimée Dorr describes three cognitive and psychosocial factors that make the child viewer unique: (a) an incomplete world knowledge; (b) an eagerness to learn; and (c) different, or limited, approaches to learning. Each of these characteristics has implications for a child's comprehension of television.[1]

A child's world knowledge, while ever expanding and evolving, is limited. Part of growing older is accumulating ever more information about the world, its inhabitants, its social, cultural, physical, and spiritual properties, its history, and its potential. When a person is young, there are a number of major gaps in this picture. Though schools and family life recognize and even embrace a child's limited knowledge, television cannot always be so flexible. With the exception of children's programming, much of television is created for a relatively experienced audience; as such, there is little need for television to "explain itself" to viewers who presumably are savvy enough to catch on. The reality is that not all of television's viewers are savvy or informed. Children, in particular, have not had the experiences or the education necessary to make them enlightened viewers. This viewing handicap can have a number of potential consequences. First, children may fail to understand or misunderstand program content if they lack the essential background knowledge. Second, they may accept program content as accurate "information" when more knowledgeable viewers know it to be otherwise. And third, kids may evaluate content without considering the means and motives for producing and broadcasting that content.[2]

Like their level of world knowledge, children's capacities for cognitive tasks are also limited. Though kids seem to make daily gains in their cognitive abilities, certain mental tasks pose difficulties at certain stages of development. Very young children, for example, struggle with verbal skills and language development. Once over that hurdle, it still takes a number of years to understand logical thinking concepts like classification, conversion, and reciprocity. And when older still, children continue to be challenged by the demands of abstract thought.

Meanwhile, kids of all ages have limited long-term memory capabilities and fairly short attention spans. As we'll see later in the chapter, each of these cognitive challenges influences how a child attends to, comprehends, and retains what is seen on television.

Finally, though children may have an incomplete world knowledge and limited cognitive abilities, they are ever eager to expand in both areas. Children put adults to shame with their thirst and enthusiasm for learning. As adults, we tend to take television's constant barrage of information for granted; after a while, we start tuning it out. Children, on the other hand, are eager to soak it all up. Kids love to learn, and by watching television they see how the world—at least Hollywood's version of it—works. Depending on the circumstances, this eagerness for learning via TV can be beneficial or detrimental. As discussed in Chapter 1, *all* television—the good and the bad—is educational. Since kids don't always have the skill or interest in making discriminations in quality or suitability, it is often up to parents and other adults to run interference. When an adult is in the room watching alongside the child, for example, confusing ideas and images can be readily addressed. Anyone who has watched television with a child knows that actual viewing is largely supplanted by a lengthy question and answer session. Though some questions can be a little tricky ("Why is that man lying on that woman?"), lucky is the child who has an adult nearby to give a responsible answer. Those children left to their own devices may have a hard time reconciling what they see on the small screen and what is expected or true in real life.

Through their incomplete world knowledge, limited cognitive abilities, and eagerness for learning, children experience television in a unique way. As adults—parents, educators, and counselors alike—it is essential that we understand this relationship between children and television before we rush to alter it. Few people would attempt the dreaded task of programming a new VCR without consulting a manual for guidance. How much more complex are our children!

A Child's Involvement With Television: Passive or Active?

One of the most heavily debated issues in the field of children's television viewing involves the opposing notions of activity and passivity. Both the lay and scientific communities have been at odds over the level and quality of children's involvement with television: Some sources say the experience of viewing television is active and involving, while others claim it is passive and reactive. This debate may be of particular interest to parents who lament the hours their children spend glued to the television set. And "glued" does seem to be the appropriate word for some young viewers. With their eyes glazed, jaws slack, and bodies hunched over, many kids seem to be stuck in a zombie-like TV trance. No amount of cajoling, tap-dancing, or arm-waving can sway their attention. It is as though television has literally zapped the life out of some children, feeding their unguarded brains the secrets of the TV world. Fact or melodrama?

Passive Kids?

According to much popular literature, this preceding scene is not far from truth. Many prominent voices in the field say that viewing television is indeed a passive, reactive experience in which the transfer of information is a one-way street. In her well-known book *The Plug-In Drug,* author Marie Winn writes, "There is, indeed, no other experience in a child's life that requires so much intake while demanding so little outflow."[3] Jerry Mander echoes Winn's theme in his book *Four Arguments for the Elimination of Television*: "In the end, the viewer is little more than a vessel of reception, and television itself is less a communications or educational medium, as we have wished to think of it, than an instrument that plants images in the unconscious realms of the mind."[4]

Such arguments reside not only in the often conjectural realm of popular culture; the scientific community offers plenty of its own support. The passive-reactive theory has attracted the support of numerous researchers, including the pioneering violence researcher Albert Bandura. Over the years it has become a subtle guiding principle in much of the scientific discussion. One of the most influential proponents of the passive theory is social scientist Jerome Singer. In a 1980 study on television's effects on cognition, he concluded that television's "powerful appeal" occurs because the "constant movement and pattern of change that characterizes the screen produces a continuous series of reflexes in us, and it is hard to habituate to the set."[5] In other words, TV's sophisticated movement—cuts, zooms, and pans—combined with its brilliant colors, sound effects, and sharp graphics, holds our attention without our even thinking about it. We simply *react* to its mesmerizing quality. Singer believes that children, who typically lack knowledgeable experience in television, are particularly vulnerable to TV's command of visual attention.

From a lay perspective, television viewing certainly seems like a passive experience. Little conscious mental energy is involved, and the brain always seems a bit sluggish after hours of viewing. In time, the inactive experience of television watching seems to create a dependence of sorts—the longer we watch, the more tempted we are to sit still and continue watching. Surely we have all found ourselves viewing programs that are either uninteresting or just plain awful; yet, even after asking, "Why am I watching this?" our inertia keeps us glued to the couch. (Television executives count on this passivity, hoping that after watching a favorite program viewers will stick around to see the rest of the station's offerings for that evening.) Furthermore, compared to activities like soccer or playing the flute, watching TV *is* passive and reactive. The extent of our physical movement is simply a deft click of the remote control. We otherwise sit still, quietly watching action on the screen rather than participating in it ourselves.

Active Minds?

Despite what both science and common sense seem to tell us, recent research has challenged traditional notions of passivity. A number of respected researchers now take the opposite view: that television viewing is actually an *active, two-way transaction.* As one research team put it, "It is the children who are most active in this relationship. It is they who use television, rather than television that uses them."[6] In this view, a young child who earlier in the day was fascinated by a cartoon show will not stare indiscriminately as stock market reports jump across the screen a few hours later; variables other than exciting movement are at work. Furthermore, according to the active theory, children typically do not gaze at the screen for hours on end; rather, most children look away frequently, perhaps turning to a toy while TV provides the background noise. The underlying assumption is that children actively control the viewing experience.

The active theory may be a more difficult notion to accept because much of the active response goes unseen, occurring in the invisible canyons of a child's brain. Many of our notions of passivity come from direct observation—a child staring blankly at the TV set hour after hour does seem to indicate a decided lack of mental effort. Yet, despite appearances, a great deal of activity in the form of information processing occurs while children watch television. With a screen filled with more sights and sounds than they can ever possibly attend to, children must decide which ones are important and which ones are forgettable.

They must then successfully decipher the information on which they have chosen to focus. Finally, they must choose which information to store in long-term memory.

According to the active theory, to make such decisions a child continuously constructs meaning based on his or her own set of experiences, motivations, cognitive abilities, and knowledge structures, or schemas. Without giving it much conscious thought, a child applies these elements to the television program at hand as a guide for attention, comprehension, and retention. Researchers Daniel Anderson and Elizabeth Lorch became convinced of the child's active role as they studied children's visual attention to television. In explaining the theory, they write

> The active theory puts control of viewing directly with the viewer rather than with the television set. The viewer does not simply respond reflexively to inherently meaningless salient features of the medium. Rather, based on his or her experience with the medium, familiarity with the specific program, level of cognitive development, and general world knowledge, the viewer applies viewing strategies more or less appropriate to the program and the viewing environment. Variations in visual attention to the television are thus seen as having a rational basis and represent an ongoing interaction between the unfolding conceptual content of the program and the viewer's understanding of that content.[7]

Though the active theory has been popularized in recent years, not everyone is ready to adopt it wholesale. Researcher Cedric Cullingford instead charts a middle course, subscribing to the practical elements of both the active theory and the passive theory. In his 1984 book *Children and Television,* he writes

> It cannot be assumed that children are constant in their attention or that they will make continual discriminations between the important and the unimportant, between the main message and the peripheral information.... Children find the idea of paying close attention to a situation comedy, or thriller, or a cartoon, absurd.
> Children's expectations of television mean that they adapt to what is offered; they do not only reflect what is

offered. [For example] they do not automatically attune themselves to the news because it demands more cerebral attention.[8]

Cullingford does believe that the formal features of television (the sights and sounds) are capable of maintaining a child's attention. On the other hand, he believes also that children are capable of exerting tremendous powers of concentration. Regardless of how attention is achieved, he holds that much of what children see on television passes them by; they simply do not catch it all, nor do they care to. Perhaps the most significant finding of Cullingford's research is that children, as a function of watching television, often seek out the *most* entertaining stimuli that demand the *least* amount of attention and reliance upon memory. Before any sense of reproach sets in, we should note that many of us grown-ups tend to rely on this very same standard.

While Cullingford's middling sensibility strikes a chord of assurance in many lay minds, it hardly puts an end to the argument. In fact, the debate seems destined to continue, as each position is founded in truth. While "TV trances" make for catchy rhetoric, perhaps we should give children a little more cognitive credit than it seems they have received. Children's television viewing can require a fairly high degree of brain activity; moreover, it is widely accepted that children actively construct their own meaning for what they see on television. On the other hand, is the existence of an active, complex, and highly individualized information processing system enough to say that television viewing is an active experience? Active compared with what? Most people consider watching television on par with resting or doing nothing. Indeed, while viewing we usually just sit and stare as television delivers its easy, instant entertainment through a flat glass screen. Though the attentional and cognitive elements of the passive theory may be losing ground in scientific community, its broader message seems to ring true.

Evaluating these divergent opinions may seem like a difficult task. For nonexperts, it is often hard to know whom or what to believe. Though scientific research has an important place in this debate, there is also room for everyday common sense. And in this case, the most common sensical questions include the following: How do my own children react to television? Are they passively "glued" to the small screen no matter what's on? Do they selectively choose what to watch and remain conversational and "loose" while viewing? Are they somewhere in the middle? Don't be surprised if the answer is different for each of your children. One family we know has three children with three very different approaches to television: Mark, the oldest at age 8, watches TV sometimes with full attention, sometimes not; it always depends on if something more appealing like a book or a game is competing for his attention. When he does watch, he makes chatty comments about the content, playing the role of the knowledgeable big brother. Ally, the youngest at age 4, is much more interested in repeatedly trying on every dress and ribbon in her closet than in sitting still for most TV shows; watching television is too sedate an activity for this whirl of pink and purple. Five-year-old Brandon presents a different story altogether. An imaginative, observant, and fairly passive child, Brandon seems powerfully attracted to those same qualities in television. When the TV comes on, everything else in his world turns off. His eyes grow like wide, unblinking blue saucers and his mouth forms a small, slack "O." As his mother says, the house could crumble around him and he'd still be sitting, chin in his hands, staring straight ahead at the TV set.

Three kids, three approaches to television. As is often the case in life, one size *doesn't* fit all. Similarly, one television-related theory rarely embraces all children. So use both your common sense and your understanding of the habits and peculiarities of your individual children. In child-centered debates like these, this is often the smartest course of all.

A Child's Understanding of Television: Attention and Comprehension

As adults, we often take television's "tricks of the trade" for granted. Without much thought, we can follow a given show's time sequence, understanding that "TV time" jumps from the past to the present to the future to the past again with little regard to the rules and conventions of linear time. We recognize that hazy, fuzzy scenes signal dream sequences and that commercials—however entertaining—are not part of the program. We also know that news events are real and that most other TV shows are not. Children, however, do not have the benefit of either our experience with television or our more developed cognitive abilities. As a result, their comprehension of television is often significantly compromised.

A child's comprehension of television is closely related to his or her age and experience. In fact, there is no better predictor of TV comprehension than a child's age and his or her corresponding cognitive abilities. To organize our discussion of comprehension, we'll start by looking at two distinct age groups: preschoolers (roughly ages 2 to 6) and school-aged children (6 to 12). Such categorization reflects the natural age break when many kids make major gains in television comprehension. It is important to note that we are generalizing here. There is a great deal of cognitive diversity within these subgroups, and rules of age are not hard and fast. A child's cognitive growth is instead dynamic and fluid, rarely bound by the strict dictates of a 12-month cycle.

Comprehension for the Preschool Set

Without having school or daycare to fill their time, preschoolers who remain at home during the day represent one of television's largest audiences. They are also among the least prepared and least knowledgeable of television's audiences, making coherent viewing something of a challenge. In examining their level of understanding, Jean Piaget's cognitive development theory serves as a useful model. Though Piaget's famous stages are no longer the sole model for cognitive development, his work gives us a helpful frame in discussing comprehension.

According to Piaget, there are four stages of cognitive development: sensorimotor (birth to 2 years); preoperational (children age 2 to 6); concrete operational (children ages 7 to 11); and formal operational (adolescents on up). Television powerfully attracts viewers from all of these stages. Even newborns—who in the sensorimotor stage are highly stimulated by their senses—can be seen attending to television's strange sounds and swirling colors and shapes. Though many babies do *seem* to be watching TV, true, purposeful viewing does not usually begin until a child enters the preoperational stage around the age of 2.

For many years it was believed that preschoolers understood very little of what they see on that small glowing screen. Despite hours in front of the TV set, it appeared that they carried away only a superficial and fragmented understanding of television's electronic action. Recent research has been more positive, indicating, for example, that children as young as 3 or 4 understand many of television's formal features like zooms, pans, cuts, and edits. Moreover, during the preoperational stage most children make great strides in areas of language development and symbolic thought; television, the eternal home of "talking heads," satisfies their delight for words. Such facts notwithstanding, do not expect your 4-year-old to sit quietly and watch *Masterpiece Theater* with you.

There are a number of cognitive difficulties that can block young children's comprehension of television. To begin, their skills in logical thinking are limited, making concepts like reversal and cause and effect difficult to understand. Without the benefit of logical thought, their reasoning instead rests on the fickle, imprecise notions of subjectivity and intuition. In addition, preschoolers are tremendously egocentric, unable to understand or coordinate multiple or different points of view; this in turn makes following television's diverse perspectives a tricky course for young children to negotiate. Preoperational children are also marked by their tendency toward centration, that is, thinking about just one thing at a time to the exclusion of other ideas. As such, they view the world—the TV world and the real world—only in terms of black and white absolutes rather than in its wide ranges of gray possibilities. The primary difficulty facing TV's youngest viewers, however, rests in the overwhelming amount of information that fills a screen at any given time. Given their limited world experience and their inexperience with the medium itself, young children can easily find themselves focusing on filler (like the advertisement's dog in our earlier example) rather than the true substance of a program. They simply do not know what to look for, nor do they (or should they) always care. Watching the movements of a marginal, but goofy cartoon character may wholly serve the entertainment needs of a toddler; the fact that the creature is in the far back corner of the screen action matters not at all.

On the other hand, many young children do wish to make sense of television. To do this, they make heavy use of the medium's formal features. Television's formal features, or forms, are the visual, auditory, and structural elements of a program. Specific forms include camera angles and movements like zooms, cuts, and pans, loud noises, background music, voices, pace, special effects, animation, and variability of scenes. As researchers Aletha Huston and John Wright describe them, forms "constitute the grammar and syntax of television. Visual and auditory techniques are used to mark breaks in content, changes in scene, connections between distant events, and as bit and program boundary organizers."[9]

Though some forms like hazy dream sequences or flashbacks might confuse young viewers, most serve as effective guides for attention and comprehension. In a review of research on formal features, researcher George Comstock found the forms best facilitating attention among young viewers include changes in character or level of audio; peculiar voices; puppets; movement; camera cuts; sound effects;

laughter; applause; colorful, active, and comically featured animals; rapid action; and high violence.[10] Repetition is also a key factor for young children. Educational programs like *Sesame Street* make heavy use of this form, frequently highlighting the day's number and letter through funny, informative skits and quick-bit highlights. Often kids provide their own repetition. Surely we all know the child who begs to see the videotape of *The Lion King* for the 568th time in a row—this time being just as necessary and entertaining as the 567 previous viewings. Though this penchant for repetition can drive parents to distraction, research suggests that repeats and reruns provide young kids with great pleasure, perhaps because they convey a sense of comfortable familiarity. More important to our current discussion, repetition allows children to anticipate content, thus rendering it more understandable.[11] Not all researchers, however, find rapid repetition to be the key to comprehension. Psychologist Jerome Singer, for example, argues that *Mr. Rogers' Neighborhood* is a better educational choice for children than quick-bit shows like *Sesame Street* because the slow, deliberative pace of *Mr. Rogers' Neighborhood* permits time for viewer reflection. Time for reflection, according to Singer, is an essential element in promoting comprehension and recall.[12]

Though tools like formal features, repetition, and reflection may aid in guiding attention and comprehension, they offer no guarantee. Meanwhile, a number of other hurdles still stand in the way. For example, young children also have trouble making inferences, or guesses, about what happens to time, people, or events not explicitly shown on the screen. In the minds of most preschool-aged children watching television, if they didn't see it, it didn't happen. Thus, a cartoon which first shows a clever dog's eyes "boing-ing" out when he sees his owner's unattended steak dinner, then cuts to him licking his chops and patting his belly presents something of a problem to the very young viewer. The fact that the mischievous mutt gobbled the meal might escape the child entirely. This is no small obstacle, as television relies heavily on inference in order to tell a full, well-developed story in 22½ minutes.

Preschoolers also tend to have difficulty determining fact and fantasy. Though even the youngest of children usually realize that little creatures do not live inside the TV set, many preschoolers cannot always determine what on television is real and what is not. As television so closely approximates real life, how confusing this task must be to a young mind. Children's judgment errors can range from believing that Chip and Dale actually live outside in a tree to assuming that limbs of a body can be handily replaced with bionic parts. As one researcher commented, "A 9-year-old girl told us she did not have to be careful crossing the street because she could always go to the hospital, as the bionic woman did, to get replacement parts better than her own completely human body."[13] Though studies show that most children by the age of 5 or 6 do have a fairly good grasp of what is real and what is fantasy, subtle errors can easily creep in. Stereotypes are easily accepted, while frightening and violent scenes, however preposterous, can cause nightmares and jitters for kids of all ages.

Finally, children under 7 or 8 years have only limited powers of reasoning and perspective, typically permitting only absolute choices between black and white, good and evil. As a result, subtleties, ironies, and inconsistencies between appearance and behavior or deed and consequence are usually resolved in the direction of the most visually obvious interpretation.[14] An example of this superficial reasoning comes from a mother we know and her experience with her 4-year-old son, Thornton. Each time they watched a videotape of the movie *Beauty and the Beast* together (he is well into the repetition stage), she asked him which character he preferred: Gaston, Belle's dashing but egomaniacal suitor, or the Beast, grotesque and angry, but tender-hearted and true underneath it all. Each time Thornton responded with the same answer: "Gaston, silly!" For his age, Thornton gave a perfectly typical response. On the surface, Gaston does look to be the catch, and in his eyes his mom *was* silly for asking such an obvious question. It probably will be several years before he discovers who the film's true good guy is.

In another example, a 6-year-old girl we know recently announced that MTV's *Beavis and Butt-head* is her all-time favorite show. The fact that this bizarre animated program is not appropriate for children is beside the matter. More to the point, this child has no way of knowing that *Beavis and Butt-head* was intentionally created as tasteless parody. Children of her age cannot make, much less understand, such a distinction; as a result, she may be earnestly carrying away a number of detrimental messages from the show. Though not all comprehension difficulties have potentially harmful results, this example illustrates the problem of children watching programs they cannot well understand.

Comprehension in the School Years

Though younger children easily misunderstand and misinterpret television, their viewing skills become more sophisticated as they grow older. For many children, the magic age in making gains in comprehension is 7 or 8, when they are well into Piaget's concrete operational stage. At this stage children lose much of their egocentrism, allowing them to see the world from more than just their own narrow perspective. Concrete operational children have also developed logical thinking skills; previously difficult concepts like classification, class inclusion, and reversibility are no longer mysteries. They also are able to think more objectively and generally and are not misled by appearances and single, standout features. Finally, their level of world knowledge has expanded dramatically; they are highly fluent in specific subjects, often to the embarrassment of less informed grown-ups.

These cognitive and knowledge gains naturally translate into improved television viewing skills. Many elementary school-aged children are quite adept at differentiating between essential and nonessential information on television, organizing and integrating essential plot information, and identifying the intent of particular TV messages. With their expanded world knowledge and experience with television, older children can also make both inferences and plot predictions with relative ease. In contrast to preschoolers, older children are also less reliant on television's formal features as cues for attention and comprehension. Rather, they provide their own cues for guiding attention through the use of *schemas*, which are frames for knowledge or models for information. In life we constantly rely on our own schemas without even thinking about it. For example, a woman who has been pregnant will know she can probably expect morning sickness, swollen feet, raging hormones, and an aching back the next time she is pregnant as well. Or, to use another example, a seasoned fan attending a professional basketball game knows precisely what to expect at the arena: Before the game begins, the national anthem is sung, the starting line-ups are announced, and then the tip-off starts the game. After tip-off, there is first and second quarter play, each 12 minutes in length; the half-time break complete with dancing women and frenzied mascots; and finally another 12 minutes each of third and fourth quarter play, with the thrilling possibility of overtime. The practiced fan also knows the rules of the game, the players' names and numbers, and the location of the nearest hot dog stand and rest room. With such a strong schema in place, this person simply is able to watch and enjoy the game's action without having to expend mental energy on sketchy interpretations or guesswork.

So it is with children and television. Whereas young children rely heavily on TV's formal features to guide attention and interpretation, schemas play this role for older children. Over time and with experience, kids begin to develop their own schemas, or expectational frames, for television viewing. For example, if they have developed a schema for an action-adventure show, they will know to expect a wild chase scene. If it is a schema for a love story, they will be on the lookout for a romantic kiss. Cognitively advanced children also are able to add sophisticated concepts like motives and feelings to their schemas. They understand, for instance, a TV character's feelings of rejection after not making the school's basketball team or another character's impulse to cheat on a test. The concept of applying schemas to television viewing comes straight out of the active theory and is often referred to as Constructionism. Researchers Anderson and Lorch explain the active, constructive nature of schemas:

> A basic notion is that ongoing processing of television is to a great extent schema driven. . . . It functions by guiding the comprehender in constructing expectations as to what information will occur. . . . We assume that the viewer, through experience with television as well as through general world experience, develops expectations about the temporal and conceptual flow of normal television programs. Importantly, we assume that visual attention to television is to a great extent driven by these expectational schemata. Fluctuations of attention to a program reflect the viewer's moment-to-moment understanding of the television content ("bottom-up" processing) as well as schematic strategies of processing television in the context of available alternative activities ("top-down" processing).[15]

In addition to increased use of schemas, older children are beginning to understand the fabricated nature of television, which in turn influences their understanding of television's realism or lack thereof. Though we have stated that children as young as 5 or 6 are capable of discerning fantasy from reality, it takes a few more years to realize that entertainment television as a whole is a made-up property and that actors portray TV's people. Though this understanding generally occurs around the age of 8, some major difficulties still surface. A 1980 study, for instance, found that third-, fourth-, and fifth-grade children had difficulty with the notion of "realistic" characters such as the "Fonz" and Mary Richards, confusing their real names (Henry Winkler and Mary Tyler Moore) with those of the television characters they portrayed.[16] School-aged children also often fail to understand television's production process. It is hard for kids to imagine that a setting that appears to be a sprawling Midwestern home is actually shot on several cramped sets on a West Hollywood studio lot. Similarly, it is hard for them to know the difference between live and pretaped television, especially with the use of laugh tracks on many sitcoms. Older children and adolescents—even many adults—also often fail to recognize the profit-making motives of commercial and cable television (or, for that matter, the educational motives of public television), as well as the bias of a message or the omission of an opposing view. For example, kids laughing hysterically at commercials that portray parents as clueless dorks are generally unaware that the advertisers are exploiting their feelings in order to sell them something. As Dorr writes, "Children who can accurately supply motives for the creation and distribution of content on each system (respectively to educate, to inform and enlighten, and to make money) can use these attributions to adjust their views of the credibility of content on each system. Children who cannot make such attributions have one less criterion to use in assessing the reality or realism of what they are watching."[17]

Finally, despite their overall gains in comprehension, older children often have a hard time understanding the abstract lessons of television programs. As the phrase implies, children in the concrete operational stage usually only think in terms of concrete or direct evidence. Thus, a program that subtly weaves in a theme of moral responsibility probably will not be understood on all intended levels by elementary school-aged children. Again, this is a temporary hurdle. Skills in abstract thinking begin to develop in the formal operations stage, usually entered around age 12. With some exceptions for particularly difficult or subtle themes, the formal operations stage marks a significant threshold in television comprehension. In fact, by the time most children reach the eighth grade, their comprehension of television is generally on par with that of adults. It would be a mistake, however, to take this as a sign that all television programs are appropriate for teenagers and preteenagers. Though kids in these age groups try hard to convince the world that they are ready for adulthood, in fact their world experience and emotional maturity are still considerably less developed. Some programs simply should wait.

Additional Influences on Understanding

The preceding description of age-related comprehension is admittedly broad. Within the age subsets of preschoolers and school-aged children there are enormous variations in comprehension as each year of childhood brings such rapid developmental and experiential growth. Moreover, children's comprehension of television cannot simply be defined by age and corresponding cognitive abilities. The process is more complex.

For example, children of all ages pay closer attention to content that is somehow familiar to them. Similarities in character and viewer age, gender, social class, ethnicity, and occupational goals, as well as features ranging from setting (city apartment versus suburban Cape Cod; newsroom versus classroom) to background music (classical versus the latest in alternative rock), all prove to be important determinants in attending to and comprehending television. As adults, we can easily recognize this tendency in our own viewing habits whether the draw is a gritty police drama or a female-driven comedy. Programs that successfully tap into widely shared experiences tend, in turn, to find wide audiences. Part of the success behind the trendy 1980s show *thirty-something*, for example, was that it offered easily identifiable characters matching many Baby Boomers' own stages in life: the stable suburban couple, the on-the-brink-of-divorce couple, the hard-to-commit male, the single urban woman. With a focus on jobs, marriages, friendships, and child rearing—the stuff of life that enormous numbers of Americans were then also experiencing—viewers had recognizable TV "companions" traveling the road with them. Kids seek similar, if not greater, identification on TV. Numerous studies indicate that children—a population fascinated by anything or anyone reflecting their own selves—attend to TV characters who in one way or another are most like themselves; in turn, their comprehension is enhanced.

It is a nearly universal rule that kids pay closer attention to shows featuring child characters, especially those close to their own age or slightly older. Moreover, girls tend to be attracted to girl characters and their traditional "girl" activities, while boys generally favor boy characters and their traditional "boy" activities. Though the factors of gender and age are most obvious, many more subtle discriminations hold similar importance for child viewers. For example, in a study among 7-year-olds, a program featuring a family of the same social class was better understood than a program featuring a family of a different social class.[18] Other studies have shown similarly enhanced comprehension when ethnicity is a shared characteristic. In discussing this common pattern, Dorr offers some explanations:

> That children look more at similar characters (when they are equally important and on screen about the same amount of time) suggests that similarity influences the distribution of attention and effort during information processing of television stimuli. That children like similar characters more and

learn more from them suggests that similarity increases arousal during viewing, which in moderate amounts would heighten attention and effort during viewing and lead to more learning. That children better understand content featuring families of similar social class and remember more from similar characters suggests that similarity allows children to draw upon their own background knowledge to help interpret and evaluate television content.[19]

The fact that children better comprehend content that features characters with familiar qualities has serious implications for children's broadcasting in general. If television producers hope to teach effectively or entertain our nation's broad range of children, diversity in casting and content is essential. Fortunately, programs like *Sesame Street* that have long featured boys and girls from a wide spectrum of racial and ethnic backgrounds have been recently joined by a small new crop of culturally diverse shows like *The Puzzle Place, Gullah Gullah Island,* and *C-Bear and Jamal,* helping to reflect a more accurate America. The great bulk of children's programming, however, continues to ignore demographic realities, potentially "locking out" a large share of its audience.

In addition to similarities between the viewer and content, another powerful determinant of comprehension is the presence of others in the viewing environment. Though watching television is sometimes a solitary activity, often there are others in the room, either watching alongside or participating in another activity. A child watching television with a group of friends, for example, may find it difficult to concentrate closely on the screen; attention and comprehension are typically reduced in favor of talking, laughing, and playing nearby games. On the other hand, when a child views with an older sibling or friend, comprehension might increase as the younger child follows the older child's cues for understanding. When an adult is co-viewing with a child, comprehension can be even more significantly enhanced. Children love to ask questions, especially about things they do not understand; when an adult is close at hand, their confusion can be quickly cleared up. Moreover, an adult can be proactive in the matter, turning the tables by doing most of the asking: "Do you think that could actually happen in real life?" (fantasy versus reality); "Why do you think that person said that?" (understanding motive); "Is there a moral to this story?" (understanding abstract lessons); and so on. Not only can such questioning give a fair reflection of a child's level of comprehension, but it also makes the viewing experience more interactive and meaningful. More about the benefits of adult co-viewing will be discussed in Chapter 6.

In addition to similarities between viewer and content as well as interaction with others in the viewing environment, there are other important determinants of comprehension. They include viewer interest (Not surprisingly, children will more frequently watch, more fully attend, and better comprehend those programs that are interesting to them); viewer needs (Kids will exert more concentration if their need is informational—e.g., to gather data for a school project); the viewing environment (Is the viewer's baby brother crawling around the room? Are toys scattered everywhere?); and the mood and physical condition of the viewer (Tired? Hungry? Bored? Hyperactive?).

It is tempting for organizational purposes to lump all of the previous variables—age, similarities, the presence of others in the viewing environment, the viewing environment itself, and the viewer's needs, interest, mood, and physical condition—into distinct, noninteractive piles. Yet, television viewing, like life itself, does not occur in a vacuum. All of these variables work together at any given time, sometimes subtly and sometimes powerfully influencing a child's comprehension. As such, patterns of comprehension are not always predictable, even with the same child. Your 3-year-old daughter who *always* catches on to Mr. Rogers' lessons might have some trouble on the day she's not feeling well. Or your 8-year-old son who has always despised public television now sits still for a program about whales after learning about them in school. Like most other aspects of a child's life, viewing patterns and levels are hardly predictable. It is also important to note that not all children fit into neat, compact categories. If your child does not closely follow the Piagetian guides for age, for example, do not be alarmed. Children frequently defy rigid adult expectations, instead taking life at their own pace.

Understanding Advertising

Actual television programs represent just a part of what children are called upon to understand when they tune in to TV. The other portion of television's airspace is swiftly filled in by commercials, which just as surely require skills in comprehension. Many beleaguered parents will say that their children understood the meaning of commercials before they learned to crawl. And indeed, children do become picky consumers at a startlingly early age. But do they actually understand the advertisements, or are they just following the cues of a larger consumer society?

Like general comprehension studies, those that focus on children's understanding of commercials are numerous. A great deal of research is generated by the advertising agencies and product developers themselves. Manufacturers are careful to not pour millions of dollars into an ad campaign that will be lost on the very minds they wish to persuade. As a result, tremendous (and typically secretive) effort goes into studying children's reception of television ads. Though advertisers like to keep their findings close to the vest, the scientific community has contributed plenty of its own research, all open to public review. In general, it appears that children's comprehension of commercials largely mirrors their understanding of television at large. However, because of the controversial, high-profile role of commercials on for-profit children's television, the subject merits a discussion of its own.

In Chapter 1 we discussed the highly appealing and entertaining aspects of television commercials. This entertainment factor leaves many observers wondering if children are capable of discerning the ads from the actual programs they are watching, especially when familiar cartoon characters and other "heroes" are used to sell products. There is some debate in this matter. Some researchers argue that young children—especially those under 3 or 4—are unable to discriminate the point at which television entertainment trails off into television advertisement. With the zippy visuals and memorable characters of today's advertisements, such a conclusion makes sense. Other researchers have found that young children do realize that commercials represent a different part of television (they are shorter and perhaps funnier) and that they are quite conversant on the subject of commercial characters and the products they sell. Researcher George Comstock, for his part, argues that children's ability or inability to recognize television advertisements is a futile debate: "If children cannot recognize their persuasive intent, their ability to distinguish commercials as different from the program is irrelevant."[20] To that end, most research concurs that it is not until age 8 or 9 that children begin to understand the persuasive intent of commercials. Interview studies, for example, indicate that a majority of children under age 8 could not explain or identify the purpose of commercials.[21]

According to Comstock and many others, this difficulty in comprehension of intent raises serious questions about advertising ethics and fairness. Comstock writes, "If we hold for children the same standards we hold for adults, then television advertising directed at them is deceptive for many children under the age of eight, and the proportion for whom it is deceptive increases markedly with decreasing age."²² To be sure, most young children consider television commercials merely a colorful romp through the world of cereals, snacks, and muscle-bound action figures. Lacking skills of discernment, youngsters become easy targets for many clever advertising techniques.

With only 15 to 30 seconds to pitch their products, advertisers have cultivated a number of sure-fire methods and features to attract and maintain a child's interest. Some of the tried-and-true tactics include snappy product brand names (Bubblicious, Cap'n Crunch, Care Bears); frequent repetition of the product's name; rapid pace; partial or full animation; live action; fantasy settings and situations (elves working in a tree factory, chipper leprechauns bounding about); bright colors (the more neon the better); catchy jingles ("Apple Jacks, Apple Jacks, 10 vitamins and minerals that's what it packs...."); and loud, bouncy music. Capitalizing on MTV's phenomenal popularity among young people, many ads now feature dizzying camera angles and kids hip-hopping across the screen.

The bottom line for any strategy is making the product seem fun. In his virtual how-to manual called *Children's Television: The Art, the Business, and How It Works,* advertising executive and author Cy Schneider emphasizes the importance of fun:

> No matter how you position the product, emphasize that special ingredient called *fun*.... Over and over again, looking at hundreds of children's television commercials, it is apparent that children respond to the fun in any aspect of product advertising. It must be fun to do, fun to eat, fun to drink, fun to wear, or fun to look at. Frivolous and simplistic though it sounds, if you don't make it fun, it won't appeal to kids. Sometimes seemingly ordinary things can be made more fun by the way you look at them, how you package them, or even the story you tell about them.²³

Children, who are not always skilled at discerning the proverbial wheat from the chaff, are easy targets for "ordinary things" in slick, bright, fun packages. In one specific study, R. P. Ross and his colleagues found that their sample of 400 boys between the ages of 8 and 14 overestimated the size, speed, and complexity of a toy race car when they viewed a commercial that included footage of live auto racing.²⁴ In that same study, the researchers also demonstrated the power of celebrity endorsements—commercials with celebrities were better liked and resulted in higher ratings. For example, when a famous race car driver appeared in the commercial, the boys' preference for the toy increased. They also found that celebrities were perceived as experts about the toy. And while the younger boys in the sample (8- to 10-year-olds) were more reliant on the endorser's advice and more vulnerable to the ad's perceptual tricks, both age groups showed a similarly strong preference for the toy. Ross et al. write, "The combination of a famous presenter with perceptually exciting and dramatic material from his 'real' world would be a powerful message for children who are prone to believe adults, aspire to emulate heroes, and are literal-minded in their interpretation of sensory information."[25]

In addition to believing real-life celebrities, children are also likely to believe those of an animated persuasion. Celebrity cartoon creatures like Tony the Tiger, Toucan Sam, and the elfin Snap, Crackle, and Pop trio exhibit big star power. Though these images are used solely for the purposes of vending, other noncommercial characters have inched over that fine line dividing entertainment and advertisement. For decades, many loved and trusted cartoon "stars" have successfully moonlighted as commercial endorsers. Though host selling in its purest form has long been banned (e.g., having a program's cartoon character vend a product during the program's commercial breaks), the concept now lives on more subtly. For example, young fans of *The Flintstones* reruns can regularly spot their pals Fred and Barney hawking Fruity Pebbles during other programs, still successfully drawing attention to a product that might otherwise be lost in the shuffle.

At the height of the endorsement game is the tangled relationship between television programs and their spin-off licensed merchandise, each effectively and lucratively reinforcing the other. In their urge to emulate and encapsulate their TV heroes, children long for products that show their allegiance. Clever marketers rush to gratify kids' longings by creating a cache of merchandise (toys, cereal, lunch boxes, stickers, sleeping bags, bed linens—you name it) based on a wildly popular TV show or movie. The profitable cycle continues when after waking up on a Batman pillow, for example, the impulse to watch the show (and, by association, its ads) begins anew. A few years back, the phenomena surrounding the Teenage Mutant Ninja Turtles proved how far a product's marketing potential could be pushed. It took only a few months for the Ninja movies, the Ninja TV show, the Ninja bedspread, the Ninja curtains, the Ninja Halloween costumes, the Ninja toothbrush, the Ninja turtle-shaped ice cream bar, the Ninja lunch box, and the tiny plastic replicas of Donatello, Michelangelo, Leonardo, and Raphael to all blend together for one big merchandising blur. The connection between program and product is so tightly woven that sometimes it's hard to remember what idea was launched first. Though the Turtles have become passé these days, the same question can be asked for any number of currently hot programs and products. Today it's the Mighty Morphin Power Rangers; tomorrow it will surely be something else.

On the flip side, there are now a number successful toys that have landed their very own programs. Check your *TV Guide* and you'll now find listings for *Barbie, G.I. Joe,* and *My Little Pony Tales;* the plots may be thin, but the ploy still works. This concept has been stretched to the point that one-shot TV specials, including those for Strawberry Shortcake and the Care Bears, were expressly conceived to launch the toys themselves. Many critics believe that program-to-product and product-to-program endorsements are manipulative for both kids and their parents. Few children recognize the profit-making cycle of this symbiotic relationship; parents, meanwhile, endure request after request after request.

In addition to offering licensed merchandising, enticing product claims, exciting features, and celebrity endorsers, advertisers have one other classic strategy that is sure to turn a child's head: the televised premium offer. Every day in grocery stores across America the same argument is heard over and over again: A child wants *this* cereal and *only this* cereal, not for its taste or nutritional qualities, but for the spiffy toy that comes inside the box. Indeed, how many boxes of cereal have been ripped and shredded in a manic search for a 10-cent glow-in-the-dark plastic decoder ring? Children—like the rest of us—are easily charmed by the idea of getting something for nothing. But unlike adults, children rarely realize that there is a catch (in this case, the purchase of a particular brand of cereal). Studies on the topic reflect the general findings of children's age-related comprehension: that younger kids, who already have difficulty selecting appropriate information from the screen, are easily sidetracked from product attributes ("It tastes scrumptious!!! And it's good for you, too!!!") with the premium offers. Older children, with more developed eyes for TV ads and their purpose, view premium offers with some degree of skepticism.

In a similar vein, young children often have difficulty understanding many of the disclaimers and qualifiers that advertisers are bound by the National Advertising Board code to include in their commercials. For example, one study found that the phase "Part of a balanced breakfast" was ineffective for kindergarten and first grade children; most in the study did not understand the message that cereal alone is not nutritionally adequate for the breakfast meal.[26] Similarly, formal phrases like "Batteries not included," "Some assembly required," and "Sold separately" typically carry little meaning for young minds. However, one study found that when sample advertisements substituted the common disclaimer "Some assembly required" with a simple phrase like, "You have to put it together," comprehension rates for young children were significantly higher.[27] Of course, such clarity is not in the best interest of the advertisers, who instead usually bury the information beneath their ads' enticing action or tag it on at the end in a low, adult male voice-over.

Though many ad tactics pose problems for young viewers, as cognitive processes grow more sophisticated with age, so does the understanding of TV advertising. The older the children are (beginning at about age 8), the more objectively and critically they view commercials. In fact, many kids adopt the same negative attitudes towards commercials as adults: In one study, over 80% of 10- to 13-year-olds said commercials did not always tell the truth.[28] In 1994, Coca-Cola went so far as to wage a multimillion dollar ad campaign for its new "OK" soft drink wholly based on this cynicism. With a strategy heavy on irony and low expectations, a Coca-Cola marketing executive explains this unconventional approach: "It underpromises. It doesn't say, 'This is the next great thing.' It's the flip side of overclaiming, which is what teens perceive a lot of brands do."[29]

Like other areas of television viewing, it takes time for children to learn to use critical and logical thinking skills when watching commercials. Though in their early years children are highly susceptible to many products' exaggerated claims and distracting devices, with time and experience they become fairly savvy commercial critics. Unfortunately, as most parents know, such heightened knowledge does not appear to diminish even the most jaded teenager's appetite for the latest must-have product. Some things, it seems, we never outgrow.

A Child's View Beyond Television: Video and Computer Technology

While it is important to understand the extent to which children attend to and comprehend television, this effort now just scratches the surface. Television — once a revolutionary force of its own — now plays the role of the poor, simple cousin to its younger, flashier relations in electronic entertainment. Though television is still at the center of the fold, it now competes for a child's attention with VCRs, cable TV, video games, interactive TV toys, computer games, computer on-line networks, interactive multimedia systems, CD-ROM, virtual reality, the Internet, and — coming soon — video-on-demand technology. Daily, it seems, the electronic options expand.

There are a number of immediate differences between each of these technologies and traditional television, especially in terms of a child's level of cognitive and sensorimotor involvement. The most significant factor in terms of our current discussion is the interactive nature of these entertainment options. The debate over television's level of passivity or activity becomes nearly moot when compared to the level of involvement offered by this new media. From the fairly simple technology of VCRs (allowing manipulation in terms of content choice, time of viewing, rewinding, fast-forwarding, and recording) to the highly sophisticated maneuverings of computer networks, children are now active participants in their entertainment options. Whether this new level of interaction translates into a higher quality experience is still up for debate.

Electronic Possibilities

There are a number of significant pluses for these more advanced technologies. Children watching television stare at a flat, one-dimensional screen; their only chance for active manipulation is switching channels or turning it off altogether. The new electronic technologies, on the other hand, offer a large measure of choice both in terms of content and viewing experience. Consider the experience of using a VCR. Just visiting your neighborhood video store is a bewildering exercise in choice: Cartoon or live action? Comedy or action-adventure? Classic or new release? Once a movie has finally been chosen, viewers can pop it in the machine at their leisure; if a scene is confusing or if nature calls, the movie can be stopped, rewound, and replayed over and over again. Video games offer even greater opportunities for manipulation. Players set games to their ability level, and then through the frantic use of buttons and levers on a handset implement their own course of action. In the end, it is the player's skill level that determines the outcome of the game. Even a device as simple as the remote control has altered the viewing landscape. Many parents find it impossible to keep up with the quick trigger fingers of children with clickers in hand: boring or nonrelevant programs and commercials are zapped in the blink of an eye. The pace of channel surfing may make grown-ups dizzy, but children love the sense of control.

Not surprisingly, the increased level of activity associated with the new media leads to higher levels of attention for child viewers. For example, children usually pay closer attention to a movie on videotape than to a traditional television program. In turn, increased attention requires higher levels of cognitive effort. Though some parents may shudder to believe it, studies have found that the playing of video games can lead to increased cognitive and sensorimotor skills. Patricia Marks Greenfield argues that video games not only increase sensorimotor skills like hand-eye coordination but that they also strengthen cognitive skills like inductive thinking (many games require the player to figure out the rules as the game is played), parallel processing (juggling a number of variables and different pieces of information at the same time), and spatial skills (coordinating visual information coming in from multiple perspectives).[30] For those who want to take advantage of these cognitive benefits, there are a number of fun, challenging, nonviolent games on the market that can be enjoyed by the whole family. If you decide to play against your child, however, be warned: You'll probably lose. Children are remarkably adept at video games, allowing them the frequent pleasure of beating an adult fair and square. Greenfield offers a theory for children's well-honed video game skills:

> If moving visual imagery is important in the popularity of video games, then perhaps the visual skills developed through watching television are the reasons children of the television generation show so much talent with the games. Children also pick up and use more information about action from seeing action on television than from hearing action described (as in radio) or from verbal description combined with static images (as in picture books). Children who watch a lot of television get a great deal of experience in taking in information about action—more so than did generations socialized with the verbal media of print and radio. Perhaps this experience with the moving visual images of television leads to skills that can be applied to playing video games.[31]

That video games and computer programs increase or enhance certain cognitive skills comes as no surprise to educators, who for now over two decades have been relying on microcomputers for CAI (computer assisted instruction). Partly because of the novelty and partly because of the active orientation, kids love to learn things through computers. Computers give color and shape to abstract lessons, allowing children the opportunity to actively manipulate variables and hypotheses. Moreover, computers grant unlimited practice, provide immediate feedback and reinforcement, allow for individualized instruction, and are nonjudgmental about mistakes. Precisely for these reasons, computers and video technology have been particularly successful in reaching learning disabled and physically challenged students who do not respond well to traditional pedagogical approaches.

Electronic Liabilities

There is much to applaud regarding the new media. It brings an important measure of interaction, allows for more active control by the viewer or player, and increases access to ideas and information by leaps and bounds. Yet despite these significant advantages, many aspects of the new media also raise serious concerns.

To begin, the benefits of the new electronic media extend to only a limited group of consumers. Despite their seeming proliferation, video and computer activities currently embrace only a carefully defined, but devoted, audience. Its consumption—both the positive and negative aspects—is held in check by two factors: gender and wealth.

It's no secret that the vast majority of video game players (and to a lesser degree computer users) are boys. Though girls do play games and use computers, there does not seem to be that all-absorbing attraction that boys commonly display. Part of the explanation rests in the fact that most games are intentionally created to attract a male audience by using violent themes and masculine images. A visit to a local video game store will show that nearly all the customers are young, wide-eyed males rhapsodizing about the latest bloody cartridge. One psychologist, featured in a 1993 *Time* article, offers another perspective:

> Unlike young girls, who seem to be able to take video games or leave them, boys tend to be drawn into the games at a deep, primal level. . . . What is going on? According to psychologist Sherry Turkle, author of *The Second Self*, the key lies in the rates of development of young boys and girls, which to their mutual pain and embarrassment are usually out of synch. Girls in their pre-teen years tend to mature faster than boys—socially and sexually. Normal day-to-day interactions with these girls can be stressful and troubling for the boys, who tend to withdraw to a safe place—sports, scouting, computer gaming—where they can hang out until they are ready

to hold their own with the girls, a process that can take years. Most home video games, unfortunately, are derived from coin-operated arcade models that were designed not to build up a lad's fragile ego but to defeat him and take away his quarters.[32]

Besides being largely the territory of males, video and computer equipment is also the private realm of the relatively affluent. Video games, computer equipment, and computer software are all quite expensive, accessible only to those who can pay the price. Despite their wild popularity in American culture, in truth only a fraction of the nation can afford to keep pace with what is being offered. There is a significant population of children for whom computers are a pipe dream and personal video games are still somewhat of a beeping, flashing mystery. Moreover, as we ogle the possibilities of the Internet and the Information Superhighway, there are many people who have never even heard of these revolutionary networks or who have no hopes of getting online even if they have. As more and more of society becomes computer driven and oriented, there is the looming risk that a large segment of America will be increasingly alienated and isolated. High cost and ever-increasing sophistication ensure that computers will continue to be the playground of the affluent. Thus, for many kids, a discussion of the possibilities and liabilities of computer and video "edutainment" represents exclusive middle-class chatterings. For better or for worse, traditional television will have to suffice.

That said, there is still a large population of kids for whom video and computer activities consume a great deal of time, energy, and devotion. And for these kids, the above-described benefits are tempered by a number of serious concerns. First, within the increased role of child-directed activity, there comes an unfortunate paradox: The greater the level of involvement, the greater control the machine seems to have over the children. Video game playing, as many parents can attest, often appears addicting. Locked in battles of seemingly eternal consequences, young players seem literally stuck to the handsets and the corresponding action on the screen. Many will play until the sets are yanked out of their hands. "Just one more game!" is their plaintive plea.

One Canadian research team found the idea of a video game "addiction" wholly plausible. Though the study focused specifically on arcade video game playing, this group's findings can be applied to home versions, as well:

The remarkable refinement of reinforcement parameters which microcomputers afford (fast timing, multimodal feedback, intricate structure) and which has been taken advantage of commercially, represents the perfect paradigm for induction of "addictive" behavior and should be of some concern especially with regard to children as consumers. The results obtained in this respect suggest that reinforcement theory has been applied to the letter by video game designers. This leaves little doubt that individuals susceptible to such conditioning may be at risk for spending inordinate amounts of money in the arcades on the one hand, and for developing an obsessive-compulsive attitude to the video games on the other.[33]

Though Patricia Marks Greenfield highlights the fact that playing video games can promote feelings of independent achievement, others claim it encourages unhealthy competition and social alienation. Lest we pick on kids too much, a prime example of an alienating and competitive compulsion can be readily found in the world of adult leisure activities. Take a trip out to Las Vegas or hop on a glittering riverboat casino and you will see row upon row of bleary-eyed grown-ups feeding slot machines buckets of quarters in search of "The Big One," a jackpot of mythic proportions. "Come on, come on," they whisper, praying that a cascade of coins will soon spring forth. It's hard to stop, as a win always seems just another pull of the lever away. The same compulsive principle operates when kids play video games. They beg to continue playing until they either beat the machine or a competing player. Meanwhile, life goes on without them. As we'll note in Chapter 3, the seemingly addictive quality of many games and computer programs can pose serious problems for a child's social development.

Besides being "addictive," the playing of video games can impinge on the freedom of one's imagination. Despite the extraordinary branching capabilities of computers and video games, a child cannot play them with total abandon. Obviously there are certain built-in limitations to computers and video games: players must play within tight parameters and rules, with only a limited number of possible responses available. Although this still is a significant advantage over traditional television, it does not fully maximize a child's ability for free, creative thinking. In contrast, when a child learns to rely on the imagination, anything is possible.

Finally, as mentioned in Chapter 1, parents should be wary of the content of many video and computer games. The potential benefits of computer activities and video game playing are severely compromised, if not wholly eliminated by harmful content and destructive game goals. Computer online networks, for example, are rife with opportunities for kids to eavesdrop on or even join in conversations the likes of which would make most adults blush with shame. Computer users can also download — often for a fee — pornographic images with such shock value that *Playboy* or *Hustler* seem tame by comparison. Most adult-oriented bulletin board systems require proof of age (usually a driver's license number) and kids who want access to sexually explicit material, or "cyberporn" as it is commonly known, must work to find it. Occasionally, however, exposure to it is unintended, the equivalent of taking a wrong turn or being enticed by candy from a stranger. In its controversial cover story on the topic of "cyberporn," *Time* magazine told the story of 10-year-old Anders Urmarcher. One day while hanging out with other kids in the Treehouse chat room of America Online, he received an E-mail from a stranger that contained a "mysterious" file with information on how to download it. He followed the instructions and was greeted by a screen filled with 10 tiny pictures of couples performing acts of sodomy and engaging in heterosexual and lesbian intercourse. His shocked mother was quoted as saying, "I was not aware that stuff like this was online. . . . Children should not be subjected to these images."[34] In addition to the danger posed by sexually explicit material, the effect of violence in video and computer activities must also be considered by parents. As discussed in Chapter 1, violence is the heady fuel for an alarming number of video games. Players are rewarded for shooting enemies, landing clean punches, blowing up mines, and destroying battleships. Even when players assume the hero role, there is enough gratuitous violence flashing on the screen that good intentions are hopelessly lost in the action.

As with television, there is growing concern that frequent playing of violent games can lead to aggressive behavior, or, at the very least, a steady desensitization to violence. The question takes on even darker dimensions when one considers the fully active role of a child committing violence through a TV-interactive toy or when sitting in a virtual reality chamber. In her book *TV Interactive Toys: The New High-Tech Threat to Children,* Pamela Tuchscherer offers her assessment of these new possibilities in electronic media:

> Sitting down with the paper one evening, I read an article describing new battlefields that were to be laid out in family living rooms. I learned of new television interactive

toys that will allow children to use hand-held weapons to shoot the bad guys on TV, toy warships which will be activated by inaudible cues, and plastic soldiers operated by flashes of light. These signals were actually going to be coming into my living room, emanating from the television set. My initial reaction was that this new power gives television programming more control over children than it already has.

Our children are no longer sideline viewers of television violence. With toys in hand, they become an active part of the program. This link-up of working war toys and violent television programming is a child psychiatrist's nightmare. The combination encourages children to actively role-play aggressors and defenders in futuristic battle scenes.[35]

Is this what we want for our children?

Summary

Children are unique consumers of television and the new electronic media. With less developed cognitive abilities and limited world knowledge, their skills at comprehension and discernment are seriously compromised. Though children's programming often considers their cognitive shortfalls, other programming efforts — including commercials, adult and general programming, and low-quality children's shows — are not so forgiving. Adults should first recognize the gap between what television offers and what a child can understand and then serve as a ready bridge for their comprehension. In terms of a child's level of involvement, despite continued scientific debate on the notions of activity and passivity, most parents realize that traditional television watching is not exactly an invigorating experience. And while more active orientation of the new electronic media is a welcome modification of the endless hours spent sitting in front of the TV set, it often allows for action we would rather not see.

Kids, of course, are not interested in hearing diatribes about their TV viewing and game playing habits. Until children are given something better to do, they will continue to give the electronic media most of their free time. And as we will see in Chapter 3, television does consume an enormous portion of many kids' lives. For excessive viewers, in particular, the costs can come high.

3

The Charm and Cost of Television

There are certain things one can count on when it comes to children: Legos and Barbies, PB & Js, sticky fingers, runny noses, messy bedrooms, and, naturally, television. To a great extent, television shapes what children do day in and day out, year in and year out. When they are very young and small, most children cut their alphabetic teeth on *Sesame Street* and learn life's sweet truths from Lamb Chop and Mr. Rogers. They graduate to dashing about the house in a Batman cape and playing house *Full House* style. When older still they beg for Power Ranger kick-boxing lessons and later copy (to mixed reviews) Blossom's funky fashion style. Throughout their years, most children delight in the bright, funny, happy-in-the-end TV world. And as a sign of their dedication, they give a better part of their childhood to learning its ways and wisdom, such as it is.

Familiar statistics reveal the tremendous amount of time children give to television: On any given day, the average American child spends 3½ to 4 hours watching television (*not* counting VCR use or video games). Such devotion quickly adds up. By the time most children become first graders, they will have watched 5,000 hours of television; by the time they graduate high school, the total rises to 9,000 hours. Kids spend four times as much time in front of the TV than doing homework (why are we not surprised?), and, all told, as much or more time in front of the TV than in school. In that now famous kicker, by age 18 the average American child has spent more time watching TV than engaging in any other activity except sleep.

Keep in mind that these statistics express *average* viewing habits. Your children may or may not fall into this range. Many kids, for example, are not particularly interested in television; other activities are far more enticing to them, and TV's impact on their lives is minimal. On the other hand, there is a significant population that quietly sits along the other extreme, watching television excessively. In fact, a full 25% of children watch television between 4 to 11 hours a day, officially qualifying them as "heavy viewers."[1]

Whether a child's viewing is heavy or simply average, parents and other individuals have cause for concern. Heavy viewing, obviously, is most troubling. As will be seen in the second half of this chapter, excessive viewing can seriously challenge a child's social, emotional, mental, and physical well-being. Yet even average viewing should send up some warning flags. As discussed in Chapter 1, television's content does little to nourish children's tender psyches. Violence, sex, stereotyping, and the overwhelming push for material consumption can leave firm imprints on impressionable young minds, making many kids old before their time. Furthermore, as seen in Chapter 2, when children spend time watching TV not created expressly for them, difficulties in comprehension may further twist already shaky messages. Finally, just because viewing is "average" does not earn it an automatic endorsement. Three or 4 hours is a significant portion of a child's day, and each hour cuts into the valuable time that kids can just be kids: riding bikes, playing dress-up, searching for worms, and making mud pies. Too often, TV takes them away from such simple, yet somehow essential, childhood pursuits.

The Lure of the Small Screen

Discovering worms and playing in Grandma and Grandpa's old clothes seem like such delightful activities. Why, then, would a child prefer to sit still in front of a small glowing box? Indeed, sitting still seems anathema to childhood!

There are a number of reasons children so regularly flock to their TV sets. First, children are quick to follow the cues of their family and society at large. Both groups, unwittingly or not, send the message that television should be a central part of all our lives. Second, television very handily plugs in to many children's needs and goals, offering easy, nonstop entertainment, information, companionship, and escape. Finally, as a leisure activity television enjoys a unique status: It's (basically) free, it requires no coordination or special skill, and it is readily available to most any child who can twist a knob or click a clicker. By these very qualifications, it invites wide usage by kids of all ages and socioeconomic backgrounds. Each of these motivations provides a powerful impetus for TV use.

The Centrality of Television

Writing in 1939, one *New York Times* reporter offered a confident prediction for television's future:

> The problem with television is that people must sit still and keep their eyes glued on a screen; the average American family hasn't the time for it. Therefore, the showmen are convinced that for this reason, if no other, television will never be a serious competitor for broadcasting.[2]

Amazing how a few years can change a person's perspective. In the decade spanning 1946 to 1956, television ownership increased from near zero to nearly three-fourths of all households. By 1960, the figure had climbed to 87%, and today a full 98% of American homes have televisions, with most turned on about 7 hours a day.[3] Somehow—surely to the surprise of our prognosticating reporter—we found the time to sit still.

A National Pastime. Though our eyes may widen when we hear the astonishing figures for children's television use, should they come as any surprise? Television occupies a most hallowed spot in our nation, ranking right alongside family, health, religion, and work in terms of our devotion and attention. Not only do we sit still for television, but we carefully arrange our lives around it. Living rooms have given way to TV rooms, and dinnertime—once a sacred family ritual—is often set around the start of a favorite show. Should mealtime actually conflict with a special program, the problem can be solved by eating TV dinners on TV trays in the TV room using *TV Guide* as a handy coaster for the drinks. As a boon for the household with more than one viewer, television has now also burst past the boundaries circumscribed by just one room. In addition to the main TV set, most American households have a spare set or two, allowing the possibility for tuning in while cutting carrots in the kitchen, repairing a chair in the basement, or dozing off to sleep in the warm comfort of the bedroom. Television is omnipresent in our lives.

And why not? Many critics and observers would argue that television has *become* our lives. As early as 1966, Louis Kronenberger, writing in *TV Guide,* had this to say about the medium:

> What I think must be said is that television is not just a great new force in modern life, but that it virtually is modern life. What, one might ask, doesn't it do? It gives us — be we rich, poor, snowbound, bedridden or slow-witted — the time, the weather, the small news, big news, spot news: now in spoken headlines, now in pictured narrative, now at the very scene of the crime or the coronation itself. It plays, sings, whistles and dances for us; takes us to movies and theaters, concerts and operas, prize fights and ball games, ski jumps and tennis tournaments. It delivers babies, probes adolescents, psychoanalyzes adults. It dramatizes floods, fires, earthquakes; takes you to the top of an alp or the bottom of an ocean or whirling through space; lets you see a tiger killed or a tiger kill. It becomes a hustings, or a house of worship; guesses your age, your weight, your job, your secret; guides you through prisons, orphan asylums, lunatic asylums; lets you see a Winston Churchill buried or a Lee Oswald shot. It teaches you French, rope dancing, bird calls and first aid; provides debates and seminars and symposiums, quizzes and contests; and it tells you jokes, gags, wheezes, wisecracks, jokes and jokes.[4]

All this, in one small screen. No wonder we are dazzled.

Yet television, it now appears, was only just the start. While TV still maintains the center spot, we must now find room in our homes for a new generation of electronic entertainment. Simple TV stands just won't do — today we need oak-paneled, glass-doored, multishelved entertainment centers to hold all the new electronic boxes, wires, knobs, and cords. Technology that once seemed outlandish when featured on *The Jetsons* is now readily available at our local electronics superstore. From video games to VCRs to sophisticated home computer systems, upper-income consumers have heartily embraced the new possibilities. Not surprisingly, America's delight for entertainment technology was immediate. From the moment the new generation of electronic equipment hit store shelves, consumption rates soared.

For most families, the first post-TV electronic purchases were the primitive, yet then thrilling Atari games like Pong, that spare pseudo-tennis game rising to popularity in the mid-1970s. As Pong became popular in the home, more sophisticated games filled video arcades and (to the chagrin of many quarterless parents) the lobbies of family restaurants. By the early 1980s, Pac-Man was the video arcade champ, creating a mass mania for the round yellow creature and his pursuers Shadow, Speedy, and Pokey. More advanced games like Donkey Kong and Super Mario Brothers soon found their way back into the home, allowing millions of kids the opportunity to play a machine for "free" in the comfort of their own living room. Today, video games seem ever present in the lives of children, creating a unique childhood subculture. Kids swap Nintendo cartridges like baseball cards, and a top Gameboy score can turn an otherwise unassuming child into the coolest kid on the block.

VCRs have also dramatically changed the landscape of electronic entertainment. Allowing viewers to either tape television shows for later viewing or play rented theater movies on videocassettes, VCRs seemed a novel way to have it all: selective, convenient viewing on the viewers' own terms. In the early 1980s, VCRs—most of the clunky Betamax variety—found their way into 1.1% of U.S. households. By mid-1986, nearly 35% of homes had adopted VCRs, a 30-fold increase over the previous 6 years. By 1989, VCRs were found in nearly two-thirds of all U.S. homes, most of which included young children.[5] While Americans were out buying the machines, VCR technology was busy spawning a number of smart, lucrative ancillary industries. Video store chains now line local highways, while palm-sized video cameras cram diaper bags and tourists' backpacks. Even that most traditional of all occasions—the wedding—has been revolutionized by the video camera and the VCR, allowing the bride and groom to relive their big day (social blunders and all) over and over and over again.

However popular, video games and VCRs just hint at our entertainment options. Cable TV is now *de rigueur* in most homes, as are remote control devices. Close to one-third of American homes have personal computers, and summertime computer camps are now a popular option among young techno-whizes. A whole new universe of communication is opening as millions of Americans wile away the hours chatting on the Internet. Multimedia systems utilizing CD-ROM and videodisc capabilities are expanding daily; meanwhile, a new generation of gadgetry is zooming in from the not-so-distant horizon. High-definition TV promises to make the screen larger than life, while video-on-demand technology and proliferating cable and satellite systems (with their 500-plus channels) are guaranteed to make our heads spin with overwhelming choice.

Who's to Blame? Given the saturation and appeal of the electronic media in our lives, a child's attraction to it seems only natural — natural, but not always acceptable. We often bemoan the amount of time children spend with traditional television and its spin-off creations, but perhaps we should first look at our own habits before confronting the kids. Though children are most vulnerable to television, they are certainly not the only ones prone to excessive viewing. Adults can be equally enticed by TV, and when they tune in, children will learn to do so, too. Researcher George Comstock notes that parents determine to a large degree whether a child will be a light, moderate, or heavy viewer of television. Their influence is expressed in three possible ways: (a) through rules and strictures, or the lack thereof; (b) by implicitly recommending television when they themselves view a great deal; and (c) if they are heavy viewers, by increasing the opportunity for a child to be in the vicinity of an operating set, which in turn increases the likelihood of the child's own viewing.[6] For better or for worse, children are great modelers of other people's actions.

Besides being influenced by parents, children are also influenced by the simple availability of television and other media in their homes. Many studies, for example, have demonstrated that the greater the number of sets in the house, the greater the viewing.[7] We have made immersion in technology even easier by providing our kids with portable video game players that they can carry with them wherever they go. It should come as no surprise that in having such a vast array of electronic gadgets, children spend time using them — this is why we buy them in the first place. So who's to blame here? Though kids do put enormous pressure on parents to buy the latest electronic "in thing," children themselves usually do not have the buying power to make such extravagant purchases. Someone else must hand over the credit card or write the check, usually Mom or Dad. On our own, we've provided a situation ripe for abuse.

Finally, our society at large must admit some culpability. The make-believe world of television has become an essential part of our own reality. Our small talk revolves around shows seen the night before. We leverage ourselves for a new Lexus because the TV ads promise we will be admired. And we worship TV stars as heroes, furiously reading magazines and tabloids that give gossipy reports on their lives. Kids see such devotion to television and successfully imitate our own behavior.

It's no surprise that children love television so dearly: We teach them well. On the other hand, children are not just mindless followers of their parents and the larger society. Television fulfills many of their own needs and wants, most notably those for entertainment, information, companionship, and escape.[8]

TV as Entertainment and Information

Asking children why they like television is a bit like asking them why they like recess, ice cream, or snow days that cancel school. It's basically a rhetorical question, and most children will reward your inquiry with an exasperated, multipurpose "Beee-caaaauuse," as if that one word held all the explanation you should need. Indeed, it is widely understood that watching television is an entertaining way to spend one's time, and, pushed for details, most kids will eventually describe this very quality in their own words: "Because it's fun"; "Because it's funny"; "Because I like seeing guns and stuff"; "Because the stories are interesting"; "Because it's something fun to do with my friends."

As an entertainer, TV has no rival. By flipping on a switch, the viewer can be led from knee-slapping laughter to nail-biting suspense to wide-eyed wonderment all in a matter of seconds. That, as they say, is the magic of television. Directors, producers, actors, and production crews all strive to create a world of sharp visuals, snappy sounds, and catchy lines that captivates an audience. Children, perhaps, are the most eager and receptive of all audiences. The elements of children's programming—simple storylines, colorful animation and scenery, lively music, humor, suspense, action, and broad, easy-to-recognize characters—combine to amuse and engage millions of young viewers.

Different features on television are entertaining to different kids. Again, age is the primary determining factor. For example, most 3-year-olds think it's truly hilarious when a show's scoundrel trips, hits his head on a tree, lands on his rear, and then grumpily looks up to see stars circling over his swollen head; such broad humor, however, would bore most school-age kids. Instead, they enjoy shows that are liberally sprinkled with sarcasm, insults, and jokes, the conversational styles in which they specialize for navigating their own social relations. Gender also influences what kids find entertaining. Despite many parents' best efforts at promoting non-gender-specific activities, clothes, and names, many little girls still seem to adore programs wrapped in shimmering pink while most boys love shows that are loaded with lightning bolts, dynamite blasts, and punches that send the villain sky high.

Though it is primarily the stock of young preschoolers, the perennial favorite *Sesame Street* may best illustrate television's power to entertain kids. For well over 20 years, kids have flocked to their local public television channel to see and hear about Oscar's gripes, Big Bird's kind, bumbling curiosity, and the latest chapter in the enduring friendship of Ernie and Bert. These characters and others have risen above the gimmicks of trendiness, making them true classics of children's television. Parents watching with their kids can be equally entertained by the inside jokes woven throughout. We laugh out loud at segments like "Monsterpiece Theater" and appreciate furry characters named Tom and Virginia Wolfe/Woolf. *Sesame Street* is clever and witty, and manages to retain loyal fans of all ages. Watching it, we understand television's entertaining pull.

Sesame Street, Mr. Rogers' Neighborhood, Shining Time Station, Beakman's World, Wishbone, and many other fine shows often qualify as informative television, as well. Most quality shows manage to offer a double billing: entertainment to please the kids, educational information to appease the parents. Most children are oblivious to the distinction between the two features, and because kids truly do like to learn new things, it is almost always a successful formula.

Traditionally, informational or educational television has been targeted at the youngest audiences. Eager young viewers learn about subjects as far-ranging as African folk crafts, street safety, fear of the dark, the importance of sharing, and the necessity of brushing one's teeth. No matter how charming and thoughtful some programs may be, however, their viewer appeal is astonishingly short-lived. As any parent of a 7- or 8-year-old will attest, certain shows are simply no longer cool among the elementary set. There seems to be a mysterious threshold for television tolerance: One day Mr. Rogers is a hero, the next day he's a wimp. The evolution of image is a semi-tragic rite of passage.

The deliberate quest to learn edifying things may not hold up for long, but this does not mean that kids don't wish to be informed by television. On the contrary, they look to television to inform them about nearly every facet of their lives. Their thirst for TV knowledge stems from two very different motivations: their natural interest and curiosity and their wavering social confidence.

Although kids don't usually like being deliberately informed by television, they do enjoy what one research team calls "incidental learning."[9] Children want to know how to do things, how things work, and why things are the way they are; television often satisfies these curiosities at the same time it entertains. As they watch a professional baseball game, for example, they might also learn how to swing a bat. When they view *Doctor Quinn, Medicine Woman,* they'll get a (cleaned-up) view of frontier life. And by tuning into *The Fresh Prince of Bel-Air* they'll incidentally discover how rich people live. Additionally, the recent crop of kid-news shows like *Nick News* (Nickelodeon) and *News for Kids* (syndicated) teaches young viewers about current events without making them lose their dignity. Whether incidentally or directly, television allows kids to satisfy their intense curiosity about the world around them.

As kids grow older, television's information also provides an important social function. From television they learn how to dress, how to talk, how to look sexy, how to be cool, and what brands and products to buy. Knowing and effectively utilizing this information becomes seemingly essential to kids as they move into the preteen and teen phase; suddenly, image *is* everything. Kids similarly try to maintain their identity among peers by keeping up with the storylines of certain programs. For some children this may just mean regularly tuning in to harmless comedy like *Family Matters* or fantasy like *Star Trek*. Image-conscious kids, meanwhile, often use television as a measure of coolness. This explains why your older children beg to squeeze in a few nonkid shows before bedtime, for coolness rarely comes before 9 p.m. Central Time. In their urge to push the television envelope, increasing numbers of kids watch shows created for sophisticated adult audiences. In recent years, for example, keeping up with *Seinfeld* and *Frasier* have been signs of "cool" among kids as young as 3rd and 4th grade. Though most surely find that the content is above their heads, few dare miss out on a chance to stay current. They want desperately to be able to report back to classmates and friends on what was seen the night before. It's the small-fry equivalent of chatting around the water cooler.

Like television, video games and computer activities provide a sort of clubby atmosphere among peers. What games are hot, what games are not—these are the important questions discussed among young players. The competitive quality of most games and the complex language of computers only enhance the sense of exclusivity in these activities. Video and computer activities also have many straightforward applications in the realms of entertainment and information. Forgetting for a moment the important questions of quality and content, most video games *do* provide intense fun and action. The competition alone can be thrilling, while dazzling sights and sounds, combined with dramatic or funny-looking heroes and villains, add a great deal of appeal. The computer, for its part, provides an avenue for information of great depth. At home or at school, personal computers allow kids to hook into an incredible number of electronic resources.

Computer networks, for example, let kids tap into special data bases (NASA is a popular computer "destination" for young users) as well as connect with other users. Sophisticated systems can allow a child from small-town Kansas to chat online with a child from Singapore, giving a lesson in cultural diversity no textbook can match. Encyclopedias, meanwhile, lose their dusty, musty reputation when stored on CD-ROM. Otherwise abstract and far-away lessons come to life as kids see vivid pictures of the solar system as space exploration is described or watch news footage of the Hindenburg explosion while listening to the reporter's trembling voice in the background. In addition to encyclopedias, which serve broad informational needs, there are hundreds of fun, educational home software programs that teach specific subjects like science, math, spelling, or history. High quality software programs like "Sim City 2000," "Storybook Weaver," "Time Riders in American History," "Millie's Math House," "Richard Scarry's Busytown," and the "Where in the World" series are terrific tools for imaginative learning. Many of these programs are so entertaining that your kids probably won't even realize that they're actually learning something along the way. It's incidental learning at its finest.

Television as Companionship and Escape

More subtle than entertainment or information is television's role as companion and friend. Like a favorite old blanket, television can often be just as reliable and comforting. Adults are not exempt from creating this type of relationship. Many just want a little background noise to keep them company; others seek to live vicariously through soap opera queens and prime-time heroes. A simple but compelling explanation for using TV as a companion is loneliness. Getting to "know" certain characters can temporarily ease those painful feelings. Moreover, TV "friendships" are far easier to sustain than interpersonal ones. Successful human relationships take work and time and are fraught with the potential for hurt and rejection. With television as a partner, the viewer is in control, eliminating the possibility of rejection. Video games and computer activities offer a new twist on the TV-as-companion role. Both technologies are considerably more interactive than television, and with the development of realistic graphics and computer-generated voices, the sense of an "other" is all the more real. In one disturbing study, 250 male and female 10th and 11th graders were surveyed about their video game usage. Based on the students' answers, the study concluded that "heavy videogame players were more likely than less frequent players to agree that arcade videogames were good companions for them, were almost like friends to them, and helped them forget they were alone."[10]

Both children and adults may be easily tempted into forging this kind of false relationship. At the very least, it is an unfortunate reflection on the human condition, but for children there are special dangers involved. Childhood is a time when socialization skills are being tried out and tested on a daily basis. And while humans are innately social creatures, the characteristic requires some practice and refinement. For those children too shy to initiate social rituals, television can be a steady companion. And for those children bruised early by rejection, television can offer safe refuge. As will be shown later, there is a serious concern that children who rely prematurely on electronic entertainment's steadfast presence will not fully develop those crucial social skills needed for relating in a highly social world.

The last major motivation for watching television is escape. Life without some form of escape would be dull and downright unhealthy. We all regularly slip from reality by daydreaming, fantasizing, charting pipe dreams, and mapping our goals. This is considered a healthy, normal response to modern life—a safety valve for stress and an outlet for creative energy. Literature, music, art, dance, and nature often serve this same purpose. These pursuits stimulate the brain, spark ideas, and carry the mind to new places. Television, however, has an edge on all these activities: It's far more convenient, it's basically free, it requires little mental investment, and it provides immediate gratification. As a form of instant escape, television is in a league of its own.

Often children who turn to television as escape are doing precisely the same thing as their adult counterparts. No doubt, it can be fun to sit back and be swept into another world. Many kids find highly creative and unusual shows like *Star Trek* or *The X-Files* to be the perfect antidote to routine living. In addition to regular television, emerging technology provides even more—and more realistic—opportunities to escape from the real world. In a 1992 article on virtual reality, a *Chicago Tribune* reporter described the experience of sailing through a different world:

> Step into our chamber, they said, and you can fly over downtown Chicago. It was very clear I wouldn't have a plane. But I stepped into the 7-by-7-foot cubicle and donned a pair of magic glasses and joined the ranks of Peter Pan, Wonder Woman, Icarus and the angels.
>
> All right, all right—I had lost touch with reality. But who needed it? . . .

(V)irtual reality is computer sleight-of-hand of a much higher level than just projecting pretty 3-D pictures. It creates interactive environments—emphasis on interactive—so that I just wasn't *watching* animated graphics. I was *right there* inside them, an avid new tourist of "cyberspace."[11]

Both the new technology and traditional television can provide broad, stimulating avenues for escape. And in small doses, using these mediums for this purpose is fine. It becomes problematic, though, when kids begin relying on TV and other technology to escape from difficult situations and stressful experiences. This appears to become a more and more familiar route as the world of a child grows increasingly pressurized. Like adults, children of all ages face jam-packed schedules, unfamiliar family roles, and a heavy load of responsibilities. Considering the toll of such demands, it is no wonder that kids like to veg out in front of a glowing box.

Less dramatic, but far more common is a child's tendency to use television to escape from simple boredom. How many times has a parent heard a child wail, "I'm sooo boooored. There's nothing for me to do!" Clever parents will suggest plenty for a child to do, like cleaning the slimy, fuzzy green fish tank, or worse, cleaning his or her now slimy, fuzzy bedroom. Not all parents are so resourceful, however, and kids usually mope around the house until something comes to mind. Television is typically the quickest and easiest answer: Flip a button and instant entertainment fills the screen. The role of boredom or lack of alternative activities should not be underestimated. It is in those empty hours—Saturday mornings and weekday afternoons and evenings—that most of a child's viewing hours are amassed. And in consistently choosing television over other activities, a child can seriously compromise his or her mental, physical, and social well-being.

The Cost of Heavy Viewing

That pesky scarcity problem—it's a fundamental lesson of economics. It is often summed up in the old adage "There's no such thing as a free lunch," meaning that scarce resources can always be put to alternative uses. In other words, if a resource like time, money, or pastrami is used for one purpose, it is unavailable for another purpose. This rule is formally known as "opportunity cost," and it applies equally to CEOs negotiating business deals and children spending hour upon hour in front of the television set.

In the case of children viewing television, the opportunity cost is the next best thing they could be doing with their time. Obviously for children who watch TV only occasionally, the overall opportunity cost is fairly low; they still have plenty of time to play outside, read a book, or do homework. For heavy viewers, however, excessive time spent in front of the TV often comes at a very high price.

There is mounting evidence that excessive viewers are hindered in a number of developmental areas including academic and intellectual achievement, physical health, and social and emotional well-being. (For our purposes, "excessive" or "heavy" viewing is viewing over 3 hours of TV a day, though this definition is not hard and fast.) Again, not all children are influenced by or respond to television in the same way. Some kids may spend every waking hour outside of school watching TV and still manage to bring home high grades just as others who are consistently exposed to junk food commercials may continue to choose carrots over caramel corn. Certainly, there are exceptions. Moreover, research does not always make clear whether the negative consequences (like antisocial behavior) are actually consequences of excessive viewing or if they are, in fact, the impetus or motivation for excessive viewing. Such uncertainties notwithstanding, common sense tells us that constant television cannot wholly benefit a developing child.

The Cognitive Costs

Fervent diatribes against television are often quick to whip up fear that excessive television has a disastrous effect on children's academic and cognitive achievement; put less delicately, many people fear that too much TV makes kids dumb. Heavy viewing *has* been negatively linked to academic and intellectual achievement in a number of studies, but the findings are often much less simple or obvious than first glance would indicate.

For example, consider that alarming headline now annually appearing in newspapers across the country: "SAT scores decline again!" Such articles typically introduce the question of whether TV is to blame for the disappointing results. Many readers and critics jump at the cue and cry, "Yes! TV is the culprit!" While it is always comforting to confidently assign blame, the fact is that research has not implicated television for this particular ill. On the whole, declining SAT scores have far less to do with television or even the quality of public education than with the changing demographics of the test-takers themselves. In the early baseline years of the test, most of the students who took it were white, college-bound, middle- and upper-class kids with every educational advantage available to them. Today, a much broader range of students takes it, including those who come from educationally disadvantaged homes and minority students whom critics claim face a test that is culturally biased. Given a more diverse test-taking population, the scores will naturally be more diverse, as well.

This SAT example points to the difficulties in randomly blaming television for academic ills. Scholastic achievement is tightly bound with a host of more fundamental issues like socioeconomic status and parental involvement. Unless television viewing is isolated from these other variables when achievement is measured, firm conclusions are impossible. And even when television viewing is isolated, complications remain. For example, heavy viewing has been positively linked with both low mental ability in teenagers[12] and with lower socioeconomic levels,[13] making it hard to determine actual causation.

Though assumptions that TV is the root of declining SAT scores are simplistic and generally inaccurate, such reserve does not mean that television earns a scholastic seal of approval. On the contrary, there remain some legitimate concerns, and the correlation between heavy television viewing and lower cognitive and academic achievement has been implicated in a number of carefully designed and controlled studies.

One of the most telling studies performed to date is the California Assessment Program (CAP). In 1980, all California 6th graders and 12th graders were surveyed regarding the amount of time they spent viewing television, reading for pleasure, and doing homework and assigned reading. The results indicated that heavy viewers scored lower on CAP tests of reading, written expression, and math than did students who viewed little or no television.[14] This was true for all socioeconomic levels. In a specific finding, the rate of decreased test performance for 6th graders was constant up to 3 hours of television viewing a day, but became significantly poorer for the 20% of students who reported watching more than 4 hours a day. A follow-up study in 1982 took into account a number of other factors including previous achievement, characteristics of the viewing environment, and the students' socioeconomic levels. Again, heavy viewing was linked to lower scores. The sharpest declines were seen in students who reported watching more than 6 hours of TV each day.[15]

Additional studies demonstrate that children who are heavy viewers are more likely to receive lower marks at school.[16] These are important findings, but they are superficial when regarded alone. For more specific answers, we must examine the reasons that children who watch high amounts of TV often do poorly at school.

Among the greatest predictors of academic success or failure are language and reading skill levels. Excessive television can negatively impact both areas. Though moderate viewing of educational programs like *Sesame Street* often results in language gains for many children (especially those from low socioeconomic backgrounds who are not otherwise challenged), an inverse relationship between *heavy* viewing and language acquisition has been found in preschool children.[17] Furthermore, once children reach elementary school, numerous studies show excessive television to impede reading skills and achievement. Researchers Michael Morgan and Larry Gross, for example, found in their 3-year study of over 200 children that heavy viewing and reading achievement were negatively associated, regardless of sex, grade, or socioeconomic status.[18]

The most common explanation for this often steeply inverse relationship is that TV viewing displaces time that children could otherwise spend reading. Important practice time is forfeited, and, as a result, children (especially those with learning disabilities and other reading difficulties who need the practice) lose fluency and automaticity.[19] Such time displacement can be particularly damaging in the early elementary school years when reading skills are being learned and honed. Kids who initially find reading frustrating and thus unenjoyable will likely continue in this vein throughout their academic careers. And since reading forms the foundation for much of a student's education, this single deficiency can have a disastrous spillover effect.

In addition to lower reading achievement, skills in listening and writing may also be at risk for conditioned TV viewers. One educational researcher has found that listening skills are adversely affected by heavy TV use because many children are used to talking over television as if it were background noise. This habit is often carried over into the schools, where kids tend to interrupt or are inattentive to teachers or peers.[20] In terms of writing, one researcher found that children's writing is frequently much like the writing of a television show's script: choppy and fragmented, jumping from here to there with little regard to the conventions of logic. Finally, heavy television viewing has been found to "dull" certain mental activities. In one study, children in grades 3, 5, and 8 were asked to write various stories. At all three age levels, children who were heavy viewers gave less complex responses and were less involved in the task than those who watched fewer hours of TV. In addition, they gave fewer details, showed less insight into characters, and placed more emphasis on superficial descriptions of observable action.[21]

This tendency toward simple, uninvolved writing by heavy viewers may in part stem from heavy viewers' program preferences. In a sample of more than 15,000 sixth graders, the 1982 CAP data indicated that heavy viewers prefer situation comedies, prime-time soaps, and action-adventure programs—all genres that require little concentration while providing maximum entertainment. On the other hand, light viewers preferred more serious entertainment (*M*A*S*H*, for example) and public affairs programming. A study released in 1996 demonstrates the cognitive outcomes of different program preferences. Following 250 children for 3 years, researchers Aletha Huston and John Wright determined that low-income preschoolers who watched educational programming, including *Sesame Street*, not only were better prepared for school, but actually performed better than otherwise would have been expected on verbal and math skills as late as age 7. On the other hand, they found that preschoolers who watched primarily adult programming and entertainment cartoons did worse on those later tests than would have been expected.[22] Taken together, this data would support Comstock's view that "television viewing is inversely related to achievement when it displaces an intellectually and experientially richer environment, and is positively associated when it supplies such an environment."[23]

Finally, heavy viewing can negatively affect not only individual academic achievement, but the educational system at large. Many children now come to school expecting only to be entertained and are unwilling or unable to invest the attention and effort required for active, thorough learning. Cedric Cullingford sees the very act of television viewing as the culprit, pointing out that the "acquisition of the habit of subconscious inattentive viewing, half-hearted attention sustained over long periods, an indifference to information and the casualness of boredom" can all profoundly influence learning habits.[24] Indeed, teachers today face a nearly impossible battle in teaching and influencing minds attuned to the breakneck, laugh-a-minute pace of television. For many kids, traditional education now seems too slow, a pedagogical dinosaur in an MTV age. Like a boring show on television, they simply learn to tune it out.

Despite the abundance of research that points to television's potentially negative effects on cognitive development, these problems are easy to overlook because television so dramatically enlarges children's vocabulary and superficial knowledge of the world around them. It is both impressive and humbling listening to many children converse today—their grasp of language and their fluency with sophisticated information is extraordinary. In his book *The Hurried Child,* author David Elkind notes, however, that these gains may not be as beneficial as they first seem:

> One consequence of television homogenization for children, therefore, is to create what might be called "pseudo-sophistication." Children today know much more than they understand. They are able to talk about nuclear fission, tube worms at 20,000 fathoms, and space shuttles; and they seem knowledgeable about sex, violence, and crime. But much of this knowledge is largely verbal. Adults, however, are often taken in by this pseudosophistication and treat children as if they were as knowledgeable as they sound. Ironically, the pseudosophistication, which is the effect of television hurrying children, encourages parents and adults to hurry them even more. But children who sound, behave, and look like adults still feel and think like children.[25]

The Health Cost

Does TV make kids fat? Not exactly: Too many calories, not enough exercise, and unfortunate genes all conspire to make kids overweight. Television, however — either by its content or by the lifestyle it encourages — spurs the process on. For those who tune in frequently, the fight to maintain a healthy weight and good nutritional habits is rendered especially difficult.

Part of the problem stems from the inordinate amount of food-related commercials on children's television. As described in Chapter 1, well over three-fourths of children's network ads vend food products. The nutritional quality in these commercials, meanwhile, is less than sterling. For example, one recent study found that nearly three-quarters (72.3%) of all network ads airing during children's programming were for foods like sugared cereal, candy, cookies, snacks, sugared drinks, and fast food.[26]

As ad after ad flashes on the screen, one can hardly blame children for being tempted, especially when friendly characters like Tony the Tiger and the Keebler elf ask little consumers to try their yummy products. Children's commercials are very effective in influencing consumer behavior, and heavy viewers may be most vulnerable to such ads. For example, Charles Atkin and his colleagues found that heavy viewers of food ads were twice as likely as light viewers to say that sugared cereals and candies are highly nutritious.[27] The same study determined that frequent viewers consumed more advertised cereals, candies, and snacks than their lighter viewing counterparts.

Besides advertisement influence, some kids just naturally flock to the refrigerator or pantry when watching TV. A slightly overweight 7-year-old girl we know recently announced, "When I watch TV, I *have* to eat. I *always* eat when I watch TV! I like ice cream and Coke the best." We then asked how often she watched TV, to which she quickly replied, "All the time!" Exacerbating the food and television issue is the fact that watching TV is a sedentary activity, one that has spawned the now common cliché for those who excel in its idle ways. Countless kids have become mini couch potatoes, sprawled on the couch with a remote control in one hand, a bag of chips in the other. (Those who substitute a computer for a TV set, meanwhile, join the new generation of so-called "mouse potatoes.") In either case, exercise is often lacking in their routines, and, sitting still for hours, they typically consume far more calories than they burn. Weight gain would seem inevitable. One study, for example, found that at least 25% of the recent increase in adolescent obesity may be directly attributable to increases in TV viewing. The researcher concluded that the frequent food-related references contained in commercials and programming may promote unrealistic conclusions regarding eating and body weight.[28] Many other studies have been conducted on this topic, and the connection between heavy TV use and heavy, physically unfit children seems convincing; however, in looking at questions of obesity and television it should be noted that causality is not always clear. Some already overweight kids might be watching more TV simply to avoid strenuous activity or to escape the social pain of obesity. The TV-obesity link may work both ways, with each habit reinforcing the other.

Gaining weight is only the most obvious sign that one's nutritional intake is off-kilter. In fact, significantly more threatening conditions may result. In one of the major research findings of 1992, researchers at the University of California College of Medicine-Irvine discovered that children who watch 2 to 4 hours of television a day were more than twice as likely to have high cholesterol levels than those kids who watched under 2 hours daily.[29] More significantly, for those kids who tune in to TV more than 4 hours each day, the odds for troublesome cholesterol levels are *four times* as high. Again, it is not the actual television that is causing these abnormal levels, but rather the fat-laden foods that often accompany the viewing activity. Although high cholesterol generally does not pose immediate danger for kids, many doctors worry that these children will face a much greater risk for developing heart disease later in life.

Excessive amounts of television can also harm children's health in more subtle ways; those kids who do not carefully critique content are especially vulnerable to trouble. As mentioned in Chapter 1, in its quest to entertain and titillate, television rarely considers the dreary world of logical consequences. Thus, ads for beer show only happy, beautiful crowds enjoying life with the help of Brand X. There are no beer bellies, no recovering alcoholics, and no DUIs. A sexy bedroom scene shows a pair of young lovers rolling passionately on the sheets. Afterward, there is no unplanned pregnancy, no venereal disease, and no AIDS. And what of TV's aloof, sophisticated characters who are seen coolly blowing smoke rings in the air? Later, there is no stale smell, no hacking cough, and no lung biopsy. For adolescents on the verge of initiating these kinds of adult rituals, television does more than a disservice; it sets before them a clearly marked path of destructive behavior.

The Social and Emotional Cost

Finally, and perhaps most significantly, excessive television viewing can exact a high social and emotional cost. The consequences affect not only the individual child but also the family and the community at large.

Television at the Child's Expense. Though television typically seems like a harmless, if not always worthwhile, pursuit, it can have serious social and emotional consequences for the avid viewer. For example, despite all the glittery attraction of television, heavy viewing has been shown to have a depressing effect on emotions. In a study of heavy-viewing adults, a research team asked the subjects to use weekly self-reports to describe their feelings while watching television and participating in other activities. Heavy viewers generally reported enjoying television less and feeling worse during the week than did light viewers.[30] Though there are a myriad of possible explanations and causations for this phenomenon, a few of the most compelling theories, all of which apply to children as well as adults, follow.

First, television can be a potent reminder of a viewer's own perceived inadequacies. Looking back to Chapter 1, the reader will recall that television carefully creates a world that is visually appealing and emotionally enticing. Shadows and wrinkles are electronically erased, and troublesome issues are always resolved at the end of the show with a climactic group hug. Contrast that with the real world, which is filled with shadows and wrinkles and lingering pain. It doesn't take long for a viewer to look from television's giddy world to his or her own seemingly average/boring/measly/pitiful existence. According to one critic, many programs widen this gulf by their insistent emphasis on happy togetherness:

> If there is one consistently dishonest element in every situation comedy . . . it is that no one . . . is isolated, alone, atomized. In a country where family bonds are dissolving, where broken marriages are increasing almost geometrically, and where the trend of living alone is becoming an important national fact of life, the world of the situation comedy depicts strong bonds between friends, coworkers, and family. No one sits home at night watching television; the most pervasive habit in American life today usually goes unrecorded even in the most "realistic" comedies because it is not funny.[31]

In addition to social habits, viewers also compare houses, clothes, smiles, cars, happiness, families, figures, hair, romances, and jobs, often to the sad conclusion that they just don't measure up.

Watching television excessively can also be depressing simply because it comes at the expense of many more invigorating, stimulating, and emotionally satisfying activities. Well-adjusted, happy individuals often cite things like friendships, good family relationships, exercise, and getting out into nature as essential components of their mental health. But glued to the TV set hour after hour, dedicated viewers have little time or motivation for such pursuits. The expense of choosing television over an active life can be enormous. A lack of abiding social relations can be particularly crippling, for the human urge to be known runs deep. And though a viewer can know every channel, every show, and every character intimately, for all of its wondrous power television can never know a viewer in return.

In addition to influencing emotions, excessive television viewing has also been found to negatively alter certain behaviors and attitudes in children. For example, researcher Michael Morgan found that heavy viewing adolescents (especially males) were more likely to express traditional sex-role stereotypes than their less-frequently viewing counterparts.[32] Researcher Charles Atkin, meanwhile, found that heavy viewers are more likely to believe advertisements than light viewers,[33] an unfortunate finding in light of television's insistence that aspirin can make the pain go away and that the right toy will bring true happiness.

The topic that prompts the most concern, however, is the excessive viewing of violence. Despite the less-than-certain results in many TV violence studies, there is *nearly universal agreement* when it comes to heavy viewers. Keeping in mind that children who watch television see inordinate amounts of violence, it only seems logical that heavy viewing would be a contributing factor in resulting aggressive behavior. Research has confirmed these suspicions. In a study involving preschoolers who watch excessive amounts of TV, particularly cartoons and action-adventure programs, there was a higher incidence of aggression during playtime.[34] Other studies show that excessive viewing by elementary students, especially those who watch violent shows, is correlated to later aggression, restlessness, and belief in a "scary world."[35] For older children, the conclusions are similar. In a study by researchers Greenburg and Atkin, the researchers gave 9- to 13-year-old boys and girls situations such as the following: "Suppose you are riding your bike, and some other child comes up and pushes you off it. What would you do? Hit them, call them a bad name, tell your parents/teacher, or leave them?" The investigators found that physically or verbally aggressive responses were selected by 45% of the heavy-television violence viewers, compared to only 21% of the light violence viewers.[36]

Finally, and perhaps most disturbing, is the finding that habitual viewing of violence appears to have a desensitizing effect on many excessive viewers. When guns are flashed and heads are blown off with such ho-hum regularity, it's hard to expect kids to see violence as anything but routine. Researchers Ronald Drabman and Margaret Thomas showed how easily children can become desensitized to violence. In their study they exposed 44 third- and fourth-grade children to either a Western with many violent scenes or to a no-film experience. Each child was then asked to "baby-sit" two younger children whose behavior they could monitor by television. Contrary to appearances, the child was actually viewing a videotape in which the two children play quietly, then become progressively destructive, and finally erupt in a physical fight that demolishes the television camera. Those who saw the violent Western tolerated greater violence before seeking adult help.[37]

In addition to *increasing* undesirable behavior like stereotyping and aggression, excessive television simultaneously *decreases* desirable behavior in children. The most common sacrifice to television is play—

unorganized, unstructured, using-your-imagination play. Many kids today simply don't know how to amuse themselves without the guidance of an electronic talking head. Board games are a pain to set up, playing tag is too tiring, and make-believe games are for babies — so go the excuses. When the kids finally do play, much of it seems to be television related anyway: "You be Blue Ranger, you be the Pink Ranger, and I'll be Lord Zedd!" With this concern in mind, one might eye suspiciously the new generation of TV-interactive toys, operable only when the television is on. Last year's big seller was the TV Teddy, a furry brown bear with all of the warmth of a car battery. TV Teddy and its main competitor Toby Terrier are wired to pick up signals from a transmitter that connects to the TV set. When certain words and phrases emit from the television set, the toys are programmed to respond with clever, smart-alecky phrases. Creative product design, yes, but the promises of interaction are a bit chilling: Though the toys have expansive vocabularies when speaking to the TV set, they cannot respond to human beings. Meanwhile, the child sits idly by, watching an electronic relationship take flight. While other TV-interactive toys are more involving, there still remains a fundamental problem: Such toys are designed to work only when the TV is on. As technology assumes an ever greater part of children's lives, more and more it seems that silly, aimless, and imaginative play — the true and magical stuff of childhood — is becoming a lost art.

Excessive television viewing also takes kids away from other important pursuits like reading for pleasure, exploring, creating art, and making music. Yet of all the behaviors that television challenges, none is so costly as the sacrifice of social interaction. Television is a solitary activity that draws viewers *into* the TV world and *away* from the real world that surrounds them. Hours spent with the television mean hours spent away from meaningful human interaction. This isolation is not without consequence. Researcher Sydney Burton and his colleagues, for example, found that 1st graders who were heavy viewers engaged in less interpersonal play than their lighter-viewing counterparts.[38]

Part of this pattern may simply be the result of time displacement (kids watching TV instead of playing), while part of it may be that children watching television all day never fully develop their social skills in the first place. A child who prefers sitting inside playing video games to heading outside for a neighborhood game of kickball, for example, loses a rich opportunity to learn about teamwork, sportsmanship, and the complex dynamics of neighborhood life. And children who prefer television shows over family interaction risk forfeiting an understanding of how to love, trust, fight, and negotiate with those who love them most.

A second factor contributing to the pattern involves the ease of electronic relationships. This is a particularly important point when it comes to video and computer technology, which is more active and manipulable than simple television. It's easy to forget that the interaction is human to machine, which at best is an artificial partnership. Even when interpersonal relationships bloom over computer networks, a machine is the medium, providing a sturdy shield for people's true selves. To say that these electronic trends foreshadow a gradual weakening of human relationships may be overstating the case; nevertheless, artificial relationships are far easier to maintain, and a quick press of the EXIT key can dissolve them in an instant.

In addition to losing out on important social interaction, children who retreat into TV on a too-frequent basis also risk alienating themselves from real-world experiences. As discussed earlier, escape is a powerful motivation for television usage. When used moderately, it can be a healthy activity; when abused, it can lead to underdeveloped relational skills and an inability to successfully cope with life's stresses. A suggestion by a pair of psychologists sparks a good example of this tenuous balance. Writing in a parenting magazine, the authors suggest that in a joint custody situation, it may be helpful for kids who are beginning a stay at one or the other parent's home to spend an hour or so in front of the TV to reduce the stress brought on by a change in environment.[39] True, a cushion of relaxing, independent activity might calm ruffled nerves, but there is an implicit danger that a child might overuse TV to avoid dealing with the ongoing pain of divorce or any other family trauma. Children need opportunities to fully experience life—along with its warts and pain—to become emotionally capable adults. Excessive television denies them this.

In their thoughtful book *For the Love of Children*, Edward Ford and Steven Englund describe the emotional issues at stake when children tune in excessively to television:

> The major social strengths of life—play, work, love, faith—will be relatively strange lands for the TV-weakened child, experiences he has tasted only vicariously, at secondhand, or partially. He will in a truly lamentable sense, remain something of a stranger to the species and the promise of his human birth. And the final twist is, he won't know these things until it is very late. Indeed, he may never learn

them, but instead will simply make do with the halfway mechanisms, surrogates, and material crutches of an affluent society. Like a baby who is born blind, the generation of the media child may never discover what it is missing, though it constantly feels the dull inexplicable ache of emptiness.[40]

Television promises children fun, excitement, and nonstop entertainment. Too many children, though, are cheated by this very appeal. Families also have been duped by the small screen; anticipating an enjoyable group activity, they often get much less than what they hoped for.

Television at the Family's Expense. At its inception, television promised to be the Great Socializer. Early advertisements featured happy families gathered 'round the set for an evening of fun and togetherness. As one writer put it, television was to be the "electronic hearth," the warm, glowing center of family life.[41] And television still does seem to serve that purpose. For many families, watching television is their most common joint activity, becoming an easy ritual: After the dinner dishes have been cleared and cleaned, family members head towards the television and settle down in their usual spots. Seats are claimed, the show turned on, and an evening's entertainment begins. Sounds normal enough, but not everyone is ready to applaud this type of family activity. Marie Winn writes

> Television's contribution to family life has been an equivocal one. For while it has, indeed, kept the family members from dispersing, it has not served to bring them *together*. By its domination of the time families spend together, it destroys the special quality that distinguishes one family from another, a quality that depends to a great extent on what a family *does,* what special rituals, games, recurrent jokes, familiar songs, and shared activities it accumulates.[42]

Dallas Morning News columnist Ann Melvin echoes Winn's theme as she discusses, with some irony, the phrase "family hour":

> See, there really used to be a family hour. . . .
> We played, we quarreled, we ate ice cream. Nobody called it the family hour or anything. We just did stuff. And when that was over, we did something else.

One summer, I spent two weeks with some relatives in Fort Worth. They had a television set. After supper, we all went in the living room and watched it from 7 o'clock until after the 10 o'clock news. . . . It was the worst two weeks of my life. I missed my mother's humming, my father's whistling out in the driveway, the shudder of the refrigerator when it turned on and the laughter of strangers driving by in the night. I missed the intent gaze of my mother as she listened when I talked and the murmur and shuffle of people talking and moving about the house.

I wasn't smart enough to know that during my two weeks of TV, I was seeing the ultimate in family viewing for which a nation would mourn 40 years later—the phenomenon that would come to be called, quite erroneously, the family hour.[43]

Television powerfully draws its viewers' attention away from each other and toward the small screen. Conversations both silly and significant seem to stop when programs begin. Commercials allow the only true break in attention, making people rather adept at talking in 30-second sound bites. Indeed, one of the most unfortunate influences television has on the family is in the area of interpersonal communication. Many critics describe families' social experience during television viewing as *parallel,* rather than *interactive,* with each viewer "alone" or isolated in his or her attention toward the set. In one well-known study, researchers observed 3- to 5-year-olds with their parents watching TV and in a family playtime when the TV was off. Though there was more touching between parents and children during TV watching (sitting on a lap, for example), children talked less, were less active, and were less oriented toward their parents than when playing.[44] Certainly, many families do talk to each other over the noise of the television though this habit can be disturbing for those members trying to closely follow a program. In one family we know, a young viewer regularly yells out her admonition to the chatty offenders: "THIS IS A TV ROOM, NOT A TALKING ROOM!"

Such frustration can naturally cause conflict in a family as can choice of program and the important question of who gets control of the remote control. These can be sticky situations and are usually resolved either by seniority, brute strength (hair-pulling, pinching, biting, punching, and eye-poking), or the comparatively civilized rule of "who was there first." Interestingly, one study found that the amount of family television viewing was related to the amount of tension in the family. Though causality was not determined, it was clear that the greater the viewing, the greater the tension level.[45] One specific area that has frequently been cited is family conflict over excessive viewers' frequent requests for advertised products. Charles Atkin found that children heavily exposed to Saturday morning commercials were clearly more likely to experience frequent conflict. In averaging reactions to toy and cereal denials, he found that 21% of the heavily exposed children compared to 9% of lightly exposed children argued "a lot."[46]

Though conflict may frequently erupt as a result of excessive television viewing, the rise of multiple sets in homes has probably served to reduce intrafamily television arguments. With two or more TV sets, family members are better able to watch what they want when they want. When families split along TV lines, the most common viewing arrangement involves the parents watching one set together while siblings gather around the other(s). Though potentially nasty wrangling may be avoided with multiple sets, the concept often defeats the idea of whole family viewing. The amount of time families spend viewing together dramatically decreases as the result of having more than one TV set in the house. One study found that in multiple-set families children viewed by themselves about one-fourth of the time, as did husbands and wives. For only one-third of the viewing time did the entire family view together.[47] In addition to generational separation, multiple set use also contributes to the rise of solitary viewing. So much for promises of family togetherness.

Computer use can further separate the family, especially along child/parent lines. Parents must assume considerable responsibility for this great divide, for they are the ones who often create it in the first place and then widen it by not climbing on board. In well-meaning efforts to give their child an educational advantage, many parents who can afford to will head out to the computer superstore and buy all the goodies that will guarantee their child's spot at MIT and later an executive position at Microsoft. Unfortunately, few parents can get past pulling the equipment out of the box, leaving it to their computer-literate child to figure out the details. From that initial starting point many parents never catch up, leaving them feeling a bit like outsiders whenever computers and their mysterious language are concerned. In an article describing this phenomenon, the "great divide" is evident as a set of parents wrangle over their concern about their son Michael's passion for computers:

> [The] wife is decidedly less upbeat, in part because she thinks her son has entered a world of which she can't be a part.

"There have been several times when I've said, 'Why don't we just get rid of the [computer]?'" she says. "Because both boys are so obsessed with it. And I'm so unsophisticated. When Michael tells me what he's doing, it's like he's speaking Martian. I have no idea what he's talking about."

One floor above, [Michael] is logging on to his Internet account. Maybe he'll visit his favorite newsgroup, rec.games.abstract, a cyberplace for fans of abstract computer games. In any case, he's flying solo, and it looks like a long trip. "If I'm up here too much, sometimes my parents tell me to get off," he says. "But mostly I'm on my own."[48]

Television at the Community's Expense. In addition to influencing the individual and the family, the effects of a child's excessive television viewing have repercussions that reach all the way to the community level. We should note that the following observations have less to do with the problems of individual children watching television excessively and more to do with the pervasive influence that the electronic media has on nearly all its young users.

First, television's mass influence contributes to an increasingly homogenized society. Nowhere is this more evident than in today's youth culture, and no force has been so powerful as MTV. One could argue that it is the cable station's music alone that drives today's style and fads (as music has done throughout the ages), but in truth MTV's carefully orchestrated *image* is what drives youth culture. To a large extent MTV determines what music kids listen to (and the messages derived therein), what kids talk about, what language they use, and what clothes they choose. This pattern has most recently been seen in the mass appropriation of urban street style. Long before rap music found a mainstream audience, MTV gambled by putting it on center stage. It worked. Today you'll find affluent white boys from the suburbs saying "Yo" and "homey" to each other; their pants dangle precariously from their waists and their sports team caps are all cocked at precisely the same angle. The sight is vaguely amusing, but there are two major problems. First, in their effort to be different and stand out in society, young style-seekers end up looking and acting exactly the same. Second, and more importantly, though shared experiences serve an important socializing function, their very popularity dilutes their original strength. This present trend, for example, has reduced the very uniqueness of urban street culture to the level of just another passing fad.

Attendant with the formation of a powerful youth culture is the decline of adult authority and influence. Part of this stems from the messages about adults that kids receive on TV. In television for very young children, adults are nearly nonexistent. Cartoon kids usually run around on their own, perfectly able to meet the challenges of life without an adult's guidance. Programs for older kids, meanwhile, do show adults but generally only in a bumbling, annoying capacity. Very often on television it is the child, not the adult, who lends the voice of wisdom and maturity. Additionally, through television, children have learned not to trust adults as they did in generations past. First, they've learned that we can't always deliver what we promise. In ads that flash day and night, seemingly trustworthy adults make promises that too often come up empty. Soon enough, children become cynical and learn not to trust at all. Second, through the proliferation of tabloid news programs and movie-of-the-week psychoanalyses, all of our foibles, weaknesses, and failings are now magnified to the nth degree. In watching today's television, children may logically wonder why grown-ups deserve any respect at all. In their compelling book *Dancing in the Dark: Youth, Popular Culture, and the Electronic Media*, Quentin Schultze and his colleagues write that as a consequence of today's electronic media, "Adults have generally lost their role as conduits for transmitting the meaning and purpose of life. Most traditional institutions now seem to have at best slight relevance for youth, who find little value in history, maturity, and wisdom."[49] In the place of traditional culture, television swiftly takes over as the prime socializing and teaching agent of the young.

Television's contribution to the decline of adult trust and authority reaches far beyond American middle-class society. One of the most poignant passages we've come across describes television's impact on a seemingly impenetrable culture:

> In the remote Amazonian rain forest villages of Gorotire, Brazil, for example, a satellite dish brings *He-Man* and *The Flintstones* to the naked Kaiapo Indian children. The villagers call television the "big ghost." The nature of their community is changing. They no longer gather at night to meet and to talk, to pass information, or to tell stories. Beptopup, the oldest medicine man, says, "The night is the time the old people teach the young people. Television has stolen the night."[50]

Finally, in addition to homogenizing society and trivializing adult authority, our persistent habit of watching television contributes to the demise of community strength and ties. The community experiences a significant loss when individuals and families consistently choose to stay inside and watch television rather than get out and become involved in their neighborhoods, making them safer, more livable, more hospitable places. It is especially unfortunate when children shun civic opportunities like scouting, clean-up campaigns, and other community clubs and events, for children are naturally invested with the energy and optimism that propels positive change. Excessive television viewing also injures the community on a more intimate scale by keeping us on our couches and away from our neighbors. A few years ago syndicated columnist Bob Greene wrote an article entitled "American Mass Media and the Backyard Fence." In it, he describes a future with 500 cable channels and discusses the shared views of two seemingly disparate individuals: Michael Eisner, CEO of the Walt Disney Company, and Sandy Marschinke, a stay-at-home mom from suburban Chicago. He writes

> Forget for a moment that television itself may have been the most potent destroyer of community there has ever been. Before the advent of television, there allegedly were real communities . . . whose citizens were reputed to once have spent long hours talking over the backyard fence. . . .
>
> Here is what Sandy Marschinke and Michael Eisner have in common, even though they've never met each other: Each realizes that the more American society becomes fragmented — the more each person becomes able to select his or her entertainment fulfillment from a virtually unlimited and unmonitored menu — the more we potentially trade off in the name of progress.
>
> Mr. Eisner worries that if there is no true national mass entertainment — if Americans become a nation of people flipping up and down a spectrum of 500 cable TV channels — it will be tantamount to what is left of the backyard fence being torn down. Mrs. Marschinke worries that the fence has already been torn down, and that unwanted visitors have stormed into her yard. . . .
>
> The main thing they seem to have in common is that they sense that whatever is coming next, it probably won't be an improvement. In a nation that stocks up on double-

strength locks and iron gates and video-surveillance security walls, the backyard fence is obsolete. Apparently it was too fragile.[51]

Summary

Children and television are tightly bound in American culture. Not only does the relationship reflect our society's own love affair with the medium, but it effectively provides for many of a child's own needs, including entertainment, information, companionship, and escape. Watched moderately and selectively, television can be a normal part of childhood. Watched excessively and/or age-inappropriately, however, television presents a significant risk. For many kids, the hours spent in front of the tube carry a high academic, physical, social, and emotional cost. Even considering television's recognized benefits, excessive viewing is a losing proposition.

How can the game be turned around? First, recognize the central role that parental responsibility plays in TV monitoring and reduction. No matter how difficult this task seems—and no matter how unpopular this task makes us with our kids—it is essential that we take charge of one of the most influential agents in our children's lives. And second, before rushing headlong into reduction strategies, we should take time to evaluate our kids' TV habits and effectively prepare them for a new way of living.

PART II

Managing Television

4

A Parent's Role

In the early blushes of parenthood we all make loud, grand promises we later find hard to keep: My child will always eat good things like plain Cheerios, bananas, and low-fat yogurt (except that Pop Tarts are so handy); my child will never be told "I told you so" (except when he or she breaks the VCR after poking Legos pieces inside); and, certainly, my child will not watch too much television (except that life keeps rushing in, leaving me too tired to do anything about it).

Life does tend to get in the way of good intentions. And today, many parents find that good intentions seem ever harder to fulfill. Indeed, if, as we stated in the Introduction, childhood isn't what it used to be, it follows that adulthood isn't the same either. Great numbers of us now juggle the stresses of divorce, daycare, work (often for both parents and most definitely for single parents), health care and insurance woes, and unemployment. Our own shifting ground creates a shaky footing for our children, making parenting today an exceedingly difficult task.

Not that parenthood was a breeze in earlier days. It has always been the most exhausting and demanding of jobs, causing plenty of worry lines and even more headaches. Yet the institution endures. We still abide by most of its fundamental rules, saying to our own children the very things that once made us roll our eyes: Eat your vegetables. Tell the truth. Tuck in your shirt. Please don't pick your nose. Wash your hands before dinner. Do your homework. Say "thank you." Today this perfunctory list seems incomplete. We are now compelled to add pleas and warnings that our own parents probably didn't consider: Stay in school. Stay out of gangs. Stay away from guns. Don't do drugs. Don't deal drugs. Don't drink and drive. Abstain from sex (and if you ignore this advice, please, please, *please* use protection). We beg our children to do the right thing because far more is at stake than germs and bad manners.

Rather than being a balance of loving discipline and loving trust, today parenthood often becomes an exercise in disaster avoidance and damage control. Why? In part it is because our influence seems to count for less these days. Though we may still pay the bills and buy the groceries, many of us are too busy or tired to maintain a stable presence in our kids' lives. Economic demands (real or perceived) keep us at work and social demands (important or unimportant) keep us on the run; time flies, and our children go on without us, spending more time on their own, in the company of their peers, or in the company of a television set or computer. These are the wobbly moral compasses that increasing numbers of children now follow. Sociologist Amitai Etzioni explains the heart of this problem: "If all that children receive is custodial care and morally careless education, their bodies will mature but their souls will not. If the moral representatives of society do not fill the inborn vacuum, television and the streets will."[1]

What then does it take to be a good parent, to "fill the inborn vacuum"? The question is too large for our small arena here. We will, however, say this: It is our understanding that successful parenting is not so much an ecstatic *state* achieved only by Mr. and Mrs. Perfect as it is an ongoing, sometimes painful *process* of decision-making. In the end, raising good and happy children is the hoped-for result of making tiny, reasoned decisions each day, each moment: a decision that they will eat a banana at lunch, that they will write thank you notes for yesterday's birthday gifts, that they will be home by dark, and that they will be loved no matter what.

The issue of moderate and appropriate television watching is just one more in the line of daily decisions that will lead to a healthier childhood for your children. Easy? No. Essential? You bet.

Our Responsibility With Television

It's really pretty simple: Either control television or television will control your kids. No cultural force has a reach so long and powerful as television, and no audience has minds so green and yielding as children. As a consequence, parents have an obligation to often bridge and sometimes block TV's seeping influence on their children. Ignoring it just doesn't work.

Parental Obligation

In the wake of the 1993 *Beavis and Butt-head* fire tragedy, then-*New York Times* columnist Anna Quindlen wrote about the issue of parental obligation. In response to the tragic accident, many public and private citizens quickly decried the inane and nasty content of the program. Quindlen took a different tact:

> The only thing missing from this discussion are the parents. Where are we? Gone. Abdicated. If the industry has given up on standards in what it produces, many of us have done the same in what we permit. . . .
>
> The truth is that neither alternative—government control, industry control—can completely take the place of parental control. Neither Big Daddy will make the choices we should make for our individual kids, if we are willing to do the hard work of making choices for them.
>
> I know that's difficult. I know from experience that it's tempting to use television as a baby sitter. I know supervision is harder with latchkey kids and adolescents. But a 5-year-old who has run of the programming? Come on.
>
> Making distinctions between what they want to do and what is good for them—that's a parent's job description. And it extends to the remote control.[2]

Quindlen doesn't hesitate in placing ultimate responsibility for control of television at the feet of parents. Her emphasis on personal responsibility sounds quaintly old-fashioned, coming at a time when fewer and fewer people look at the idea with any seriousness. Responsibility, though, has never been just a fleeting fad or the sole account of Eagle Scouts and other do-gooders. Parents, especially, must embrace the idea in order to raise young children to become healthy, productive, self-reliant adults. Moreover, our efforts must go beyond what Etzioni called "custodial care." Just as we try to monitor what our kids eat and how long they sleep, so too must we ensure that they use their mind and time in ways that are healthy and beneficial. Watching television excessively and in age-inappropriate doses is clearly not healthy and is rarely of lasting benefit to a child's mind and day.

Importantly, in her column Quindlen recognizes the difficulties that parents face in monitoring their kids' television habits. Though we all know it's the right thing to do, the thought of limiting a child's television viewing is often as overwhelming to parents as it is vexing to the children themselves. We hesitate to admit it, but television can serve a mighty role in our quest for sanity. Lofty goals of providing our children with stimulating experiences tend to fly out the window when reality charges into our lives. The laundry pile has become a mountain, the dog needs to go to the vet, and that report is due at work tomorrow, no excuses. Suddenly the television seems so convenient, a sure-fire way to occupy the kids for an hour or 2 (or 3 or 4 . . .). It's a familiar scenario: We're busy and stressed. Our children are wild and crazy. Set them in front of the television and magic happens — they grow quiet. Then the guilt sets in. But the telephone rings. And round and round it goes.

One young mother we know explains the temptation to rely on television to provide those infrequent moments of quiet and calm in her life:

> It's just so hard to grab moments of peace. Not for lounging around, but for cooking dinner, ironing clothes, writing notes, and whatever else needs to get done. I have a toddler who's into *everything* and an always-hungry infant who's into spitting up. Peace is hard to find. Bribing my 2-year-old with *Sesame Street* seems like the only way I can get things done.

Faced with the demands of real life, the idea of limiting television can be hard to swallow. It requires a great deal of determination, stamina, and watchfulness, as well as a sacrifice of time, energy, and some well-entrenched habits. It will also surely result in a few loud, pouty protests from your kids and perhaps your spouse. Such challenges might explain why few parents actively monitor and regulate what their children watch. As researchers Jerome Singer, Diana Zuckerman, and Dorothy Singer found, few parents are willing to seriously invest time and interest in their children's television viewing habits. In the course of studying a group of middle-class elementary school children's understanding of television, they discovered that the subjects' parents were reluctant to participate in the TV workshops offered and that they even lacked interest in the research results concerning their own children. Most of the parents involved seemed to think that television was a problem for *other* people's children, especially those children less privileged than their own.[3] Such passivity is not unusual. When asked about the extent of their TV mediation, most people seem either embarrassed ("I know I should be doing *something* . . . ") or defensive ("We do the best we can . . . "). Please note that it is not our intent to instill guilt in our readers about past inaction. Monitoring children's television viewing is hard work. Television's overwhelming presence in our lives and society make it a difficult, often unpopular endeavor. Moreover, we recognize that certain family situations—when toddlers are toddling about or when kids are sick—make television reduction significantly more difficult. Parents faced with such taxing (and fortunately temporary) situations should keep in mind that TV reduction is not a race for severe perfection. Flexible, loving efforts are preferable to a rigid iron fist.

In addition to parents' hesitations to ease back with television, others further challenge the effort. Libertarians, freedom-of-speech defenders, and network executives are often quick to cry "censorship!" Limiting television for children is not censorship. In their compelling book *Abandoned in the Wasteland: Children, Television, and the First Amendment,* former FCC chairman Newton Minow and journalist Craig LaMay speak to this issue:

> For half a century, anyone who has questioned the American commercial television system has been shouted down as a censor. Instead of talking seriously about how to improve television for our children, Americans argue to a stalemate about broadcasters' rights and government censorship. We neglect discussions of moral responsibility by converting the public interest into an economic abstraction, and we use the First Amendment to stop debate rather than to enhance it, thus reducing our first freedom to the logical equivalent of a suicide pact.[4]

Censorship stops the actual transmission of an idea, and that is not our present suggestion. Indeed, most parents don't mind that the occasional adult-themed program exists, they just don't want their kids tuning in to it at seven o'clock in the evening. And as parents, that is their prerogative. Limiting television is not a subtle form of tyranny, either. There are those who will say that children must have the freedom to make choices for themselves. This is a fine philosophy when it comes to deciding on a science project or in choosing a sports team to join but not when it comes to television. With their greater experience with the medium and in life itself, parents simply have a better vantage point from which to make television-related decisions. Finally, some will argue that children should not be artificially protected from the real world, that forcing them to watch only innocuous shows like *Lamb Chop's Play-Along* will produce neurotic, incapable kids when the real world knocks at their door. Of course, this argument first presumes that television presents a real-world view, which is hardly the case. More to the point, we argue that children do need—and do deserve—parental protection in many matters, television included. With careful guidance and direction, they will gradually, naturally learn what to expect from the world and what the world expects of them. Meanwhile, childhood is too short and too precious for rude interruptions from adult life. Far from censorship, tyranny, or coddling, limiting television is simply responsible parenting.

Industry Obligations

If on one side of the fence we have libertarians arguing for a child's freedom of choice, on the other side there are those who would like nothing more than to shut down Hollywood and start all over, this time with family values firmly in place. It's hard to argue with good intentions though their effectiveness in this arena is limited. With the important exception of public television, the goal of the television industry is not to guide the moral and intellectual development of your children. Nor does it have to be. As a business, its chief goal is profitability, and if high ratings and profitability are achieved through the propagation of raunchy stereotypes and bloody bullets, so be it. As long as it stays within the bounds of FCC guidelines, the industry is under no real obligation to provide stories that warm the heart and soul.

Such moral immunity does not mean, however, that the government is assuming a hands-off approach to television. Television was granted its hallowed status in part through the government's largess. The gift of airwaves came with one stipulation: that broadcasters would use them "for the public good." To the extent that the networks ignore this mandate, the government has cause to step in. As discussed in Chapter 1, the lightning rod for Congress and the Attorney General is excessive violence in programming. In answer to governmental hearings, reports, and threats of further action, the networks agreed in 1993 to air warnings on shows that contain excessive violence or adult themes. The Children's Television Act of 1990 further circumscribes broadcasting efforts, requiring, if somewhat vaguely, that television stations increase the airtime and educational quality of children's programming. Positive change in this area has been slow in coming.

At the least, television's heel-dragging pace of improvement has sparked renewed consumer interest in the quality of TV. Launching high profile public relations campaigns is the specialty of increasingly sophisticated advocate groups. Though television's most persistent watchdog, Action for Children's Television, disbanded a few years ago, a number of newer organizations have stepped in to keep issues involving children and television before the public. Groups like Viewers for Quality Television, the Center for Media Education, and Children Now are actively pressuring both the industry and the government for higher quality television. Positive results can also be achieved through spontaneous individual efforts. When viewers were upset that the family drama *Brooklyn Bridge* was being canceled a few years back, letters and phone calls poured in to the offices of CBS. Under pressure, the show was (very briefly) reprised. Publicly boycotting corporate sponsors can be another effective approach. When viewers gather steam and threaten to boycott sponsors of excessively violent shows, for example, the usual speeches about creative license grow strangely quiet. Indeed, if the industry feels their profitability will be hampered by the airing of a questionable show, it will respond to public demands.

In response to public pressure, other forms of electronic entertainment have also begun policing themselves. Video game companies now include ratings on game cartridge boxes much like those used for feature films. Moreover, some of the most gruesome versions of games like Sega Genesis' Mortal Kombat require a "blood code." Those seeking maximum gore must obtain the code from Mortal Kombat retailers, who are under Sega Genesis' orders not to give it out to kids under age 17.

As for computer technology, new products and services continue to be developed in an effort to help parents control the messages popping up on the computer screen. For example, a wide range of software products is now available to parents leery of letting their kids surf unsupervised through an increasingly dicey Internet. Most screening products limit Internet access either by filtering out preprogrammed keywords, phrases, and banned sites or by adhering to a system of ratings for violence, sex, offensive language, bigotry, and the promotion of illegal drug use developed both by the Recreational Software Advisory Council (RSAC, the council responsible for rating video games) and SafeSurf, a parents' organization. Among the most highly rated Internet screening programs are Cyber Patrol 3.0 (voted "Best of Test" in *Internet World*), CYBERsitter 2.1, Specs for Kids, Intergo 2.1, and Surfwatch 1.0v10.[5] In a related effort, CompuServe has started seeking out the family-friendly market through their new Wow! online service. As an option, families can sign on for Wow! Kids, an easy-to-use online service created expressly for children. In addition to offering special versions of games, messaging, E-mail, and reference services, it also offers restricted Internet access and other safeguards. If successful, CompuServe's competitors can be expected to quickly follow suit.

Though stations and networks don't seem terribly eager to comply with new FCC demands, some — perhaps recognizing the benefits of good public relations — began advancing their own independent efforts for change. For example, in the fall of 1994 ABC introduced a new logo which appears in place of the network's logo at the beginning of a designated program and several seconds after commercial breaks (see-through style, in the lower right-hand corner of the screen), signaling programs that are "particularly enjoyable for family viewing." This strategy, at the very least, is a shrewd marketing move. Many local news affiliates are putting their own spin on this kinder, gentler trend, offering family friendly news in their early evening broadcasts. The news is delivered without bloody corpses and the other graphic footage we have come to expect from ratings-hungry newscasts. While cynics again point to the marketing angle (today's parents of young children are most valued by advertisers), at least parents can now watch the news without fear of their 5-year-old seeing a gruesome massacre in the latest war-torn country. Finally, some network affiliates are flat-out refusing to air certain controversial programs. WFAA in Dallas-Fort Worth, the eighth largest ABC affiliate in the nation, opted not to carry *NYPD Blue* for its first two seasons despite the fact that the show was a critical and ratings success.

While some people heartily applaud such bold and unconventional decisions, others are loath to have their news and entertainment screened and sanitized. There are a few industry options that might placate both sides, allowing for individual choice in matters of television taste. Cable companies have long offered "locks" on cable boxes, blocking out stations that parents might find offensive or inappropriate for their children. Also, most television manufacturers now produce TV sets that will air only certain channels (for predetermined programs) at certain times. Finally, for those families who insist on having two televisions but can only keep tabs on one, there is a device called VisionLock. Working through the antenna to block the necessary electronic impulse, VisionLock can, on demand, cut the signal for the extra set.

Any previous options for quality control or parental control, though, must now seem like chump change compared with the latest development in viewer choice. Early 1996 broke with the startling news that the networks, cable operators, and syndication companies had "voluntarily" offered to develop a ratings system for the programs they air beginning in early 1997. This unprecedented move was sparked by the 1996 Telecommunications Act and its requirement that television manufacturers include in their televisions a V-chip ("V" for violence) by 1998. As discussed in Chapter 1, the chip will electronically read encoded ratings, allowing only those shows that fall within a parent-programmed range of acceptability. Recognizing the futility of a V-chip that has no ratings to read, lawmakers crafting the Telecommunications Act empowered the FCC to organize a standard-setting panel to rate television programming if the industry did not create their own system within a year. In a move that caught most pundits and analysts off guard, television industry executives—a group that usually breaks out in hives when confronted with options for parental control—met with President Clinton and swiftly hammered out a ratings agreement. Indeed, the usual foot-dragging, finger-pointing, and cantankerous debate that typically marks any governmental encroachments on hallowed television ground was notably absent. Why the sudden change of heart? Some observers claim that public pressure, enflamed by a 1996 presidential race in which nearly all candidates claimed the moral high ground by lambasting television's fondness for sex and violence, had finally reached a recognizable boiling point. Others saw the quick response as an opportunity for the industry to take a stab at the inevitable before potentially more punitive governmental measures were enforced. And finally, other commentators have suggested that the move was an attempt by the television industry to get on the government's "good side" as Congress debates how to dole out newly available spectrum space for digital broadcasting and additional channels. Regardless of the motivation, the television industry—along with its viewers—should be bracing for some major changes.

As announced in late 1996, the ratings plan will be a variation on the system currently in place for motion pictures. In fact, the leading negotiator for the television industry in the ratings discussions is none other than Jack Valenti, famed head of the Motion Picture Association of America and original designer of the MPAA's ratings system. The television industry, taking a cue from its big screen counterpart, announced that the following ratings will appear on TV screens and in TV listings in early 1997: TV-Y (for all children); TV-Y7 (inappropriate for children under 7); TV-G (for general audiences but not specifically children); TV-PG (parental guidance urged); TV-14 (not for children under 14); and TV-M (adults over 17 only).

Once word leaked out that the industry opted for an age-based rather than a content-based system, a noisy round of testy debate erupted. Parent groups, Congressional leaders, children's advocates, and many others argue that the vague categorizations are not informative enough, that parents want and need very specific information regarding the levels of violence, sex, and rough language on particular shows. They advocate using a system (similar to the one used in Canada) that rates each show with both a letter indicating the potentially offensive material ("V" for violence, "S" for sex, and "L" for language) and a corresponding number indicating the level on a scale of, say, 1 to 10. The industry counters that such an approach would be too confusing and arbitrary both for the producers of television shows (who have been pegged to do their own ratings) and for parents trying to make sense of an "alphabet soup" of ratings. The federal government is currently remaining fairly hands-off in the debate, taking the "wait and see" course by advocating that the industry be given a set amount of time (10 months, for example) to see if their system is workable and acceptable to parents.

This immediate content-versus-age debate aside, the general V-chip discussion raises a host of other questions that should be considered. It doesn't take long for the waters of this debate to grow murky:

- How will television producers charged with formulating the ratings handle the nuances of television? In terms of violence, how do the no-pain antics of *The Three Stooges* reruns compare to the gritty but consequential violence of *Homicide*? Or what about sexually suggestive material: How will a joke about achieving orgasm stack up against a fleeting shot of a married couple in bed?
- How will traditional kids' cartoons, with their unrealistic and consequence-free violence, rate? Will they fall into the same TV-Y category that would presumably include very high quality kids' shows like *Sesame Street* and *Reading Rainbow?*
- If news programs will be nonrated (as it presently appears), how will the industry handle shows like *Hard Copy* and *Inside Edition* that routinely ride the thin line between news and exploitation? Moreover, though sporting events also fall into the nonrated category, what about the swell of raunchy commercials that tend to air during games or the increasing possibility that post-game interviews will be laced with the players' own heated profanity?

- How will advertisers respond to a ratings system? Do critics have a point when they argue that a vague, age-based system is more advertiser-friendly?
- If adult-oriented, substantive programming earns consistently prohibitive ratings, will this lead to a further "dumbing down" of television?
- On the other hand, might the existence of ratings give producers the green light to just go ahead and plow through all small-screen taboos, opening up the small screen to big screen-style sex and violence?
- How can parents be assured that their kids, who are potentially more fluent in the language of technology, won't be able to override the V-chip system with a little electronic wizardry?
- How will the V-chip technology work in families that have children with widely varying ages? Will a 16-year-old be compelled to only watch shows acceptable for his or her 7-year-old sibling?
- Most important to our current discussion, will the existence of a ratings system lull parents into a false sense of security concerning their children's television viewing habits? Television viewing without blood and sex is still television viewing, keeping children from the real world and the lessons it offers.

The questions raised previously are not meant to discredit the V-chip concept, for it will give interested parents a much-needed sense of control over the material now appearing in their family rooms. *New York Times* columnist Frank Rich did, however, make an interesting point when he called the whole ratings discussion "an escapist sideshow deflecting attention from any real discussion about the coarsening of our culture and the growing stranglehold of video in all its forms (including video games and the Internet's own junk) over the young...."[6]

Indeed, as much as we'd like instant, painless solutions to the television dilemma, they are not — and will not — be forthcoming. Working toward a reasonable, healthy approach to television takes time, initiative, and personal responsibility. No plan — government or otherwise — will be a fully satisfactory substitute.

A Time for Action

Whether you are concerned about the *quality* or *quantity* of your child's television viewing, now is the time to get involved. Comfortably secure in their habits, your children probably won't change on their own. Yet much is at stake when they continuously tune in. Moreover, as technology becomes increasingly refined, the role of electronic entertainment in our lives will continue to expand, further sapping our time, energy, and resolve. We need to get a game plan together now, when we're not yet overwhelmed and when it's not too late.

In Chapter 5 we will examine and evaluate several tried-and-true methods for scaling back the role of television in the lives of your children. Some methods will appeal to you, others will not; some will work for your kids, others will fall flat. Though it may take a bit of trial and error, soon you will recognize which strategies are most effective with your particular kids, with your particular circumstances, and with your particular style of parenting. Regardless of the route you choose, some preparation is needed. In the remainder of this chapter you'll find a preliminary plan for action.

Getting Started: Understanding Your Child's Viewing Habits

Before yanking the plug on the TV set (or even announcing to the kids that you are considering it), some investigative work is in order. Though it may *seem* as if your child watches television nonstop or, on the other hand, only tunes in to educational programming, careful record-keeping is the only way to find out for sure. To that end, we encourage you to maintain a week-long written log of your children's television watching habits. Keeping a log serves three important purposes: (a) It will indicate how much and what kind of television your kids actually watch, (b) it will show the level and type of involvement your kids have in non-TV activities, and (c) it will later serve as a record of old TV-directed habits that can be compared to new post-TV endeavors and adventures.

Using either a log like the one found in Appendix A (pp. 221-224) or one of your own design, chart your children's activities for one full week, including weekends. In hour increments jot down how your children spend their time, using a separate log for each child. Try to be specific. When they watch television, for example, be sure to include the specific programs viewed, or, if playing video games, which particular games they played. Somewhere in the log include daily totals of TV viewing, videotape viewing, video game playing, and time spent on the computer. Also, be specific in describing other activities. Rather than just writing "played outside," try to include the names of the kids with whom they played and what games they played. Finally, note the activities that seemed especially fun and enjoyable for your child; this extra step will be a great help when you later try to plan alternative activities.

Those parents who work away from home may find it difficult to keep tabs on their kids' activities throughout the day. As we'll discuss in the following chapter, being away from your kids does make mediation somewhat trickier, but not impossible. In the case of record-keeping, you can either ask your children's caregivers about their activities or, if they are old enough to be on their own, just ask your children themselves. Another option for working and stay-at-home parents alike might be to encourage older kids to keep track of their own activities. If this is the case, explain to them that you're interested in discovering how they spend their days, but try not to elaborate on your reduction plans since this may influence what they write down. Let them also have a hand in designing, decorating, and maintaining their own log. Their record-keeping may not be as accurate as yours, but they will probably appreciate having your trust in the matter.

Though your children will probably catch on to your increased interest in their day, try not to make a big deal out of it—for yourself *or* your kids. This is not a spy game, nor should it turn into a suburban version of the Inquisition. If kids feel they have a roving eye constantly turned on them, they will probably grow self-conscious and exaggerate or withdraw certain typical behaviors. If instead you allow their week to naturally and quietly unfold, they will show their true selves. And this is when true change can begin.

The Benefits of Record-Keeping

Though such detailed record-keeping may seem like an unnecessary hassle, maintaining a log or diary is a good idea for a number of reasons. Most importantly, it offers perspective on how your children spend their time, specifically, how much television your children actually watch compared with their participation in other activities. Seeing things on paper can quickly bring things into perspective.

Keeping a log can also be a great source of motivation. Diet gurus are on to something when they tell their followers to maintain a record of what they eat in a typical day. Whether at home or at work, it's easy to fall into the habit of snacking all day long. Spread throughout the day, a few Ho-Hos here and there don't seem so bad. Reading on paper that you've actually consumed the equivalent of an entire box, however, does have a certain shock value to it. When it's in print, the truth is hard to ignore. The same principle applies to your children's television viewing habits. An hour here, an hour there — at the time it doesn't seem like much, but the hours quickly add up. Before you know it, childhood has rushed by and your kids only have memories of *Ren & Stimpy* to show for it. Writing down and reviewing the amount of time your children spend in front of the television can be a quick spur to action. In one family we worked with, the simple act of record-keeping cut a 3-year-old boy's 8 hour a day viewing habit to between 2 and 3 hours, a level that remained even 6 months after the initial weeklong monitoring period. The parent reported that the feedback from the record-keeping alone prompted the reduction, stimulating her to find alternative activities to television for her son.[7]

Maintaining a record also helps keep track of day-to-day fluctuations in your children's activities. For example, on days when they have many organized activities planned, television will likely not play a large role and vice versa. You might also discover that the days you *thought* your children were watching too much TV were actually pretty benign. Saturday mornings — the only network time slot now devoted entirely to children's programming — have long had the reputation of stealing kids away from more productive activities. In fact, most kids today spend just as much time watching prime-time weekday programs as they do on Saturday mornings.

Additionally, if you have more than one child, record-keeping will highlight differences in their viewing habits. No two kids are exactly alike in their television viewing habits, even if they hail from the same family. Personality, gender (boys generally watch more than girls), disturbing events (bad grades, a best friend moves away), and cognitive abilities all factor into a child's viewing patterns. Age differences also account for much of the disparity. Though your kids may easily differ from the norm, researcher George Comstock discovered that children's television viewing falls into fairly predictable, age-related patterns.[8] For younger children (ages 2 to 5) who spend their days at home, television patterns revolve around lunchtime, naps, dinnertime, and bedtime. For example, while 20% of preschoolers watch TV between 8 a.m. and 11 a.m., the percentage dips to 10% between 1 and 2 p.m. The proportion viewing increases again to about 45% between 5 and 6 p.m., then decreases for dinner. It then rises again to an even higher peak between 7:30 and 8:30 p.m., after which calls for bedtime start ringing out. The viewing patterns of older children (ages 6 to 11), vary somewhat. Certainly there are few in the TV audience during school hours (except those who are home sick or pretending to be sick, huddled under blankets watching scratchy reruns of *Gilligan's Island* and *I Dream of Jeannie*). Beginning in the afternoon, though, older kids' patterns begin to mirror those of their younger counterparts, with a peak of about 60% watching between 8 and 9 p.m. This later peak likely reflects the hard-won bonus of having a later bedtime. Teenagers represent the third main group of young viewers. Their viewing is substantially less than the other two groups. Like older children, their ranks are thin during the day. Their peak comes a bit later, between 8 and 10 p.m., and a smaller percentage — 40% — tune in at this time. With increased scholastic and work responsibilities as well as budding social lives, many teenagers find that television holds less appeal and importance as time goes on. Indeed, the last thing most 16-year-olds want is to admit that they were home last Friday night watching TV.

Your own children may or may not reflect these norms. Record-keeping, however, will give you a solid idea of their habits. You are likely to discover that your individual children have different approaches to and uses for television: While your toddler adores TV, your 8-year-old cares little about it. Should this be the case, you'll know to adjust your strategies accordingly.

A final benefit of record-keeping is that it puts you in closer touch with your kids. Closely watching their activities for a week, you might see your kids in a slightly different light; sweet quirks and silly mannerisms that you never before noticed might surface, either to your delight or dismay. You'll also better understand the ebb and flow of your kids' moods, recognizing more quickly the things that make them hurt and the things that make them happy. Such emotional proximity is especially important to maintain in a child's school years, when kids begin to cling less to their parents and more to their peers and the offerings of the larger world. Parents should not be afraid to get involved in their kids' lives, especially as they grow older. Underneath their calculatingly aloof veneers ("It's sooo embarrassing to be seen with you, Mom/Dad. Drop me off a block away."), our kids still long for parental love, acceptance, and involvement.

Evaluating the Data

At the end of the week, take some time to assess the records of activity. For each child in your family, consider the following questions:

1. How many hours did your child spend watching television?
2. How many hours did your child spend playing video and computer games and/or using the Internet?
3. What time of the day/week was most of the viewing and/or game playing concentrated?
4. What kinds of programs did your child watch on TV and/or what kinds of games were played? Were they age-appropriate? Educational? High quality? Low quality? Violent? Filled with stereotypes?
5. Was your child reluctant to break away from television or games when asked? Was he or she highly engrossed in the action or just casually involved?
6. Was your child ever frightened or made anxious by what he or she saw on television?
7. If your child is school aged, how much time did he or she spend on schoolwork? Extracurricular activities?
8. How often did your child read for pleasure?
9. How much time did your child spend in the company of friends?
10. Did your child have a high level of physical activity?
11. Did your child spend time simply playing or using his or her imagination?
12. When your child was not watching television or playing video games, what kinds of activities seemed particularly enjoyable?

In looking at the records and reviewing your own answers, do your children—one, some, or all of them—watch too much television? Keep in mind that this is a personal judgment. Though many experts will say that television in excess of 12 hours a week is too much, it is hard to put an exact number on it. The question of appropriate levels of viewing is really based on the extent to which significant activities like playing with friends or reading are being sacrificed to the television set or a solitary computer screen. Your own weekly or daily standard should reflect your kids' habits in this regard. In addition to possibly watching too much TV, do your children watch many less-than-edifying programs? Does the television seem to be instilling less-than-desirable attitudes in your kids?

If you answered *Yes* to any of these questions, we hope you'll seriously consider taking action against television's top spot in your family. But rather than being a nasty series of tirades and dictates, the act of reducing television can be an engaging adventure for the whole family.

The Rules of the Road

In reducing the role of television in your family, the going may be a bit rough and bumpy at first. Following a clear set of rules or guidelines as you tackle excessive television watching will help to smooth the path.

One rule leads all the others: Whatever intervention technique you finally decide upon, sit down and discuss the plan with your children before taking action. It would be unfair, punitive, and counterproductive to slap a lock on the TV or announce a set of ironclad rules without first discussing the idea with your kids. The following are some additional suggestions to help ensure the greatest level of success and the least amount of sulking.

Keep It Fun

This guideline is essential, for one of your primary goals is to teach children that life without constant television can be far more exciting and entertaining. If you present the idea in anger, disappointment, or end-of-the-rope frustration, you've immediately created an antagonistic situation. This approach will quickly breed resentment, and many stubborn children will make it their goal to defy you. Instead, when you initially present the idea to your children, keep the mood positive and light. Stress to your kids that limiting their television is not a punishment but rather an exciting change for the whole family. This might take some marketing ingenuity on your part because kids are nothing if not savvy consumers who can quickly spot a poorly executed snow job. Let them know that you'll have a number of other activities planned and available, so that very soon they will hardly miss television at all. Since the first thing out of many skeptical mouths will be, "Yeah, like what?", be prepared to name *specific* activities that your children can participate in. Equally important, make sure they are activities your children will truly enjoy; this *would not* be the time to push for longer practice time at the piano. Referring to their activity log may spark some ideas on the things they consider fun.

Invite Response

Second, allow your kids to have a say in the matter. When you've gathered the entire family together to set out your game plan, invite response from your kids. Why is television so important to them? (Pay close attention to this answer; in it may lie the key to their excessive viewing habits.) What are their concerns about reduced viewing? Do they think the plan is fair? How, within reason, can the plan be made more fair? What will be the hardest part about not watching television or not playing video games as frequently as they are used to? What are some fun things the family can do together to make this experience a little easier? (Don't fall for their suggestion that only a trip to Disney World will make it better. Do, however, congratulate them on Thinking Big.)

It is doubtful that your kids will accept your plan with a smile. Being told that television will henceforth be limited will probably make them feel victimized, put-upon, cheated, and much maligned, quickly earning you the honor of being the Meanest Mom/Dad in the Whole Wide World. Your children's resistance and anger should come as no surprise especially if they are seasoned TV watchers. Indeed, in limiting television you are limiting one of most influential and seemingly essential parts of their lives. Call it withdrawal, call it a temper tantrum. Whatever you call it, know that such conflict is inevitable — and, thankfully, only temporary.

Providing a forum for honest conversation and response will go a long way toward smoothing ruffled feelings. While they may continue to pout and whine, at least they know that they've been included in some of the decision-making. To enhance this cooperative spirit, it may be helpful to share some of your own concerns and planned strategies for coping with less TV. If kids understand that everyone is in it together, they will feel less like a victim and more like a contributing member of a team.

Play Fair

Nothing will more quickly undermine your efforts than not playing fair. Most importantly, you must ensure that the entire family participates in the venture. For example, it would be unfair to single out just one child for reduced viewing even if that one child is the only one who views excessively. Such equity does not mean that you must take a one-size-fits-all approach to the family rules — older children, for example, might be allowed to watch a particular program not suitable, and thus not permitted, for younger siblings. Such equity does mean, however, that everyone in the house must be a part of the game — including parents.

This last point gets tricky. It is one thing to say that a young child needs to be guided in television watching and quite another to slap those same rules on a mortgage-paying 39-year-old who has long since learned to take care of himself or herself. Yet, while we rant and rave about children's excessive television watching, our own habits often rival and even surpass those of our kids. Our habits are also more entrenched, having had years and years to perfect and hone them. Despite our own possible discomfort with the idea, it is imperative that we parents lead by our example, abiding by the same rules we set for our children. How unfair it would be to have the kids engage in non-TV activities while you or your spouse sits in front of the TV set flipping through the channels; it would be like banning junk food from the kids just as you break open another bag of potato chips for yourself. Children are astute observers of those around them and are quick to sniff out hypocrisy and double standards.

It is possible that one parent will be far more enthusiastic about television reduction than the other. Just as kids may bristle at the thought of making such an adjustment in their lives, so too might many TV-loving parents. Because it is important to present a united front when discussing the idea with your kids, be sure you have already cleared it with your spouse *beforehand*. Though some degree of spontaneity and surprise is good for a marriage, this is not one of those times. Imagine sitting around the dining room table eagerly presenting your case when your spouse suddenly cries out, "We're doing WHAT?" You will have lost your most powerful ally while your kids, thrillingly, will have gained one.

A united front is also important even if parents are divorced. Though it may require reaching new levels of civility, try to discuss the plans with your ex-spouse and encourage his or her support. By keeping the focus both on the welfare of the kids and on the hard facts of excessive television, he or she should agree to enforce similar rules. Such consistency is particularly important in joint custody arrangements and for noncustodial parents who have a regular visitation schedule. Even as kids beg for lenience, they don't function well when there are wildly inconsistent rules in two different households.

Finally, you must teach your kids to play fair. Obviously you cannot, nor should not, monitor their every move. When they are visiting friends or other family members who do not have TV rules in place, chances are they will probably watch some television. Before attaching a mini-cam to their backpacks, realize that this is to be expected, and, in small quantities, this is not a big deal. Television is still a strong socializing agent, and to expect your child to shield his or her eyes from TV at a friend's house is unrealistic and unnecessary. Besides, in time many rule-bound children will realize that there are plenty of more exciting things to be done with friends than watching TV all afternoon; often they become neighborhood leaders in conjuring up imaginative TV-free activities. Some kids, however, are so resistant to the idea of limiting their television viewing that they will head over to friends' houses with the single intent of watching television. If this becomes the pattern, you may need to sit down and chat with said child about the meaning of being responsible and playing by the rules.

Write It Down

For those who plan to limit television viewing through rules, it is often a great help to put them in writing. Though some parents may see this step as unnecessary and somewhat legalistic, it can be beneficial for a number of reasons: First, if done in detail, it makes the rules explicitly clear. There will be no more haggling over the question of whether you said "2" or "3" hours of television allowable on the weekends. Kids can be enormously creative in developing excuses for not following rules, the least being the timeworn, "But I didn't *hear* you say that. . . ." If the rules are clearly expressed, they will have to learn to funnel that creativity elsewhere. Additionally, having written rules allows you to express them as they apply to your different kids. If your kids range widely in age, you might allow older kids a bit more flexibility than your young ones. Writing it down keeps everyone's rules straight and keeps day-to-day resentments at bay. It is also helpful to have rules written out so that when the baby-sitter comes, the day or evening does not turn into a marathon TV-fest. Kids can be enormously believable in claiming the things that their parents really, truly, honestly let them do. While your kids may dupe the baby-sitter into thinking that Gummi Bears can be substituted for dinnertime fish sticks, at least the TV rules will be incontrovertible.

When you develop the rules, be as detailed as possible and keep an eye out for loopholes; if they exist, your kids will find them. Also, be sure to include the *logical consequences* that will result if the rules are broken. For example, if your kids watch more than is allowable on a certain day, don't withhold allowance or make them help in the yard. Though effectively punitive, these consequences are arbitrary and do not reflect the original infraction. A better consequence would be to revoke TV privileges for the following day. Give thought to your consequences, and be sure your kids know what they are ahead of time by including them on your rule list.

Once your rules and consequences have been established, let your kids have a hand in writing them down. Kids with passable handwriting would probably appreciate being given this grown-up job (and if you have a home computer, this would be a great opportunity for your kids to show off their word processing and computer skills). Rather than putting the rules on a boring sheet of plain white paper, use brightly colored paper and allow your kids to decorate it; this will make the rules seem less "mean" and dictatorial. Finally, post the rules in a central spot such as on the refrigerator or near the television itself. Be sure, also, to save a spare copy of the rules in a safe, kid-proof place. It's amazing how quickly such a valuable document can get "lost."

In reducing television watching in your family, we can't promise a trouble-free trip. But by keeping it fun, inviting response, playing fair, and writing it down, the journey will be a much more positive one.

Summary

Parents today have enormous responsibility for guarding and enriching the welfare of their children. Not the least of these responsibilities is monitoring their television viewing, for few cultural forces so fully impact young hearts and minds. Reducing your children's TV habits may not be easy (few actions of lasting value are), but there are a number of steps you can take to make the going a little smoother. First, take time to assess your children's current level of viewing and participation in other activities. Then, as you introduce the idea of change to your family, try to heed the following four guidelines: keep it fun, invite response, play fair, and write it down.

It's now time to decide which route to take in reducing the role of television in your home. Chapter 5 will address the strategies on the Low-Tech Road, the High-Tech Road, and the Middle Road. No matter which one you choose, you'll be guaranteed an adventurous road trip to a more stimulating and fulfilling family life.

• 5 •
Options for Change

Traveling with the kids usually involves the best and the worst aspects of family life all rolled into one frazzled, sticky, exhausting, entertaining, memorable occasion. Car travel, in particular, has its own unique drama: overheated engines, ABC games, cries of boredom, spilled drinks, unending camp songs, carsick kids, squashed ketchup packets, and plenty of back-seat fights. If parents can survive the journey, the destination just might be worth the trouble.

Reducing your children's television viewing is a somewhat similar experience. Think of scaling back television as the journey while achieving your goal is the destination. As with a true family road trip, the "getting there" may not be a snap. It would be misleading to suggest otherwise, for difficult changes are almost always painful in the beginning. When well-known author and lecturer Jim Trelease and his wife Susan announced that television would henceforth be banned on school nights, their two children did not accept the news with much fortitude or grace:

> Their reaction was predictable: they started to cry. What came as a shock to us was that they cried for four solid months. Every night, despite explanations on our part, they cried. We tried to impress upon them that the rule was not meant as a punishment; we listed all the positive reasons for such a rule. They cried louder.[1]

The crying/pouting/whining phase is part and parcel of nearly every family's journey, though to greater or lesser degrees depending on the circumstances. As parents, you should probably brace yourselves, for just as on a true road trip, your kids will find new ways to be irritable and crabby. They will try hard to make you feel guilty and mean; they'll also milk their discomfort for all its worth, pointing out every other unfairness you've ever thrust into their lives. For a short while your kids will also be more dependent on you for direction, looking to you for answers to their "forced" boredom. Meanwhile, as you shift the focus of your children's attention away from television and on to new activities, you might need to do some shifting of your own. Priorities and habits long-entrenched must be reassessed, and perhaps your own television viewing habits will require some adjusting.

Though tiring and not always pleasant, this initial phase is only temporary. Slowly the scenery will start to change. In time, your children will learn how to independently entertain themselves. Your house will probably become messier, with plenty of crayons, game pieces, and crumbs of Play-Doh underfoot. You'll see and hear more playing, laughing, and horsing around. And together your family will do more chatting, reading, and imagining than ever before. Television, meanwhile, will have quietly faded into the background of family life. You've arrived!

Here our road trip analogy falls a bit short. In reducing television, the destination (i.e., success) is an altogether different experience from that found in a true family vacation. In the latter case, once the vacation's over, it's time to crawl back into the car and return to real life. On the other hand, in reducing television watching, upon "arrival" the destination turns into a whole new journey of adventure and discovery—lifelong, we hope. Moreover, the thrill of this destination is guaranteed. While the sight of yet another colonial Williamsburg candle shop may fail to inspire your kids ("Can we go back to the motel pool now?"), having learned to live beyond television is a sure thing. This is true even in seemingly "worst case" scenarios. Despite their inauspicious start, Trelease, his wife, and their kids did survive their journey; in the end, the initial bumps and tears were worth the trouble:

> After three months my wife and I began to see things happen that the Woods [family friends] had predicted. Suddenly we had the time each night as a family to read aloud, to read to ourselves, to do homework at an unhurried pace, to learn how to play chess and checkers and Scrabble, to make plastic models that had been collecting dust in the closet for two years, to bake cakes and cookies, to write thank-you notes

to aunts and uncles, to do household chores and take baths and showers without World War II breaking out, to play on all the parish sports teams, to draw and paint and color, and — best of all — to talk with one another, ask questions and answer questions.

Our children's imaginations were coming back to life again.[2]

We believe that all families who truly put forth an effort will be greeted with similar success. Finding that success, however, will be a different experience for each family who makes the attempt. First, the length of the transition will vary from family to family. In the Trelease's case, it took 3 months for true change to appear; in other families, a week or 2 might be all that is needed. Don't despair if your family doesn't seem to be "on track." Every family is different.

Second, different families will have different goals. Though presumably all families who embark on this journey hope to scale back television viewing, specific interpretations of how much television is ultimately appropriate will vary. Much of it depends on the content of the programming being viewed as well as your children's personalities and their previous viewing habits. For this reason we hesitate to offer a hard and fast rule of how much TV is too much. If kids are die-hard viewers, racking up 5, 6, or 7 hours a day, reducing viewing to just 2 hours of age-appropriate TV a day may spell victory. In another family, more than 5 hours in an entire week may seem like too much; their short-term goals will be more conservative. You know your kids better than anyone; by keeping their best interest in mind you should be able to come up with a reasonable, achievable goal.

Finally, different families need different approaches to television reduction. In a survey study on the topic of parent strategies we found great diversity.[3] For example, some indicated that they limited their kids' viewing by requiring chores before viewing, while a few honest souls admitted to relying on arguing and fighting about TV (surely a far more common strategy than our survey suggested). This same study indicated that few families met with any lasting success; fighting, for example, did the trick in less than 10% of the homes. Perhaps one reason for the overall lack of success was that many parents chose a strategy ineffective for their particular family situation. Again, one size doesn't fit all. Family values, temperaments, time available, work schedules, and other factors ensure that television reduction will be a highly individualized pursuit. Fortunately, there is a broad range of viable options for you to consider. Finding the right path is what Chapter 5 is all about.

The chapter is divided into three sections, each with a different strategy for television reduction. We suggest beginning with the simplest, least involving methods, moving on to more sophisticated techniques only as necessary. The simpler methods will be found on "The Low-Tech Road," which focuses on developing straightforward family rules. Techniques that require external control ranging from locks to credit card computers will be detailed on "The High-Tech Road." Finally, on "The Middle Road" we will describe a highly successful behavior modification technique. We've placed it at the end of the chapter not because it is least desirable, but because it falls squarely in the middle of the two other approaches. It requires more time investment than the Low-Tech Road but none of the gadgetry of the High-Tech Road. Though behavior modification is the strategy with which we have the most experience, we recognize that what works for one family may not work in another. Again, as stressed in the previous chapter, choose an approach that will actually work with your kids and that is in line with your values and parenting style. Then take a deep breath, pack up your nerve, and start your trip.

The Low-Tech Road: Family Rules

Even if you already *know for sure* that you will have to bring in the National Guard before your children will give up television, we encourage you to try this path first. It is the easiest, simplest, and most straightforward of all approaches. In fact, the "Low-Tech Road" might be more accurately termed the "No-Tech Road," for all it requires is communication, trust, and determination on your part and some self-discipline and cooperation on the part of your kids. No outlay of cash. No plugs. No programming. Just plain, old-fashioned common sense. You might be surprised at how far this valuable commodity will go.

Start by De-Emphasizing Television

No matter what route you ultimately take, de-emphasizing television is the place where everyone should start. In order for any mediation plan to succeed, television must be downgraded from being a major player in your family to assuming just a minor, occasional role. If there is a television in every room in the house, if the arrival of the *TV Guide* continues to be greeted with gusto, and if TV trays are still unfolded each evening, children will have a hard time monitoring their own behavior. It would be akin to regularly bringing a chocolate cream pie into the home of a perpetual dieter: thoughtless and counterproductive.

On the other hand, subtly chipping away at television's omnipresence in your home will make it much easier for the entire family to succeed. Often by simply removing the stimulus (chocolate pie, television, or whatever the temptation is at hand) behaviors will change. How, then, do you de-emphasize television? The first step seems the most radical, but it is also one of the most important: Get rid of all of your extra television sets, keeping only one for family viewing. If a television is available in every major room in the house, you can hardly expect kids or even adults to try to entertain themselves with more demanding or involving activities. Keep extra sets out of two rooms in particular: the kitchen and your children's bedrooms. As the natural focus of any home, the kitchen is where dynamic family conversation and interaction can take place as members make meals, eat dinner, and share about their day; if a television is blaring continuously, these opportunities are lost. Meanwhile, if TV sets are in your kids' rooms, you'll have little idea of what or how much they are watching. This arrangement also gives kids an excuse to avoid family interaction. Given the option, many teens and preteens would just as soon close their doors, flip on their TVs, and stay inside until college. This does not bode well for family togetherness. So sell those extra sets (use the money for a special family treat), give them away to charitable organizations, or store them in the far back corner of your attic. They won't be missed for long.

As for the remaining set, shift it from center stage. Though some critics suggest moving it to the least desirable place in the house to further avoid temptation (a damp, spooky basement, for example), we offer a compromise plan. Keep the set in a comfortable place, for there are times you will want to watch TV without catching a cold or being harassed by crickets. However, it's important to *physically* de-emphasize the set. In some homes, especially newer custom homes, the television is practically set up as a shrine, so prominent is its location. Buck this trend by preventing the TV set from becoming the focal point of the room. Buy or make an entertainment center with doors that hide the set when not in use. If you are short on funds or talent, throw a nice-looking sheet or tablecloth over the set. Top it with a vase of flowers and — presto — you have an instant piece of furniture. Fashionable or not, such a tactic sends an important message: Television no longer rules this home.

In addition to physically limiting the television, you might also consider giving away your remote control devices. For all of their easy appeal, remote control devices make television watching too convenient and too habitual. With dozens and dozens of channels to surf through, the options for viewing are unending. Even commercial breaks now fail to give reprieves. By jumping and dodging a station's commercial breaks, nimble viewers can follow two, three, even four shows at the same time. And when a program grows momentarily dull, rather than sticking it out or turning off the television altogether, the viewer need only click a button to find something more appealing. In a startlingly swift fashion, remote control devices have created a generation of young Americans whose first reflex is to zap something that doesn't instantly entertain, an unfortunate trend that already reverberates far beyond the family TV room. Though few people (kids *or* adults) will want to give up this now seemingly necessary accessory to television viewing, it can make an amazing difference in one's viewing habits. Without the remote control, television viewing becomes a deliberate, defined activity, rather than one that rolls along haphazardly for hours at a time. Ironically, it is our natural laziness that works *for* us in this case. Few people would click through the channels so frequently and enduringly if it meant getting off the comfy sofa to make the switch the old-fashioned way. Though it's an admittedly reactionary suggestion, eliminating or limiting use of the remote control can go a long way toward de-emphasizing television in your home.

Finally, parents can de-emphasize television by de-emphasizing it in their own lives. As mentioned in Chapter 4, this effort is essential for whole family success. That may mean thinking twice about watching TV in the bedroom late at night, saying no to morning news programs at the breakfast table, and kissing good-bye the idea of spending entire weekend afternoons watching sports from the brown plaid recliner. For many ardent sports fans, this last rule seems especially brutal. As we must tell our kids, though, there *is* life after television.

The lesson of discovering alternative activities—however simple they may be—was made clear in a study we conducted in a nursing home.[4] When we began our study, most of the residents visiting the lounge area either passively watched television or stared off into space. But when residents were provided free access to coffee and cookies, television watching was eliminated and the residents began to interact with each other. Such a simple step produced such wonderful results. Parents and kids alike can find equally appealing activities. One father we know keeps up with sporting events on the radio as he putters in his workshop. Not only does he still hear the action and keep up with the scores, but he also often has something productive to show for his time. Other parents become voracious readers or gourmet cooks. For those who argue that they absolutely must see the evening news, there are a number of other options for keeping up with current events. Reading the newspaper is the most obvious choice. Not only is the news delivered much more thoroughly, but the very act of reading a paper sets a great example for your kids. Since reading the paper can take a chunk out of your day, those pressed for time have other options: for well-written stories and analysis either subscribe to a weekly news magazine like *Time, Newsweek,* or *U.S. News and World Report* or listen to the news on the radio as you are getting dressed in the morning or driving home from work. National Public Radio, in particular, does an outstanding job of in-depth reporting.

Just as you would find alternative activities for yourself, you must do the same for your children. In de-emphasizing television, you must concurrently emphasize positive activities. Leave piles of books and magazines *everywhere.* Designate a central, easy-to-reach cabinet or chest to house board and card games. Put photo albums out in the open. Encourage your kids to help in the kitchen. Make sports equipment readily available. As will be shown in Chapter 6, the key to reducing the role of television is to increase the role of positive, fun, engaging activities. Be creative in these endeavors.

De-emphasizing television is an important first step in reducing your family's television viewing. If families employ such a strategy when their kids are very young, excessive television habits will probably never develop in the first place. Meanwhile, some habitual viewers may respond positively to this one simple action, having never before considered the range of other things they could be doing with their time.

Try Talking

In conjunction with de-emphasizing television, your first direct approach in working with your kids should simply be to talk to them about your television concerns and ask for their help in solving the problem. Explain that they can take steps to reduce and monitor their own TV habits. Even if you doubt that your kids will respond to this approach, give it a shot. First, it demonstrates your trust and confidence (however secretly flagging) in their own abilities for self-discipline and responsibility. This trust alone can go a long way toward positive results. Second, it's a logical place to start because it is the simplest of all remedies.

Sit down with your kids and explain your concern about their television watching. Pull out your kids' completed activity logs and go over the results together. Point out specific areas of concern such as too much TV on Saturdays or inappropriate shows on weeknights. Then discuss with your kids how they can solve the problem on their own. For example, they might want to keep a TV diary to keep track of their viewing or further their involvement in an outside activity like sports or clubs. Give them a goal to work toward, say, reducing their television watching to under 2 hours a day within 2 weeks. To expect miracles overnight is asking too much; give them a reasonable, but finite period of time to make changes.

To head them in right direction, be sure to mention those things on the activity log that you particularly admired, like reading a new book or doing artwork. Try to also encourage other activities that you think they would enjoy or at which they might succeed. Often just a few encouraging words can help in the formation of new, positive habits.

Mature, self-motivated kids will probably respond well to this approach. Yet even if your children do not fall into this narrow category, give them a chance to succeed or fail all on their own before getting more involved.

TV Rules

If your attempt at reducing television through talking has turned out to be a flop, don't lose heart. While self-monitoring is an important place to start, it does call for more self-restraint than many kids can muster. Especially for older, more TV-habituated kids, de-emphasizing television may not be enough to sway them from the set. If after a few weeks neither of these approaches has led to a reduction in television watching, press forward with a new tactic. Formulating a few television rules may do the trick.

Having worked with numerous families over the years, we've heard of a wide variety of rule systems, some simple and straightforward, others that are Byzantine in structure. Despite their lack of drama, the simplest methods are often the most effective. Many families, for example, find great success in just verbally limiting the number of hours children can watch television each day or week. If this rule is established when kids are young, it becomes a normal, accepted part of family life.

For nearly 12 years now, the Hewes family has had one television rule. Their daughter Abby, now 16, and their son Josh, age 13, are allowed to watch 1 hour of television *or* play 1 hour of video games (not both) each weekday. On the weekends, the limit is increased to 2 hours. Though basic and old-fashioned, the rule has led to exceptional results for their kids and their family life as a whole. Abby and Josh are both highly verbal and interactive kids who regularly read magazines, newspapers, and books. The Monopoly game is a permanent fixture in the family room, setting the scene for the family's long-held tradition of playing board games and cards. As their mother says, "Limiting their television has made them much more able to entertain themselves. They don't require electronics to have fun." Such engaging self-direction seems infectious: When Josh's good friend David comes over to visit, he only wants to play board games. Though David watches TV frequently at home, it holds no appeal for him when he's visiting the Hewes.

Barbara Hall Palar, writing in *Better Homes and Gardens,* came up with a slightly more complex, yet still workable system for her family:

> My husband and I tried a variety of strategies with our three kids, ages 12, 8, and 6, before we found the one that works. This is our plan:
>
> No TV on school nights. Sunday through Thursday, the TV is turned off at 5 p.m. Friday is family movie night — a rental or a favorite from our collection. On Saturday evenings we watch Nickelodeon. The kids can watch cartoons or a video until 7:30 a.m. on school days, which gives them an hour to get ready for the bus, and until 8 a.m. on weekends. During the summer the set is turned off from 8 a.m. until 4 p.m., when they can watch until I arrive home at 5. All shows need to be parent-approved.[5]

Palar goes on to write that while the new system did not turn her kids into overnight creative geniuses, it did give a number of impressive returns. Her kids' overall behavior, especially where it related to TV watching, improved (no more "gymnastics on the furniture" or TV-related "bedlam"); bargaining for delayed chores diminished; and, most notably, her son's school performance improved within weeks of implementing the rules.

Variations on TV Rules

As the Palar family demonstrates, families can be creative in developing their rules. Limiting the number of hours that kids are allowed to watch television is probably the most common TV rule, but there are a number of variations you might also consider. A similar rule many families employ is *picking one day of the week when the TV set will be kept off* completely. Without the noisy interference of television, families can more easily find time to simply enjoy each others' company. The day of the week depends on your family's taste and schedule. Some families pick Sunday as their No TV day. A day that is often reserved for family time, Sunday has the added benefit of being the lead-off to each new week. Beginning the week after a restful and enjoyable day with your family can bring a great boost to Monday morning blues. One drawback to Sundays, however, is that it frequently offers special evening programming geared toward quality family viewing. Either use your VCR to record those special programs for later viewing or pick another night of the week. If you decide to employ this rule, be sure to have a number of alternative activities available. One family who bans television on Sunday nights has a game night tradition instead. Another always orders pizza and then everyone cracks their current favorite book. Whatever you choose, try to make it special.

Like the Palars, other families have a *No TV on school nights* rule. A reader of a popular family magazine sent the following letter to its Reader Solution column:

> A new rule, "No television on school nights," has improved my children's school grades and their interest in reading. As a compromise, I let them tape a favorite program, which they can watch during their free hour after school. They now find many of the shows they thought they had to see aren't worth the time to set up the VCR.[6]

Other parents declare rules that their *children must first complete certain tasks* like homework, practicing an instrument, or chores before turning on the TV. Such a practice sends the firm message to kids that pursuits in education, self-discipline, and home responsibility hold more value than a fleeting television program. Another rule we particularly like links television privileges with reading. Some families stipulate that for every hour a child spends in front of the television, the same amount of time must be spent with a book or magazine; others allow kids to earn a half hour of TV time for reading a certain number of pages or chapters in a book. Be creative in your rule-making, but also remember to be fair. After all, the point of rule-making is to provide your kids with positive, rewarding experiences they might not have the motivation to discover on their own.

In a slightly different vein, some families tie television watching to *responsible decision-making* on the part of the kids. As one mother described, at the beginning of each week she gave each of her kids 16 poker chips, allowing them 8 hours of television to be spread throughout the week. Each chip could be redeemed for one-half hour of TV (news shows were free). At the end of the week, the kids earned 25 cents for any unredeemed chips.[7] This system, a distant relative to the behavior modification system detailed later in this chapter, teaches kids the art of budgeting their TV time.

Finally, one rule all parents would be wise to consider involves *TV-related fighting*. There is surely no greater source of television conflict than different kids wanting to watch different shows at the same time. Eliminate much of the attendant yelling and punching by instituting rules that have consequences for all involved parties, regardless of who "started it." For instance, you might declare that *anyone* heard arguing about the television will lose TV privileges for a specified period of time. If the rules are made clear ahead of time, your kids will probably learn to weigh the consequences before screeching at the top of their lungs.

It's important to give your kids the tools to succeed in this endeavor. When you first present this rule to your children, well before any arguing has set in, have them brainstorm ideas that seem fair and equitable to use if a sticky situation starts rearing its head. For example, if conflicting shows come on, kids can draw straws, take turns choosing, compromise and trade off in other areas (doing a sibling's chores in exchange for watching a particular show), or use the VCR to tape the other program. If tensions further escalate, *in advance* teach them how to diffuse anger positively (count to 10 before saying anything, walk around the house to get rid of extra energy, and so forth), how to listen carefully to each another, and how to disagree politely with one other. Consistent use of this rule can post a number of terrific benefits. Aside from eliminating the source of a great number of household arguments, this approach promotes creative problem solving, civility and respect, responsibility, and the waning art of thinking first and acting second. Let us also consider the hopeful possibility that your headaches, finally, might now go away.

Content Rules

In addition to time limits, some parents may also want to establish concurrent rules about the *types* of programs their kids watch. More about content control will be discussed in Chapter 6, but a few of the important points will be highlighted here as well. First, don't assume that what your children are watching is intended for or is appropriate for kids. For example, just because a program is animated does not mean that children should be in the audience. Many kids flock to *The Simpsons,* first because of its animation—a traditional signal for children's shows—and, second, because of the antiestablishment charm of the show's antihero, Bart. Though *The Simpsons* can be wickedly funny for adults who understand its irony, its messages often run counter to the simple "be good—work hard" lessons parents try to instill in their kids.

On the other hand, make sure you've actually sat and watched a program before banishing it from the house; some programs sound a lot worse than they actually are. Parents should become familiar with the content of shows popular with their kids and then judge the merit of the content for themselves. If you are still uncomfortable with a particular show's content, take action. Watch the program with your child, countering questionable messages with your own comments, questions, and discussion. If you can't be there to watch alongside or if you've concluded that the show is truly terrible, simply disallow it until your kids reach a certain age. Be sure, however, to give reasons for your action so that it does not seem like a punishment. You might also want to post a running list of off-limit shows to keep communication and expectations clear with your kids.

It may also be helpful to take a few minutes at the beginning of each week to scan the TV listings, letting the kids pick out the programs that they positively, absolutely must see and that also fall within your standards. Not only does this give you some input in their choices, but it teaches kids to be selective viewers. Given only a few hours of TV time each week, kids will probably carefully consider their choices. This approach also catches TV conflicts before they escalate into all-out war. Planned ahead, there's less of a chance for conflict throughout the week.

Determining programs to be viewed in advance offers some important secondary benefits, as well. A woman who participated in one of our adult television reduction studies watched over 6 hours a day before our intervention. Though the focus of the study was on the use of metered feedback in reducing viewing, this woman added a strategy of her own: She checked the *TV Guide* before turning the television on, and then turned it off when the program she was interested in came to an end. In describing these changes in her viewing patterns, she said, "I felt like I was using television instead of it using me, and I liked it better." For the record, after our intervention the woman reduced her daily viewing to well under an hour a day.[8]

General Guidelines for Rules

There are four general guidelines to follow in constructing specific rules for television viewing: First, keep them simple. Rules that require a flow chart to understand tend not to work well in real-life situations. Kids better remember and better act on simple instructions. Second, as we've earlier suggested, write the rules down. This may not be necessary in families that institute TV rules when their children are very young, but for other families it can be an important step toward success. In addition to providing clarity, writing rules down also signals the seriousness with which you approach the problem. Third, back up your rules with consequences. Often when kids break rules, a parent's first recourse is to nag. But nagging is unproductive and is annoying to both the "nagger" and the "naggee." If logical consequences consistently follow an infraction, there will be no need for whiny pleas and wimpy threats. As a fourth guideline, remain flexible. There will be times when a special program or TV event falls outside the bounds of your strict rules. Many video tapes and TV-aired movies, for example, run over 2 hours. It would be a mistake to forever ban such programs, for some can provide great learning experiences. In the Hewes family, for example, Abby and Josh recently exceeded their daily limit when the two-part mini-series "Gettysburg" was aired on a cable channel. The family watched the movie together, and, though long, it sparked many valuable discussions about the Civil War. Sporting events like the Olympics, the World Cup Soccer Championships, the World Series, and the NBA Finals also tend to be worthwhile exceptions. Kids will appreciate seeing your flexible side, and the occasion will probably be considered a special family event.

Hold a "No TV" Week

Holding a "No TV Week" is another low-tech option. It is the cold-turkey approach to reducing television watching, and at first glance it sounds more radical than it actually is. TV does not have to be forever abandoned; it's just a temporary good-bye.

The idea of a "No TV Week" was developed and popularized by Marie Winn, author of several books on children and television. In her 1987 book *Unplugging the Plug-In Drug* she offers both parents and schools a very practical guide to ousting television for a finite period of time, typically 1 week.[9] The goal of the TV-Turn Off is to let kids discover *on their own* that television need not rule their lives. The hope is that after 1 week (or a month or even a year) without television, kids will be so involved in other activities that TV will naturally become only a bit player in their lives.

In her book, Winn presents a number of ideas to help make this seemingly daunting project a success. Serious planning is a must, for in many families a week without TV is cause for near revolt. First, look for a week in your calendar that is free of major events like a holiday, a major television special (the Olympics, for example, or a long-awaited mini-series), or unusual school or work demands. The proposed date should be at least 2 weeks in the future to allow for thorough planning. Next, when you present the idea to your kids, try to put a fun, adventurous twist on it ("It's an experiment," "We're all in this together," "This will be something new and different for us," "Let's think of a fun reward for when the week is over."). No matter how good your PR campaign, be prepared for a less than enthusiastic response. For many kids, this plan is tantamount to cutting off their supply of oxygen. Older children may be especially bitter; long used to unlimited access to TV, they will likely respond with comments like: "You've *got* to be kidding," "Yeah, right, this will be fun—not!" or "You guys are such geeks. I wish I had parents like. . . . " Take it all in stride; before the end of the week, they'll probably be singing a different tune.

Also, as we've earlier suggested, keep a week-long log of typical family activities, paying special attention to how much television is watched and what other activities are engaged in. This will serve as a good benchmark for when your family resumes television watching after the Turn-Off. Finally, be prepared to have an abundance of alternative activities planned—search under beds for pieces to old board games, put air in the bike tires, and have the piano tuned. For years television has entertained your children. It might take a while for them to learn to entertain themselves.

To make the thought of the week more bearable, Winn suggests preparing for it with specific rituals and rewards:[10]

1. Have each child sign a contract spelling out the conditions of the Turn-Off (no TV, video games, or video tapes; make a positive effort to engage in other activities; and keep a diary of the week). The contract signing may be done a bit tongue-in-cheek to maintain some levity, but the importance of sticking to the plan should be stressed.
2. Next, each child should come up with a personal "battle plan" for dealing with TV withdrawal, brainstorming possible activities that will make the week more palatable and fun.
3. Pack the family in the car and head to the library. Winn calls the library trip "indispensable." Stock up on fun, engaging reading material to fill those long TV-less hours. As an activity during the week, kids might want to make and decorate their own bookmarks.
4. Younger kids might enjoy making and wearing buttons and badges proclaiming their No-TV Week. You'll probably lose a lot of credibility, though, if you suggest this to any child over the age of 8 or so; they will think you are very uncool.
5. All family members should keep No-TV diaries, describing what they did, how they felt, and how their lives changed during their week without television. Younger children may verbally contribute to one main family diary, though you should encourage kids who can write to keep their own. Small spiral-bound notebooks work best, and kids might want to decorate the covers and jazz up the inside to give them more importance.
6. Last, but certainly not least (especially as far as the kids are concerned), families should together determine a special reward for the end of the week. Completely eliminating television is no small feat, and the kids will probably be more motivated knowing that there will be a reward to mark their achievement. Kids should have a hand in choosing the treat. Perhaps you could go to a local amusement park, the zoo, or a favorite restaurant. Other rewards might include having later bedtimes on weekends for a month, or if you are especially brave and ambitious, adopting a family pet from a local animal shelter.

Once all of the plans are in place and the designated week has arrived, it's time to hold a Kick-Off ceremony. Everyone should gather 'round to bid the set adieu. Though Winn suggests that families come up with their own unique ceremony, she offers a number of silly, but fun suggestions: Melodramatically read good-bye poems and speeches. Have an older child ceremoniously unplug the cord to the TV, then let everyone help in shrouding the set in a dark blanket or sheet. Affix seals (bright stickers or stamps) to the contracts to make them "legally" binding and pass out the diaries. Then walk away to begin your weeklong adventure without TV.

The week is sure to be interesting—one that merits preservation in writing. Winn strongly emphasizes diary-keeping throughout the week, and it does serve a number of good purposes. It helps kids stay actively involved in the project; it serves as a daily reminder of the project; it provides them with an outlet for their frustrations or new discoveries; it keeps track of the alternative activities they engage in; and it provides a lasting record of your family's achievement. In *Unplugging the Plug-In Drug*, Winn includes entries (complete with the original spelling and punctuation) from actual diaries from kids in some of her test families. Despite what you or they may think, your kids *will* find something to do to occupy their time. It might not be the most productive pursuit, but that's not always necessary anyway. Following are some of the entries listed in the book. In hilarious and poignant ways, the simple honesty of children shines through; unlike many adults, kids are not interested in embellishing the truth to make themselves sound more noble than they actually are:

1. Dear Diary: Friday—It was a pretty boring day until I had a fight with my sister who played the piano and she kept on kicking me.
2. Friday—After school, since I didn't have anything to do because of No-TV I did my homework. After that I took a long bath. Then I brushed my hair. Then I swept my grandmother's house.
3. Today when I got home I finished 2 drawings that I did. After that I started organizing my room. The thing I did was fix my bed, sweep, and fixed the teddy bear. Then I heard the radio. When I started to hear the radio I was thinking about going to the movies and seeing *9 Deaths of the Ninja*. When I finished that I did a lot of exercises. After that I cleaned the bathroom. It took me almost an hour. Then I started to read a book. It is called *The Sedai*. I read half of the chapter of my book.
4. 4/28: What I did instead of TV: sweep my house, did a 3D flower; played board games with my friend; made

Options for Change 163

play-dough for my 3D flower; in evening, had a party; played games with my friends; went to sleep.
5. No TV Journal—Friday: I did knitting 5 times. The first time it came out not that good. But then I got used to it. I played jump rope outside the balcony. Then I tooked a bath. After I tooked a bath I ate supper. . . . When I finished eating, I sat down on the sofa and talk to my friends. Then I did more of knitting. When I finished knitting, I read some books. . . . After that I was hearing the TV. That wasn't fun at all, so I did exercise.
6. Instead of watching TV I helped make dinner, and I usually don't.
7. I came home from school and I didn't watch TV. I just took a little rest and I was talking to my Mommy.
8. 8:p.m.—Looked for batteries. Stared into space. Didn't miss television.
9. I went to bed a half hour earlier.
10. Dear Diary: I was at my uncle's house and everybody was watching TV. I stayed in the kitchen and read and made a cake.
11. I have taken funny pictures from the *New Yorker Magazine* for a scrapbook.
12. Instead of watching TV I had a long talk about school.
13. Dear Diary: I got up at 6 a.m. Then I just sat there.
14. 11:43 to 12:15—I fought with my brother Kevin. 6:30 to 6:45—I counted my money.
15. Dear Diary: first I moped the bathroom. Then I talked on my CB for a while.
16. After supper I thought about things for a long time.
17. Today instead of watching TV, I washed out my thermos.
18. Today instead of watching TV I wrote on my brother's feet and stomach.
19. Today I went to the YMCA, came home, ate dinner, got fed up and went to bed.
20. Dear Diary: tried to kiss Arielle but I could not. But I will try Monday."*

---

*"Twenty-Four Desperation Time-Fillers from No-TV Diaries," from *Unplugging the Plug-In Drug* by Marie Winn. Copyright © 1987 by Marie Winn. Used by permission of Viking Penguin, a division of Penguin Books USA Inc.

At the end of the week, having successfully passed the No-TV test, it's now time for a celebration party. Make a special meal, go out to a favorite restaurant, or fix the family's favorite dessert and toast with milk glasses the family's success. A celebration party, however, should not include a mad dash to the TV set. Indeed, the point of a No-TV Week is to teach families that life can be richer and more enjoyable *without* television. Hopefully at the week's end, after discovering new hobbies and activities, children will naturally be less interested in television. On their own, kids will likely set new and reduced viewing patterns for themselves; otherwise parents can set them for them, probably without much complaining. While it is unrealistic to assume that the TV set will remain permanently off, TV Turn-Off families often learn that television need only play a minor role in their lives.

In case you're still leery of going cold turkey, take a look at the diary entries of a mother whose family gave up television for an entire summer. Of the family's two daughters, ages 7 and 10, one very much liked television, and the other seemed truly hooked. As Winn relates them, the mother's words should give hope and encouragement to wavering, unconvinced parents:

> "It was painful at first . . . but after the first week we were off and running. I've been teaching Tammy to sew. Kate's been trying her hand at some cooking. One cake pan turned upside down in the bottom of the stove—ooh, that was messy. That has to happen once when you're learning. And we're still all laughing our heads off when we look back at it."

As the summer progressed, the catalog of improvements continued. "The kids seem sort of proud of the fact that they can really entertain themselves. They both like to draw a lot and they made a request to Santa for some pastels this Christmas. We already have watercolors and oils. They both show an inclination towards art. They may not be good but they get a lot of pleasure from it," wrote the mother during the fifth week of the experiment.

"Music, too, has become more important without the competition of TV. Both girls spend more time practicing their instruments (piano and violin) and now they even spend time playing together. . . .

"I really feel the family is pulling together tighter as a result of our Turn-Off. I know my husband feels this way just as strongly as I do. When we see the girls doing something new we'll say to each other: 'See if we had the TV they wouldn't be doing this.'

"And there's a real difference about going outside. In the past we couldn't get the kids outside to save our souls unless my husband held the door and I booted them out, practically. Now they're going out in all sorts of weather, we have to yell after them to put on their boots. It used to be that *we'd* go out and build a snowman and they'd watch us from the living room. Now, I don't know, they just seem a lot hardier."[12]*

Besides being a great testimony to life without television, this entry also demonstrates that families can fiddle with variations on the No-TV Week. Some families, like the previous one, shoot for a month, a season, even a whole year. In one of those bizarre cases that juxtaposes life and art, the *Oprah Winfrey Show* challenged families to give up television for 1 month. For those brave families who agreed, moving vans arrived at their door to remove all TV sets from their homes. When the actual program aired, the show cut back and forth between pretaped excerpts of participants expressing their pre-TV Turn-Off jitters and live, in-studio coverage of post-TV Turn-Off experiences. While many of the program's most entertaining moments came from participants fessing up to cheating, some families did find lasting change. One couple who previously had no time for each other rediscovered their "passion" for each other. Another participant, a mother, found benefits that were both practical and social. As a boon for her, the kids started getting involved in her day-to-day activities like grocery shopping and cleaning the house. As a bonus for the kids, they found time to pursue neighborhood friendships by hosting slumber parties and simply hanging out. In the most memorable segment of the program, one mother described how the absence of television turned family misfortune into something special:

Two weeks ago my dad died. And as the kids came home from school, we told each one what had happened. We let them finish their day. And I know I would bet that if this happened when we had TV, they would have each gone

---

*"A Good Family Gets Better," from *Unplugging the Plug-In Drug* by Marie Winn. Copyright © 1987 by Marie Winn. Used by permission of Viking Penguin, a division of Penguin Books USA Inc.

to their own room and turned the TV on or gone to a TV. In fact, I did cheat and read [daughter] Colleen's journal and she said, "Grandpa died today. I wish we had TV, it would take the pain away." And I was saying, "It doesn't take the pain away. It just hides it." And we were stuck around the kitchen table and we were talking. And it was—it was—for something so tragic, it was really a wonderful experience.[13]*

In addition to the social and emotional payoffs, another benefit of a longer TV Turn-Off is that it allows enough time for the symptoms of TV withdrawal—crankiness, boredom, and plain old anger—to rear their troublesome heads and then fade away. For some dedicated viewers, it might take over a week for this process to take place. If most of a No-TV Week has been spent in a bad mood, chances are that the participant won't look back on it fondly. Longer turn-offs, on the other hand, provide enough time for positive experiences and discoveries to take place. Also, longer turn-offs can make for more lasting change. For some families, a week without TV represents just a semipainful aberration from normal life. Once the week has passed, many participants quickly revert to their regular habits. Allowing for a month or more provides enough time to let stubborn TV habits die and for new, more productive habits to take shape.

If the idea of a No-TV Week or Month appeals to you, find a copy of *Unplugging the Plug-In Drug*. The book is packed with terrific ideas on making this strategy a success.

The High-Tech Road: Electronic Tools

Low-tech approaches such as rules, de-emphasis, and total TV turn-offs work for many families, but not all. The most common complaint about the preceding "low-tech" methods is that they generally require having an adult around full time to keep them enforced. Though parents can often monitor TV watching in the evenings, guiding the after-school hours tends to be problematic when parents work. Single parents have long felt neglected in TV reduction techniques, and as more and more married mothers also head into the workplace, this becomes an issue for the majority of families in America.

New developments in the area of TV reduction techniques seek to improve this situation. Through electronic locks, switches, and com-

---

*Reprinted with permission of Harpo Productions, Inc.

puters, your children's viewing can be restricted or monitored even when you are away from them. Parents who are at home with their kids also find appeal in these devices. In some families, despite parents' best efforts, rules simply don't work. Though we would encourage you to first carefully analyze *why* your rules might not be working (some possibilities include not following up on consequences; illogical consequences, or no consequences at all; not consistently enforcing the rules; or not providing enough alternative activities), some parents still find they need more back-up and support. As an additional benefit, the employment of such devices helps to de-personalize the often touchy act of reducing TV watching. Parents must still set up the system and remain responsible for it, but they find they are not constantly yelling at their kids to "turn that darn thing off!" Rules frequently invite cheating (or at least some dedicated testing), which brings on nagging, which in turn builds up a deep reservoir of resentment. With locks and switches, nagging and its attendant annoyances are eliminated.

We should note that many people fundamentally disagree with the idea of TV locks and related devices. Critics complain that parents should be able to control their kids without the aid of locks. Moreover, they claim that locks are punitive and can crush the fragile issue of trust in a family. Another potential deterrent to these devices is that many are relatively expensive, which can be prohibitive in itself. Families on tight budgets might continue trying more old-fashioned approaches or try the behavior modification techniques outlined later in the chapter.

In weighing the philosophical issues, your best strategy will be to simply put your child's best interest first, for that is what reducing television viewing is all about. Consider the personalities of your kids, your philosophy on parenting, and the success or failure of your approaches in the past. As for the comparatively straightforward question of efficacy, we have tested several of the following TV reduction products, with most posting very positive results. Read on, then decide for yourself.

The Switch

In 1981 an otherwise chipper suburban mother named Addie Jurs had finally had it with her three boys' nonstop television viewing. Her patience was depleted, but not her ingenuity. With the help of her husband, she designed an electronic lock that controls when the television can be turned on. A 1991 article in the *Chicago Tribune* describes the inception of The Switch:

> "I would try to be real nice," says Addie Jurs. "I would try to work out a plan. My boys would always tease me that I say 'From now on we'll do this. . . .' " Playing the role of the Enforcer upset her. "You feel like an ogre, like you're not being a nice mother."
>
> It's a familiar story, and Addie Jurs didn't want any part of it. So she locked the TV and kept the key. The homemade device her husband Jerry, an investment counselor, concocted 10 years ago from a switch box and an electrical lock has led to her new life as crusader, saleswoman, and would-be author. . . .
>
> But do not call her an anti-TV crusader. She bristles. A die-hard optimist . . . she says positivism underlies her approach to the lock. . . . Jurs thinks of the lock as an insurance policy for a TV philosophy called "selective viewing," an approach long-advocated by psychologists who believe children should learn to choose what to watch. The Jurs family discussed how much time the children would spend watching TV and unlocked it only at the agreed-upon times.[14]

Today The Switch is manufactured by an outside firm though Addie Jurs continues to market it herself. Costing $21.95 plus shipping, The Switch is a small child-proof box (approximately 4" x 3" x 2") that attaches to the electrical cord of any television set. On top of The Switch is a key lock, which operates the On/Off switch. Television can only be viewed when the key is turned to the "On" position; when the key is turned to the "Off" position, the flow of the electrical current is blocked, cutting the power to the TV. Also, when in the "Off" position video games cannot be played and video tapes cannot be viewed, though the VCR can still record programs. To prevent tampering by determined young viewers, The Switch has a security door, accessible only with a specially designed tool. The only true security problem for parents is the question of where to hide the key. Many kids who cut their teeth on egg hunts and Hide and Seek will relish the challenge of finding it.

In her guide *Becoming Unglued,* Jurs advocates selective viewing and whole-family planning.[15] After determining how long the television will be in use each day, family members should then decide which programs and video games will be seen and played. Selections will probably have to be updated weekly, noting carefully the start and stop times for each show. If a program airs at an inconvenient time, flip on the VCR to record it for later viewing. As Jurs notes, The Switch does not have to be a lifetime commitment. As with many of the strategies we've been discussing, after some consistent intervention children learn to entertain themselves, relying on television less and less for their needs. After children develop positive viewing habits, The Switch can be left "On" for extended periods of time. If, however, the family starts falling off the wagon, The Switch can always be used again to help them climb back on.

From a practical perspective, The Switch does appear to work. In 1992 we tested the product with two families, with one child subject in each.[16] The first child was an 8-year-old girl named Amanda, who usually watched 2.5 hours of TV each weekday and about 4 hours on Saturdays and Sundays. The mother reported that Amanda's television viewing caused frequent arguments and tension within the family. Even with countless suggestions for alternative activities, it seemed as if nothing would stop her from watching television.

The second child was a 9-year-old boy named Robert, whose parents estimated he watched 2 to 3 hours of television on weekdays and a full 9 or more hours each day on the weekend. TV arguments were also commonplace at his house, and Robert frequently threw severe temper tantrums when asked to turn the TV off.

For 2 weeks each family recorded the total amount of time their child spent viewing TV, playing video games, and watching video tapes. In order to compare before and after totals, The Switch was not used for the first week as a baseline. During this first week, Amanda watched an average of 3.6 hours of TV per day, decreasing when The Switch was in use the following week to an average of 1.7 hours a day. In her family The Switch was activated to allow for 2 hours of viewing during the weekdays and slightly longer amounts of time on the weekends. At the beginning of the week, the parents, together with Amanda, determined which programs she could watch each day.

Robert averaged 5.3 hours of television each day during the first week. Using The Switch during the second week, this average fell to 3.3 hours of TV per day. The Switch in his family was activated to allow for 3 to 4 hours of TV each day.

Six months later, decreased viewing levels for both children still held. Amanda's parents reported that she watched an average of 1.6 hours per day, while Robert tuned in 1.5 hours each day. Meanwhile, a number of important secondary changes took place for Amanda and Robert. Though both children were reported to be angry at the outset of this experiment, within 2 weeks they became accustomed to the idea and learned to occupy their time independently. Although Amanda did not engage in any new activities while The Switch was in use, her parents reported that she was concentrating more and spending more time on those activities that she already enjoyed like reading and drawing. Robert, for his part, learned to control his temper though his mother noted that she had to carry the key to The Switch with her to prevent him from unlocking it. In time, Robert did not have to be reminded to stop watching TV each day; rather, he would simply turn the TV off himself and move on to other activities. During the week he began spending more time completing homework assignments, reading, and playing with friends.

On the basis of our research, The Switch proved to be successful in reducing the number of hours Amanda and Robert spent watching TV, with results lasting even 6 months later. Perhaps your family will have similar results, though there are a few drawbacks to consider. First, as with most control devices, The Switch does not (at least initially) encourage kids to develop self-discipline. The lock does all the work. Second, it is unclear how well this device would work with families with more than one child, as it requires that all children stick to the same viewing schedule. Given kids' fickle and ever-changing tastes in television, this may prove to be an obstacle. **For more information about The Switch, call 1-800-535-5845.**

SuperVision

SuperVision is the high-tech '90s answer to TV reduction. For parents entranced by technological gadgetry, SuperVision may be just the thing—not only does it limit television viewing, but it also allows for plenty of button-pressing and frequent reprogramming. Flexible features allow parents to build and change their viewing patterns to suit their family's growth and lifestyle.

Manufactured by Cintel, Inc., SuperVision is a small unit with an internal computer that fits behind the television set, allowing parents to program the times when their family can watch TV. Measuring approximately 3" x 2" x 1", SuperVision attaches to the antenna or cable TV input of the set, and is operated by using the TV remote control and on-screen menus. The connection to the TV set is protected against removal, and any attempt to bypass the unit is reported on the TV screen. SuperVision costs $139.00, plus shipping, handling, and tax.

There are three settings parents can use to limit viewing times: Daily Allowance, Weekly Allowance, and Daily Schedule. Daily Allowance allows the parent to set a maximum amount of TV the child is allowed to watch during the day. If, for example, you decide that your child can watch 2 hours of TV a day, you simply program that number into SuperVision using the TV remote, and your child, entering his or her password also via the TV remote, decides when to watch those 2 hours (the hours do not have to be continuous, but each time the password must be reentered to keep a running tally). After a child's allotted time is used up, the TV will turn off automatically. The daily allowance can be set in 15-minute increments for a total of up to 24 hours, with a different allowance for each day of the week.

The second setting, Weekly Allowance, is similar to Daily Allowance except that it allows parents to set maximum viewing for an entire week, giving a child more discretion on how he or she wants to "spend" his or her allowance. The third setting, Daily Schedule, is somewhat more complicated as it allows the parent to set up a specific viewing schedule each day. Up to two different periods can be scheduled each day. For example, if you've decided with your child that he or she can watch *Where in the World Is Carmen Sandiego?* and *Family Matters* on Friday, SuperVision will allow you to program those two time settings so that the television turns on only when those shows are aired. The benefit of this setting is that the parent can decide with the child which programs will be viewed. In contrast, Daily Allowance and Weekly Allowance function more as meters that keep track of TV time.

As with The Switch, we found through testing that this product was effective in reducing television viewing.[17] Our study this time focused on a family with two children, both admitted TV "addicts." Emma, age 6, and Kevin, age 9, loved nothing more than plopping down in front of the TV for an afternoon of easy entertainment. Their parents wanted nothing more than to involve their kids in other activities. In addressing their differences, they took the traditional, if unproductive, approach of most households: They fought about it. And fought and fought. They fought nearly every day until finally the parents took the dreaded "We mean it this time" action, removing all TV sets from their home. Though this step clearly eliminated the original problem of excessive television, it created a few others: total removal punished non-TV abusers (namely Mom and Dad) and it meant that even very special television events would be missed by the whole family. Not ready to make such a sweeping sacrifice, the parents allowed the television to make a comeback, this time with rules. Television would only be a reward for things like completed homework and chores or good grades. Sounded reasonable, but the parents' consistency wavered and soon the old habits were back in full swing. And so was the fighting.

After a second major conference on the issue, the family decided to try a different approach. After reading about SuperVision in their local newspaper, the parents called the manufacturer and bought the device. We had previously told the manufacturer that we were looking for a family to participate in a study to evaluate the effectiveness of the product. This family was agreeable, and we began our study.

Before SuperVision was installed, the parents were asked to record Emma and Kevin's viewing times for 2 weeks. During this initial period, Emma watched an average of 2.4 hours per day, while Kevin viewed 2.1 hours each day. Though not overwhelmingly excessive, their viewing still concerned their parents. During the next 4 weeks, SuperVision was put to use. The Daily Schedule setting was selected, allowing the parents to select appropriate viewing for the kids. During weeks 3 through 6, both Emma and Kevin watched an average of 1.7 hours of TV per day. For the next 4 weeks (weeks 7 to 10), we asked the parents to take SuperVision off the TV, allowing the kids to watch as much television as they wanted (as a verification that their reduced viewing was due to SuperVision's influence, not other circumstances). During this period, Emma and Kevin watched an average of 3.2 hours a day, up from all other averages. For the final phase of the study, SuperVision was again installed. For this last 3-week period with SuperVision, Emma and Kevin watched an average of 1.5 hours each day.

Though limited, our study demonstrated SuperVision's effectiveness in reducing the number of hours our subjects spent television viewing. Equally important, SuperVision also provided a consistent pattern of viewing. During the study, the parents allowed 1 to 2 hours of viewing per day on the weekdays; they allowed slightly more time on Fridays and weekends, provided the kids had completed all homework and chores. Such consistency dramatically reduced the number of TV-related arguments.

After installing SuperVision, the parents also noticed an increase in the amount of outside activities for Emma and Kevin. Over the course of the study, Emma posted a significant increase in time devoted to physical and social activities, spending much more time reading and playing with friends. Kevin, likewise, showed a great increase in physical and academic activities. He joined a soccer team and seemed to enjoy reading more than usual. Having found such success with SuperVision, the family decided to continue using the device in their home. As with The Switch, Emma and Kevin's parents will probably be able to gradually scale back SuperVision's use as the kids become even more self-directed.

SuperVision worked well in shifting Emma and Kevin's viewing patterns, and it would probably be a good choice for many other families, as well. It brings the advantage of being functional for more than one child, and its very techno-orientation will probably appeal to kids easily enticed by buttons and flashing lights. Parents, meanwhile, will probably appreciate SuperVision's flexibility—its options can adapt to a wide range of family needs.

As a final option, the manufacturers of SuperVision are now offering parents another device called VisionLock. Sold for $59.00, the locking device allows parents to stop the use of television at their discretion. **For more information about SuperVision and VisionLock, call 1-800-845-1911.**

TV Allowance

Fed up with his three children's excessive viewing, photographer and self-described "tinkerer" Randal Levenson one day headed down to his workshop, determined to create a device that would put some muscle behind his and his wife's admonitions for less TV. Two years and a few generations of refinement later, Levenson has now introduced this small black console to the mass market. A number of recent newspaper articles have generated publicity and interest in TV Allowance; as a sure sign of his new status he was invited on Oprah Winfey's "The Great TV Experiment" to explain the invention. As he pitched on the show, "It never gives up and it can't cheat."[18]*

TV Allowance is a not-so-distant cousin to SuperVision. The two devices share the same operating theory, a similar size, and a similarly high price: $99.79, plus shipping (a scaled-down model sells for $59.00, plus shipping). Like SuperVision, TV Allowance creates an account for each child in the family, rationing the child's TV viewing each week. Using a master code, parents key in how much television is allowed per child each week. They can also select up to three regular time periods when the TV can't be turned on, such as late night hours and homework time. In a non-Block-Out time, if a child wants to view television he or she enters a personal four-digit code to turn the set on. As chil-

---

*Reprinted with permission of Harpo Productions, Inc.

dren watch, their accounts are "debited;" once the time limit is reached, the TV shuts itself off. TV Allowance also works with VCRs and Nintendo, locking on to the power cord of any television set.

As a result of a great number of positive media profiles, Levenson has sold thousands of TV Allowances to families across the country. Though we have not yet tested TV Allowance, we hypothesize that it would have a positive effect much like that produced by the use of SuperVision. A 1993 article in the *Chicago Tribune* seemed to indicate as much. The reporter highlighted a number of families who have found success with TV Allowance. Among them was the following:

> Mary Kay Ayers of Northbrook has four children ages 10, 8, 6, and an infant. She has had TV Allowance for three months and finds she doesn't need to go through the old routine of bribing her kids not to watch television.
>
> "What I like about it is I can regulate how much TV they can watch without actually standing over them saying, 'You can't watch that!'"
>
> Ayers is surprised that after a relatively short amount of time, the children are cooperating better since sharing viewing time with siblings. The kids are also more discriminating about the programs they choose.[19]

As with SuperVision, the price is a bit steep; those families who can afford it, however, might well consider this technology. **For more information about TV Allowance, call 1-800-255-6988.**

TimeSlot

Once again, invention was the child of frustration. Bill Stewart, one of TimeSlot's three inventors, explains its origin in their promotional literature: "I was tired of coming home from work to find chores and homework undone and the kids planted in front of the tube." In 1991, Stewart and two long-time friends and associates, Leland Poole and Steve Smith, finally took action on an idea they had been kicking around for years. Using their respective professional skills (Poole is an industrial designer, Smith is an electronics engineer, and Stewart a marketing consultant) the trio formed a company to manufacture and market an electronic device that would limit how much TV kids can watch. Hence TimeSlot was born.

About the size of a Sony Walkman, TimeSlot uses a different technological approach than either SuperVision or TV Allowance. The underlying premise is basically the same, though, providing TV "credit accounts" for each member of your family. Parents serve much like credit managers here. Armed with a thin plastic "master" card, parents swipe it through a barcode reader to set the unit to its programming mode. Parents can then set up individual accounts for their children by passing the master card followed by each child's card through the device, crediting each child's card with a certain number of daily viewing hours. To activate the set (which is plugged into a locked outlet in the TimeSlot unit) children pass their own cards through the barcode reader. As long as the TV is on, time is deducted from the card. An LED monitor shows how much time is left, teaching kids to be good budgeters of their TV time. Once the account has been "depleted," the TV will not turn on again until the card is reprogrammed by a parent.

TimeSlot offers two other features. In addition to allowing parents to specify the number of daily viewing hours for each child, TimeSlot can automatically "lock out" specific time blocks (e.g., while a parent is at work) so that no viewing is possible regardless of how much time remains on a child's card. Also, TimeSlot has an "Auto Credit" function, automatically allotting time to each child's card on a daily basis; this eliminates the need for day-to-day resetting. TimeSlot comes with a users' manual, one parent card, four child cards, and a security door key.

The thought of giving kids practice at using credit cards is cause for giving some parents a nervous tic. Nevertheless, TimeSlot appears to be a good way to teach kids how to budget their TV time. With a time-remaining display ever flickering, kids may quickly learn to be more cautious TV consumers. Moreover, it solves the problem of monitoring while parents are at work.

Like the other technologies we've described, at $79.95, plus shipping, TimeSlot represents something of an investment for most families. As a bonus, though, a portion of the sales goes to the North Carolina Public Television Foundation. Currently, TimeSlot is no longer being manufactured. The developers, however, hope to have it available at a future date. **For more information about TimeSlot, call 1-919-829-3525.**

Earn TV

Earn TV is a product currently being developed by this book's first author. Though similar in function to many of the previously described devices, Earn TV offers a slightly different twist to TV reduction. The goal of Earn TV is not merely to restrict TV viewing, but also to prompt kids to realize that TV viewing is a privilege to be earned rather than a natural-born right.

Earn TV is activated by a key that enables 30 minutes of TV viewing (or use of computers, video games, or other electrical devices) with every turn of the key. Each evening parents can decide how much TV viewing will occur the next day. The parent can then use one of the following systems with this invention. Some parents will simply indicate that their kids can view a predesignated number of hours for the next day. This is the simplest system as it controls overall TV viewing time with the least amount of intervention. For more ambitious families, the meter could also be tied to certain contingencies. Parents can impose tasks to be completed or responsibilities to be assumed before the key earns its fateful turn. Though kids typically are individually responsible for particular chores and tasks, we encourage families to head in a different direction when using Earn TV. In the spirit of community building, try to find jobs or responsibilities that can be assumed by the whole gang; in other words, focus on group, rather than individual, tasks. For example, if all children in the family spend 1 hour on homework or 1 hour working in the yard, the next day 1 hour of television is earned. Such a system helps the family learn to set goals *together,* creating an approach that requires the prickly but essential arts of compromise, negotiation, and problem solving. This tactic also works against the traditional fend-for-yourself ethic that commonly prevails among kids and provides all the children with a group reward. An added benefit of both of the preceding approaches is that kids can be encouraged to work together the night before to determine what programs will be watched the next day. If disagreements develop over what to watch the next day, parents can simply not put any time on the meter for the following day. This rule, when followed through consistently, tends to get kids hustling to put on their best faces and work out a quick compromise.

A final variation of Earn TV is designed to counteract some of the health concerns associated with excessive viewing as discussed in Chapter 3. As adults, we often marvel at the energy of kids; we watch them jump and run for hours on end, a feat that would leave us—the adults in the crowd—gasping for air. Most avid exercisers know their secret: Expended energy is curiously replaced by more energy. Conversely, as most couch potatoes know, laziness begets laziness. For kids, laziness is more than a mild moral vice: In short order it can contribute to obesity, poor physical fitness, and a host of other health-related problems. Earn TV can be used to steer kids in the right direction, getting them off the couch and into the world to run around, breathe fresh air, and pump their hearts and lungs.

Children who utilize this variation of Earn TV accrue TV privileges through physical activity. The operating principle behind this system involves a bracelet-style meter to be worn on a child's wrist, ankle, or waist that records movement and activity. Kids can activate the meter through deliberate exercise like jumping jacks and jogging or — more to the point — simply by climbing a tree, riding bikes, or playing tag with kids from the neighborhood. When a preestablished level of activity has been achieved — say, 20 minutes — the meter will beep. After the activity quotient has been fulfilled, the meter can then be plugged into the TV.

Parents can preset the television to translate our example of 20 minutes of activity into one-half hour or more of television viewing. The meter will trigger power for the television for the allotted amount of time, much like the Daily and Weekly Allowance technology behind SuperVision. In addition to activating the TV set through the activity meter, parents always have the option of overriding this system and controlling the television with the earlier described key.

Early experiments at DePaul University connecting physical activity with TV viewing privileges have been promising. One experiment involved requiring the viewer to use a stationary bicycle rigged to a small, locked control box that attached to the electrical cord of a television set.[20] Two sensors attached to the wheel and corresponding wheel rim of a stationary bike. Each time the wheel made a complete revolution, a magnet on the tire activated a pulse on the reader located in the wheel rim. In theory, if a child pedaled the bike so that the tire made one revolution per second, then for 15 minutes of pedaling enough pulses would be accumulated to allow 30 minutes of television viewing. The time-earned data was stored in the device's small computer, and an electronic light on the exterior of the box indicated to the child when enough television time had been stored. The television could be turned on only after viewing had been earned through the biking activity.

The subject of our preliminary study, a 9-year-old boy named John, watched TV and played Nintendo between 6 and 7 hours daily. His mother reported that John was waking up in the middle of the night to watch television and would often miss his school bus in the morning because he would not stop watching TV. Based on reports from his mother, John watched a daily average of 6.4 hours of TV during the 20-day baseline for the experiment (3.9 hours with TV; 2.5 hours with Nintendo). During the next 30 days the program was put in place. Using a setting in which 15 minutes of exercise powered 30 minutes of viewing, John reduced his TV use to 2.7 hours a day (1.5 with TV; 1.2 with Nintendo). Immediately after the program ended and John again had free access to television, his total viewing went up to 3.5 hours a day (1.5 with TV; 2.0 with Nintendo), though at a 5-month follow-up it was down to a low of 1.8 hours. It should be noted that the Nintendo set was broken during this follow-up time, perhaps contributing to John's reduced viewing time; still, his mother considered his new viewing habits a significant victory. In addition to reducing John's overall TV viewing, use of the device also led to a surprising secondary effect. After the study ended, John often rode the stationary bike even though it was no longer hooked up to the television, indicating that the riding had become a reward in itself.

Earn TV's activity meter allows considerably more opportunity for natural child play as opposed to deliberate exercise like in the preceding example, giving it broader appeal. As with our subject, John, we are convinced that kids who begin to spend time playing active games and sports will likely find them rewarding in themselves — more rewarding, in fact, than the sedentary pastime of watching television.

Earn TV is still in the early stages of development. If you are interested in more information or have suggestions regarding Earn TV, please contact: **Leonard A. Jason, PhD, DePaul University — Department of Psychology, 2219 N. Kenmore, Chicago, IL 60614, or through E-mail (Ljason@wppost.depaul.edu).**

The Switch, SuperVision, TV Allowance, TimeSlot, and Earn TV are just a few of the many TV-reduction products now entering the market. Some brand-new devices to also consider include TV Cop (an adjustable timer controlling TV and video games; call 1-800-391-9295), TV Time (a small computer that controls access to TV and grants kids a weekly TV "allowance"; call 1-503-452-4541), and Toll-A-Vision (a token-activated viewing timer for TVs and video monitors; write to P. O. Box 972, Springfield, MO 65801-0922). Surely each year will bring new entries and new advances. Keep your eyes open, for one might be right for your family.

The Middle Road: Behavior Modification

A final method of reducing television viewing theoretically belongs in the "Low-Tech Road" section, but we are taking a few liberties here. Though behavior modification requires no gadgets or high-tech equipment, it does require a bit more day-to-day involvement than the other low-tech/no-tech methods. Behavior modification has for a long time been our primary focus of study. For over 15 years at DePaul University in Chicago we have been testing and refining behavior modification approaches to reducing kids' reliance on television. One of our earliest efforts involved training parents from local elementary schools in reducing their children's TV viewing. Spearheaded by Patty Rooney-Rebeck, then a doctoral student in our program, this pilot parent program earned DePaul much media attention. Back in 1981 syndicated columnist Bob Greene wrote about these efforts in the *Chicago Tribune:* "Psychologists at DePaul University have begun a pilot program aimed at curing an addiction that may harm as many people as alcohol and tobacco combined. The addiction is television viewing, and the DePaul psychologists are in the midst of their first formal sessions designed to help eradicate it."[21] Since those early days we've found great success; if you are willing to invest the time and energy, it's likely that you will, too.

Long a staple topic of Introduction to Psychology courses, behavior modification focuses on changing behaviors by implementing a system of rewards for positive behavior. Behavior modification is often used to curb smoking, overeating, gambling, and any number of addictions or unfortunate habits, including excessive TV viewing. The goal of our 4-week program is to help you teach your children responsible decision-making. With this approach, positive behaviors like playing with friends, reading, creating art, and making music are rewarded. Children are then able either to use those rewards to "purchase" television viewing time or to save them for a special treat.

Rather than approaching this program like some sort of clinical social science experiment, try to treat it like a fun game for the whole family. For our present purposes, we'll refer to the program as the TV Ticket Game. Surely by putting your heads together your family can come up with a snazzy name of your own. As with many other games your family plays, you'll need a few game pieces: a roll of tickets (movie theater or raffle style tickets will work best; you can find these at most office supply stores) or a stack of tokens (in which case you might change the name to the TV Token Game or something along those lines); a container for the tickets or tokens (a coffee can with a slit in the plastic lid works well); a set of instructions (each child's contract); and several enthusiastic players (your family, of course).

Here's how and why all these items come together: One of the underlying themes of this book is that when children learn about the more engaging and fulfilling ways they could be spending their time, television loses its appeal. The trick is getting them involved in outside activities in the first place—not always easy for dedicated viewers. The TV Ticket Game helps kids get over this hump by offering them tangible rewards for participating in outside activities. Based on a prearranged schedule of rewards, a child will earn, say, one ticket for every hour spent playing with friends, reading, drawing, and participating in sports and other prosocial activities. Throughout the week, children can either spend their tickets on television watching (one ticket is worth one-half hour of TV watching) or save them for a special treat at the end of the week (a trip to the zoo, a later bedtime on Friday night, etc.). In this way kids are taught that television is a privilege to be earned, one that also comes at the expense of other, perhaps more enjoyable activities. Within limits, kids are free to choose how to spend their tickets, making them very active participants in this TV reduction technique.

Like any other game, it pays to first read the instructions. Following, then, are some guidelines on how the TV Ticket Game should be played:

1. *Keep a log of activity.* The first week of the game simply involves recording observations of how your children spend their time. This log should be similar to the type we described in Chapter 4, paying close attention to your kids' television viewing and their involvement in outside activities. During this first week, do not attempt to reduce or influence your children's television viewing. Life should go on as usual. Be sure, however, to take time at some point in the week to discuss the game with your kids; build up excitement for the game, as their involvement begins in Week 2.
2. *Draw up a contract stipulating the rules, ticket values, and rewards.* Towards the end of Week 1, sit down and discuss the upcoming game with your kids. This should be a time to generate enthusiasm for the TV Ticket Game and to explain the rules. Since this experience will probably be quite unlike anything they've ever done before, we strongly suggest you put everything in writing to avoid confusion. The most effective

approach may be to draw up a contract with your kids, detailing the rules, ticket values, and end-of-week rewards (see Appendix B on pages 225 and 226 for a sample contract). Children and parents should sign the contracts, indicating on the children's part their understanding of the rules and their intent to play fair, while indicating on the parents' part their intent to follow through with rewards.

Work with each individual child to determine fair ticket values and rewards. Custom-designing the game may take a little more work, but it will help guarantee that children actually participate in it. Activities that earn tickets might vary from child to child, reflecting their ages and abilities. A 4-year-old child, for example, might earn a ticket for drawing and coloring for a half hour, while a 10-year-old would receive a ticket for spending an hour writing letters to friends and far-away family. Also consider the child's personality. If you have a child who is especially shy, make playing with other children particularly enticing: a ticket can be earned for playing alone for *1 hour,* but with another friend for just a *half hour.*

Additionally, you should consider the level of involvement a certain activity requires before assigning ticket values. Though it is easier to keep most values similar (an hour's worth of an activity equals one ticket), there may be some exceptions. Reading, obviously, takes more concentration and effort than playing in the yard. Perhaps a half hour of reading could equal one ticket. Likewise, some activities take a great deal of time and physical energy. Joining a sports team, for example, might be worth several tickets. Finally, consider adding a bonus category somewhere on the contract's reward schedule. Tickets may be earned for work activities like raking the yard or helping prepare supper. It is best, however, to avoid giving more than one or two tickets each day for work activities since the goal of the program is the development of new interests and relationships.

Just as children should be consulted in determining ticket values, so too should they get involved in choosing end-of-the-week rewards. Once the rewards have been chosen, together the family must decide how many tickets each will cost. For example, having a later weekend bedtime may cost just four tickets, while going to the zoo may cost eight. Some parents may also choose to assign a monetary value on tickets, offering a dime or a quarter for each unused ticket. You might also let the kids pool their tickets for a larger reward, like a trip to an amusement park. Watching such negotiations should be an amusing lesson in group dynamics.

The only area not open to negotiation is that of rule-making. Parents should develop just a few general, overall rules to guide fair play of the TV Ticket Game: First, determine how much television will be allowed each week. Though children will presumably be involved in other activities, television may still elicit a strong pull for some kids; for this reason you might want to guard against TV bingeing by also limiting total time allowable each day. The second rule pertains to content. Earning TV time does not mean earning the chance to watch anything and everything on the tube. If content is a concern, make sure kids know which programs fall within your standards and which ones do not. Finally, make sure there are consequences for watching television without depositing a ticket. Most kids will want to test the limits of this game, even to the point of cheating. One way to minimize this potential problem would be to disallow television watching until at least one parent is home to supervise. Also, make it clear in your contract what the consequences will be should any cheating occur.

Though the contracting and preplanning sounds like lots of work (and it is), consider it an entertaining family activity in itself. Keep the mood fun and the discussion lively; after all, this is a game!

3. *Begin play!* At the start of Week 2, play begins. To prevent a sneaky midnight raid, keep the tickets in a secure place and whenever possible hand them out immediately following a ticket-earning activity. Not only will this immediately reinforce the activity, but it also keeps record-keeping to a minimum. After a while it will be hard to keep track of how many tickets are owed to whom. If you can't be there to watch the activity take place, encourage your children to "show" you the fruits of their labor and energy. If they read, they can tell you about their book; if they practiced piano, they can demonstrate their new achievements. Also, as Weeks 2 and 3 progress, you and your kids may discover more activities for which tickets can be earned. Simply add them to the contract, having each party initial the amendment just as in a real contract. You may wish to continue entering your children's activities in their logs, noting progress and positive changes where applicable.

If children choose to use their tickets to purchase television viewing time, make sure they put a ticket in the designated container. Also, it may help kids keep track of their viewing time by setting a timer at the beginning of each half-hour viewing session. When it "dings," their time is up. Used tickets may be recycled by emptying the container each night. If you'd like to keep track of how much television each of your children views during the game, consider having different tickets for each child. You can either buy different colored tickets at the outset or have kids put their own special mark on them. When you empty the container, you'll know exactly who watched how much.

Don't forget about the rewards at the end of Weeks 2 and 3. (Actually there is little danger of this happening; your children will be only too happy to remind you.) Set aside a time at the end of the week to allow each child to announce his or her spending plan; then plan accordingly. Always follow up on promised rewards.

4. *Maintain your winning streak!* As Weeks 2 and 3 progress, you will probably notice your children developing new interests and relationships and/or deepening the ones already in place. Gradually and naturally, television will have faded in importance. By the time Week 4 arrives, your family will be ready for a revised reward schedule. This will mark the beginning of an indefinite period of time known as "maintenance."

In preparing for the wind-down of the game, the contract should be changed to include only a few activities. The main purpose of this change is to create a more streamlined system that is easy to live with after the formal game ends. The new schedule should reward only activities like hobbies, music practice, and schoolwork—all are important learning experiences and they frequently require a little extra encouragement. Many of the other activities like playing with friends and reading for fun have probably become rewarding enough to stand on their own.

When the program ends after Week 4, the contract will no longer be in effect so you'll no longer need to monitor the program in the kids' daily records. However, in order to maintain the gains your family has achieved, you may wish to continue the Week 4 reward schedule indefinitely, and, if desired, sign a new contract. Regardless of whether you continue the reward system during the maintenance period, you should keep using TV time limits to prevent old habits from returning. Equally important is your continued encouragement of your kids' participation in outside activities.

Evidence of Success

Over the years we have had numerous opportunities to test behavior modification techniques in reducing children's television viewing. Experiments both large and small have yielded positive results.

In order to make our studies as valid as possible, we introduced a few variations to our tests. The programs, however, remain identical in spirit. The most significant difference was our use of tokens and token-actuated timers instead of tickets and coffee cans. Children still earned tokens for participating in prosocial activities. If they wanted to watch television, though, instead of dropping a ticket into a can or a basket, tokens were dropped into a token-actuated timer box. Connected to the TV set, this timer activated the television when tokens were deposited in it (an infra-red detector read the token). Once a token was deposited, television could be viewed for 31 minutes; after this time, the TV shut itself off. Despite the technological advances in this approach, the program was otherwise identical.

In several studies we found that children reduced their viewing through the behavior modification technique of reward schedules. One of our subjects, an 8-year-old boy named Charles, reduced his viewing from an average of 6.4 hours a day before the program was initiated to 1.6 hours during the program. More importantly, his lower viewing levels became a habit; 4 months later, he tuned in only 1.1 hours a day.[22] In another study, our 13-year-old female subject, Keisha, watched an average of 8 hours a day before the program began. During the first intervention, her viewing decreased to an average of 0.8 hours a day, but increased to 6.2 hours a day when she again had free access to TV. We reimplemented the program and Keisha's viewing decreased to 1.6 hours a day, a level that she was able to sustain for the remaining months of our study.[23] Some victories are harder won! To encourage larger families, we performed a similar study involving a family with seven children.[24] The average amount of viewing for all children was 7.5 hours a day before the token game, then dropping to 3.7 hours during the program. Even at the 6-month follow up, reduced viewing behaviors held for all the children. It is important to note that this particular experiment was conducted not with the sophisticated token-actuated timer, but with the simple ticket methods described previously. High technology is not essential to your success! Finally, we should point out that studies conducted independent of DePaul University's efforts have confirmed the success of behavior modification approaches. The research team of David Wolfe, Maria Mendes, and David Factor in 1984 implemented a program in which children were given 20 unearned tokens each week that could be exchanged for either a total of 10 hours of television viewing or alternative reward activities.[25] They reported that children's television viewing time decreased by more than 50% during their program.

Reduced television viewing time is only one of two major benefits of this behavior modification approach. The other is the natural increase of outside activities that coincides with and further aids TV reduction. In a DePaul University PhD dissertation study involving three families, Michael McCanna found significant postreduction increases for all participants in activities like reading, sports, and homework. The most significant gains, however, were in activities requiring interpersonal contact like playing with friends and parents.[26] Though it is encouraging to see such positive changes in the lives of individuals and entire families, the true measure of success is the ability to sustain these new activities over the long haul. We have found much evidence that enduring change is possible. In a series of two studies involving several families, for example, we found that outside activities had gained their own importance over the course of the experiment: "Time logs indicated that at postintervention, alternative activities (playing with friends, developing hobbies, reading, etc.) had continued even when the tokens were no longer contingently provided."[27]

Though science offers fairly hard proof of the effectiveness of behavior modification, some of the most convincing words come from the participants themselves. One of the most gratifying aspects of our research was receiving parent and child reports on the positive changes that resulted in their lives. Our first subject, 8-year-old Charles, said the following at one point: "I want to save my tokens so I can go somewhere with Dad." Soon after, the most rewarding activity for the child was earning time in which the child and his dad could be alone together. Many important ripple effects were also noted. The mother reported that her child now enthusiastically did chores around the house and completed homework assignments. Also, the child's teacher, who was unaware of the experiment, unexpectedly called the mother and reported that she noticed considerable improvement in his schoolwork;

among other things, the child had quickly progressed beyond an entire reading book.

In the second study described earlier, 13-year-old Keisha wrote the following: "I think the program was very helpful because it helped me stop watching TV a lot. It helped me to raise my grades. I think every kid should try it because it helps." Keisha's mother echoed these positive sentiments: "It geared her into other areas that she wouldn't have gone into without the program (swimming, musical instruments, interviewer at church). Her grade in science increased from D to A and she recently won the second prize in a science fair."

Convinced? We are.

Summary

In your quest to limit television, there are a number of routes you can take. The Low-Tech Road is the common sense approach, employing simple family rules and regulations, all in a spirit of adventure. The High-Tech Road is a true sign of the times; its technological orientation helps monitor viewing when parents are unable to. Finally, the Middle Road, featuring reward-based behavior modification, relies little on technology but requires a high level of involvement. Consider carefully your own children and family situation; then pick a road and start your journey.

Road trips, as we well know, can be bumpy experiences. To make for a smoother trip, it pays to be prepared. Chapter 6 offers some solid tips. First, learn the best way to approach and watch television. Because TV will still likely be a part of your family's life, it's helpful to know how best to utilize it to everyone's advantage. And second, find out what goes in a useful survival kit—in this case, the storehouse of alternative activities that can occupy your family's minds and time while the TV is off. Advance planning of outside activities will bring sanity to adults, great joy to children, and fun, lasting memories for the entire family.

6

Family Life
(With and Without Television)

Turning off the television for your family can be a bit like participating in a thrill sport. In contemplating an immediate go at bungee jumping, skydiving, rock climbing, or any other daredevil activity, some healthy fear and doubt arises. And though your odds may not look good, you finally get up your courage (or succumb to peer pressure) and take a deep breath. Then off you go (maybe with a little push) into the great wide open. Inevitably, in the doing you discover the thrill.

So it is with reducing your family's television viewing. It may seem like an impossible task, but once you get going you'll find the great stores of fun and discovery that await. While reducing television viewing in your family is a most important step, it's really just the start of a new way of life. Now it's on to learning how to live *with* TV some of the time and *without* TV most of the time. This, truly, is the best part.

With Television: Co-Viewing Strategies

Except for those very few brave and pioneering families that decide to forgo television altogether, TV will remain a part of most families' lives. And it can be a fine way to spend some of your time once you've learned how to live with it. The trick is in knowing how to maximize television's power for good programming and how to mitigate its deliverance of the bad. There is still plenty to admire on television—it holds great power and potential for delivering informative, insightful, and entertaining programming. Seek out such shows for your family. As for the raunchy ones, simply turn them off or use them as occasional object lessons on how *not* to go about life. If you make smart content choices and keep your family's viewing active and informed, you'll find that television can still be a civil, if now less frequent, guest in your home.

What to Watch (Be Choosy)

Choosing television shows should be like picking stock purchases—which ones will give the greatest return? Like any good investor, viewers young and old should think first and act second, doing some investigating (via the TV listings and critics' reviews, for example) and giving it some thought before turning on the television. This is often harder than it sounds, especially for children. For starters, kids often make lousy investors—too impulsive, too impatient, and much too risk-friendly. And much like the New York Stock Exchange listings, television's offerings are overwhelming at first glance. Here is where you can use your age-old wisdom to guide your children toward smart choices. Aid them in particular by narrowing the options, either by mutual decision or pure veto power. There is a place for both in the great television debate.

Family Democracies. When possible, try to work *with* your children in choosing what television shows to watch. As discussed in Chapter 4, it's a good idea to sit down at the beginning of the week and figure out *what* will be watched *when*. Not only does this tend to eliminate arguing over claims to the television set, but it also teaches your kids how to make decisions given limited resources. Give your children an early lesson in economics, explaining that with less time to watch television they may want to consider carefully how they allocate it. Kids who understand this concept will probably try to avoid wasting valuable TV time by aimlessly channel surfing or fighting with each other over the remote control.

Taking time to pick shows also reinforces to kids the idea that their parents take their television watching seriously. Together you can discuss and debate the merits or faults of the upcoming week's programs. Though you can guide your children toward quality programming, resist the urge to push your own specific preferences on your kids. Just because you think *Reading Rainbow* is a terrific show doesn't mean your 6-year-old will be similarly impressed, and forcing the issue is surely a lost cause. Recognize that your kids' taste in TV shows will surely differ from yours, and depending on their age and gender, will probably differ from each others'. Meanwhile, because you are asking your kids to make television choices in advance, to be fair and keep things fun you should take time to make your own program choices; since turnabout is (usually) fair play, be prepared to defend or explain them to your kids in return.

Finally, getting together on a regular basis to choose TV shows can be a good organization and communication tool for your family. Setting aside 20 or 30 minutes each Sunday night for a general family pow-wow will give both parents and children the chance to talk about schedules, events, and concerns about the upcoming week. Also, it will give you a chance to brainstorm alternative activities for the times when the TV must be turned off.

If there is a program that you are leery about but your kids absolutely adore, watch it at least once with them. Discuss your objections, but be sure to allow your kids to have their own say, too. Though they may still be angry if you still decide to nix their favorite show, at least you've earned points (if only with yourself) for credibility. If the show in question airs while you are at work or otherwise regularly occupied, you can either ask the opinions of other parents you trust, tape it to watch together at a later time, or make a simple rule: No television until Mom or Dad is at home.

For owners of VCRs, video tapes of movies and specials offer a fairly reliable way around the content problems that crop up on network and cable TV. Give your kids a number of good options and then let them choose the ones to rent or purchase. If the quality is high, video tapes can be a good investment. They have the important benefit of being played when it is convenient for the family as opposed to when broadcasters will get the most bang for their buck. Moreover, the content is guaranteed. Having viewed it at least once, parents know what to expect on the tape and need not worry about interruptions by bikini-clad women cavorting around in a beer commercial or a special news report flashing images of blood and carnage.

Just as you would take time to choose video tapes carefully for your kids, be similarly discriminating with video and computer games. It is amazing how many parents decry the violence of the games their children play, forgetting that they are the ones who probably bought or rented them in the first place. If your kids make constant appeals for video game cartridges, learn the amazing power of the word "No."

Purchase only the games you have seen and approve, and buy them only for special occasions like birthdays or holidays. Beyond the games received for special occasions, one family has an agreement with their 12-year-old son that he can buy "preapproved" games with money from his own allowance. Inevitably by the time he has saved the money, an entirely new interest has come along.

Parental Autocracies. Though it's often best to try to work with your kids in choosing content, there are a number of circumstances in which parental veto power may be used without a speck of guilt. For example, you and you alone can make the decision on what cable channels will be allowed into your living room. You pay the bill, you make the choice. Besides, having cable TV with children is a risky venture. Though some of the child-oriented channels like The Disney Channel, the Family Channel, and Nickelodeon provide plenty of quality entertainment for kids, others are not so interested in that tender market. Though HBO airs many first-rate films and has produced some outstanding made-for-cable movies, would you want the channel on when your kids are in the room? Can you trust that it won't be turned on when you are not?

Also, if there are some specific programs — network or otherwise — that you absolutely despise or you think are inappropriate for children, simply declare them off limits. Though we have suggested watching programs with your kids before giving a program the ax, this is hardly necessary with a show you already know hovers over the extremes of taste and decency. Be aware that banning certain shows for your kids may impinge on your own viewing habits. For example, though few parents would want their children tuning in to *NYPD Blue*, many count it among their own favorite shows. Yet if you have taken a family stand on a particular program, you should expect to make some adjustments of your own. Either rethink your need to watch it or tape it to watch long after the kids have gone to bed.

On the other hand, if there are shows that you truly abhor both for yourself and your kids, take your action a step further and write the network or local station that airs the show. Write a brief letter (or an E-mail or fax) that addresses your specific complaints, keeping in mind that it will probably receive more serious attention if it is typed and written in a professional tone. You'll find network addresses in Appendix C (pp. 227-228). To truly get at the heart of the matter, another option is to write the network sponsors to express your dismay and possible intentions for a product boycott. If too many letters about a questionable show pile up, fiscally conservative corporations are likely to put their resources with a safer, less offensive program. If an appeal targeted at finances doesn't work, try an appeal to the conscience. Find out who is on the board of directors of the sponsor in question and send a letter directly to them. Seeing the issue in more personal terms (and seeing that they are being called to task) may have more of an impact. Though letter writing does not always bring about the desired results, it is an important tool and right for consumers. (On the flip side, also be sure to write if there is a show you think is particularly fine. This is an equally important act, convincing networks and sponsors that there is an audience—a living, breathing, *buying* audience—for quality programs.)

In addition to offensive or inappropriate shows, another area that parents deserve the option of veto power is that of news programs. The decision to allow or not allow TV news is often a tough call, opposing our desire that our children understand something about the world around them and our urge to shield them from the news' often harsh and context-less images. In March 1994, *TV Guide* asked several well-known TV journalists (an admittedly biased lot) how *they* handle the issue with young children at home. Stone Phillips, co-anchor for *Dateline NBC* answered in this way:

> With the news, a parent is torn between two issues: You want to protect your children from emotionally harmful images, but at the same time you want to introduce them to some of the things that happen in the world. As long as it's not a frightening experience for a child, the news brings opportunities to help children develop empathy and start looking beyond their own world, to see those going through really difficult times. When I watch the news with Streeter [his 6-year-old son], I'll split my time between watching the screen and watching him. If I think it's a little rough, I'll say "Listen, let's do something else." I don't hesitate to do that.[1]

Nancy Glass, host of the syndicated *American Journal* has a different view:

> I don't think young children should watch the news. My [6-year-old] son Max and I do watch TV together, but the news worries me, because the only things he'll understand are the images.

And the images are not always pleasant. He won't understand the context. The news is made up of two things—hyper-reality, which is the most extreme form of reality, and fantasy—and neither is appropriate for little kids to watch. . . . Should Max know about the world? Yes, but I think that reading is the best way to learn. Kids don't have to learn all the heavy things. That comes later.[2]

The decision over whether to allow your kids to watch the news cannot be made by books or experts. It is filled with shades of gray, the place where tentative judgment calls reign. This is true, in fact, for much of television's content, be it TV news or Saturday morning cartoons. In the end, what you decide for your children should reflect two highly personal factors: your own values and child-raising philosophies in addition to your children's ages and levels of emotional maturity. Because neither of these elements are precise and static, your approach may need some fine-tuning for a while. It should also probably change over time. As your children get older you may want to re-evaluate your choices for them or give them increasing voice in the matter. If you thought a highly satirical show like *TV Nation* or a high-quality, but adult-themed program like *Law and Order* was not suitable for your junior high-aged child, you might reconsider it now that he or she has become a mature 10th grader. Be sure to remain flexible and fair, but also stay informed and involved. Though it may seem like a hassle, taking time to monitor television, video games, and computer choices is just plain common sense. Most parents go to great pains to screen baby-sitters coming to their home. We should be just as cautious with television, for it is a medium that tends to have a far more enduring influence on the lives of our children.

How to Watch (Get Involved)

As discussed in Chapter 3, television has a great tendency to disrupt or suspend active family life. This can be true even after you've taken pains to reduce television's role in your family. Though you might have succeeded in scaling back the hours, the time in front of the television set may still remain silent and isolating. It doesn't have to be that way. Families can learn to use television to enhance, not inhibit, their time together. There are two simple rules: First, make television special, not routine. And second, make it active, not passive.

Make It Special. Limiting any desirable commodity almost always makes it more valuable. One result is that the consumer is often more cautious about using it. Another result is that the consumer is almost always more appreciative of the commodity, vowing never again to take it for granted. For example, if coffee prices skyrocket, devoted coffee drinkers might be forced to reduce their morning intake from six cups to four. And perhaps more than usual, they will relish and savor every single drop of deep roasted caffeine. Reducing television is likely to have a similar effect. It will prompt young viewers to choose more carefully what to watch, and it will make those times in front of the television set significantly more appreciated and more special.

There is nothing inherently wrong with gathering around the television set for an hour or so of entertainment. The key is to make it seem like a specific planned activity rather than an idle, ho-hum way to pass the time. Planning your viewing ahead of time as discussed earlier will go a long way toward making television seem like an authentic activity. It's also helpful if your family's viewing time has a definite beginning (say at 7 p.m.) and an end (at 8 p.m.). Once the show ends, turn off the set and move on to other activities. The same holds true for computer and video games. In advance, plan specific times to log on and log off. Not only will this define such activities as a special privilege, but it also addresses the very practical issue of drawing game-addicted kids away from their handsets and keyboards. When their allotted time is up, ring a bell, wave a flag, or run the vacuum cleaner near their ears—anything to get them moving on to other activities. Though they may give you sullen looks now, years later they will thank you for giving them a life beyond the glaring video monitor.

In addition to making television, video, and computer activities seem special, try to do the same for watching rented movies and video tapes. It's easy to fall into a weekend habit of renting movies; as a family event it's cheap, it entails few hassles, and the kids don't have to keep their shirts tucked in. Yet if the VCR is turned on every single Friday night, the excitement and expectancy of seeing a new film starts to fade. Additionally, the quality of films rented is fated to decline as a family's consumption goes up. Since there are only a limited number of good films available, people soon find themselves renting one-star, thumbs down, straight-to-video movies in the effort to see something new each time—a painful way to be entertained, it seems.

Instead of the same old thing, make movie night an occasional, yet standout event. Once or twice a month pick out movies your family truly wants to see. (Don't forget those old Disney classics like *The*

Parent Trap or *The Absent-Minded Professor* when you start running out of options.) Pop popcorn, spread out the blankets, and turn the lights down low. Even bend the rules a little and let the kids stay up past their bedtime. For kids with parents who are normally sticklers about bedtimes, this is a guaranteed sign that the night is a special occasion.

Make It Active. Making television watching an active experience seems to go against our very nature. When the TV gets turned on we often respond by turning everything else off—conversations, the clanking dishwasher, the reading of the paper, and anything else that competes with the small screen. While there is the not slight matter of actually being able to hear the television, why do we automatically follow those old codes of silence and stillness? Furthermore, why must television—the most powerful of educators—have the last word? Too often in watching TV we shut down our brains and shelve our opinions, silently accepting every notion from the minds of Hollywood. In the realm of human conversation, if someone says something outrageous we feel perfectly comfortable saying, "That's the craziest thing I've ever heard in my whole entire life, and I disagree 100%." Why not do the same with television? Make it a three-way conversation. Let the TV have its word, then talk back to it and talk with each other. Applaud funny or insightful things and boo or counter those things that are objectionable or offensive.

While the act of watching television interactively certainly makes it more enjoyable, far more significant is the fact that the asking of questions and the clarifying of content gives television much-needed context for child audiences. Though it's not a bad idea to forget your inhibitions and talk back while you watch television alone, talking out loud is imperative when you are watching with children. Remember that children, depending on their ages and cognitive abilities, understand only bits and pieces of what flashes across the screen. They do, however, absorb many of the images, an uncomfortable fact when the extremes of television's visual content are considered. Having an adult in the room is like providing an interpreter, translating brief but powerful images into something children can grasp. Harry Smith, then co-anchor of *CBS This Morning*, stressed this point in his response to the earlier question of TV news for children: "If your kid is going to see news, he absolutely *has* to see it with an adult, because there is so much that has to be explained. Without a human dictionary to explain what's going on, I think the news can be potentially harmful."[3]

The same can be said for a great deal of general programming. Who knows what children will believe about family life if they watch made-for-adult satire like *Married . . . With Children* or what they might think about violence and its consequences if they see a police detective who was last week shot in the stomach and is this week back on the force munching a cheeseburger? And what would they think if you, watching with them, remained silent as a popular TV character threw a punch out of frustrated anger? Would your kids then assume such action was okay? Would they think *you* thought it was okay? Without your even knowing it, your silence may be condoning what you really believe is a perfectly awful act.

To avoid misunderstandings and misinterpretations, stay active while watching television. Even shows that contain violence or spout nauseating messages about women or minorities can be used to your children's benefit if they are used cautiously and selectively as springboards for discussions. The very best way to do this is to ask your children questions that serve to gently counter, clarify, or support a particular program's messages. Since most kids will be thoroughly annoyed if pelted with questions while the show itself is airing, you might use commercial breaks as your forum. Without being overly serious or sanctimonious, turn down the volume during ads and casually discuss the previous segment's messages.

Depending on the nature of the program, some of the following sample questions or comments may be helpful conversation starters. Some are intended for younger children, some for older ones — find your own wording and the emphasis that will work for your kids. Keep in mind that these sample questions are not a formal script to read to your kids at each and every free moment of television; they are just a guide for what should be a casual, natural, and surely engaging conversation.

Violence

- Do you think that shooting that guy was the only way for him to solve the problem?
- How else could he have gotten similar results?
- If someone in real life was shot in the arm (leg, belly), how long do you think it would take to heal? Do you think it would hurt very much? Did it look like it hurt him very much?

- Why do you think there is so much violence on TV?
- Do you think there is this much violence in the real world?

Stereotypes

- In this show, all the bad guys speak with foreign accents. Do you think most people from foreign countries are mean people?
- Have you noticed that almost all of the characters in this show are boys? Why do you think there are not more girls? Can girls solve problems just as well as boys?
- Do all old people act as silly as this show portrays them? How do you think your grandma would feel if she were watching this?
- It seems that this show portrays Hispanics as being lazy. Do you think it does? What's the problem in doing that?

Fantasy Versus Reality

- In real life, can men with blue capes fly through the sky?
- In real life, do most women dress that way or always (even in the morning) look that beautiful? Are men always that tough, muscular, and good looking? In real life, are these the most important qualities in a person?
- In real life, can a person drink that much, that often, without becoming an alcoholic?
- In real life, do problems always get solved in 30 minutes?

Values and Feelings

- It seems like people put each other down a lot on this show. What do you think about that? How does it make you feel when someone makes fun of you?
- The boy in this show really seems like he's in a bind. If a friend asked you to lie to his or her teacher like that, how would you handle it? Do you think it's ever okay to lie?
- I really like the way that girl handled the situation. Do you think it was hard for her to make that choice?
- It seems like all the kids on this show dress like they are in a style show. Are clothes and looks the most important part of a person? Does watching these shows ever make you feel like you don't measure up?

Advertising

- Do you like ads on television? Do you usually want the things you see advertised on TV?
- What is the purpose of TV advertisements? Why are there so many on TV?
- Toys and food always look so fun and yummy on TV. In real life are they always that good? Which toys or other things that you've gotten have been disappointing?
- Do you think that the toy truck in this ad is as big in real life as it looks on TV? Why would advertisers make something look better than it actually is?
- How much do you think that toy costs? How many weeks would it take for you to save your allowance and then be able to buy it?

News

- Did that story give you both sides of the story? If not, which side were they favoring? Why might the news sometimes be biased or slanted in one direction?
- Why is it important for us to know what is going on in faraway places like Ireland or Ethiopia? Do you think our government is doing the right thing in that particular situation?
- How does seeing those (violent, sad, etc.) pictures on TV make you feel? Do you understand what they mean?
- Do you think the news sometimes makes a big thing out of nothing? Why do you think news programs sometimes tend to make a big deal out of small news events?

Because television offers such a broad arena for discussion, be prepared for some interesting conversations to follow. Kids are curious consumers, and they are notoriously unafraid to ask questions. If you were saving that big sex talk for a few years down the road, it may need to be introduced (perhaps in an abridged version) earlier than anticipated. When sticky issues do arise—and they inevitably will—give honest but careful answers. Kids do not need to know every single detail, be it sex or a bloody terrorist act. Again, be sensitive to their varying levels of emotional maturity and adjust your answers accordingly. Though television may lead into some uncomfortable territory, it can be an important vehicle for difficult conversations (sex, AIDS, racism) that might otherwise go unsaid. Also, talking with your kids about troublesome issues tends to be easier on both parties when something neutral and impersonal like the television set is the focus and source of a discussion. For all of its problems and drawbacks, television can provide a great number of classic teachable moments. Try very hard to take advantage of them.

There is, of course, a fine line between using television as a teacher and letting television trample on your family's values and beliefs. If language gets too rough or bedroom scenes too steamy, simply explain to your kids that you don't approve of the content. Then turn the TV off and suggest something else to do. Also, don't forget that television can easily frighten children, causing great anxiety and undue fears. Coverage of wars, for example, can spur some kids on to practically obsessing about death. Again, try to keep potentially disturbing television to a minimum. Switch it off when it comes on and spend plenty of time allaying your kids' fears. If war scenes are frightening, show them a map that illustrates how far away the fighting really is; if it is a scary monster, explain that it's all made up (and maybe let them sleep with the lights on for a few nights); and if it is a high-profile but relatively infrequent event like a child abduction, explain the need for caution without creating an atmosphere of paranoia in your home. Discussing these troubling issues requires a delicate balance of truth-telling and calm assurance. Finding that balance is an imprecise art.

Be aware also that such content problems can pop up when they are least expected, another reason for trying to watch together with your kids. For example, more and more frequently, television programs are being interrupted by special reports of breaking news, not all kid-friendly. No incident better illustrates the danger of this trend for young viewers than the O. J. Simpson murder investigation and subsequent trial. While the Knicks-Rockets NBA championship game was in full swing on a June evening in 1994, with millions of basketball fans young and old gathered around the television to cheer their team, the game was preempted for coverage of O. J. Simpson's infamous chase down a California freeway. In between live shots of the cruising white Ford Bronco was footage of his ex-wife's blood-stained terrace and interviews with various experts on Simpson's seemingly suicidal state. How to explain all this to a 6-year-old? It may be best to just shut off the TV and pull out Candyland than to continue watching and then have to tackle the ills and psychoses of modern life on a Friday night.

Fortunately, these difficult situations generally represent the exceptions in television. Much of television is simply silly entertainment that may need occasional clarification or comment. Avoid heavy-handedness as much as possible, relying instead on humor and a light touch to make your point. Also, be sure to give your children space for their own opinions, which may or may not reflect your own. It's okay to disagree with each other so long as your kids understand precisely where you stand and why. Remember, too, that kids (especially older ones) will often say things that are outrageous and contrary just because, well, you're the parent. Don't make a big deal about it (that is probably what they are hoping); deep down they likely share the same convictions as you though at a certain age it becomes appalling to admit such a thing.

In addition to providing an arena for discussions both serious and silly, actively discussing television teaches your kids to become good TV critics, an increasingly important skill in our broadening television age. Given time and practice, your kids will learn to spot a show's intended audience, to watch commercials critically, to catch and dismiss stereotypes, and to recognize abstract concepts like production motives and bias. To increase these skills and make television watching even more lively, you can turn to a number of books that describe creative television activities and games for families. From role-playing to scripting your own show, the suggestions in the following books are sure to make television watching a memorable experience for your family:

- *The ACT Guide to Children's Television: How to Treat TV With TLC,* by Evelyn Kaye (Beacon Press, 1979).
- *A Parent's Guide to Television: Making the Most of It,* by Michael R. Kelley (John Wiley & Sons, 1983).
- *Taming the Wild Tube,* by Robert L. Schrag (University of North Carolina Press, 1990).
- *Teaching Television: How to Use TV to Your Child's Advantage,* by Dorothy Singer, Jerome Singer, and Diana Zuckerman (The Dial Press, 1981).
- *TV On/Off: Better Family Use of Television,* by Ellen DeFranco (Goodyear, 1980).

Just as you should make television an active and interactive event, try to do the same for video games and computer activities. Instead of encouraging your kids to go off and play video games by themselves, have contests within your family, giving everyone a turn. Encourage unlikely players such as grandparents to join in on the action. Who knows, Grandma could have an untapped zapping skill! Also, if you have a personal computer, try to use it with your kids. For example, if your family invests in a new software package or takes a plunge into the Internet, set about learning or exploring it together. Let them take the helm at the keyboard, but chart the new territory together. Since kids often know far more about computers than adults, let them show off their skills for you. Set aside time to allow *them* to teach *you* how to open Windows and maneuver through cypberspace. It will surely be a thrill for them to know that you trust and admire their knowledge and abilities.

Television, video games, and computer activities are not necessarily bad ways for your family to spend time together. The trick is learning how to make the most of what they have to offer.

Without Television: Alternative Activities

Despite the cozy benefits of watching television as a family, they represent only a slim fraction of enjoyment a family can find together. Similarly, in spite of the entertaining hours television can provide an individual child, they represent only the barest level of intellectual and emotional excitement that a child can find. Indeed, only after the television set has been turned off can life be truly tasted. That said, we must seize the small, daily chances for our children to experience wonderment, love, joy, discovery, even pain — all necessary ingredients for a full and fulfilling life.

It's a nice suggestion, you might think, but where does one come up with the time for tasting life? No doubt, the act is made more difficult by the demands of work and an overly committed calendar. It is this perceived lack of time, however, that contributed to the rise of a generation raised by television in the first place. If things for our children are to change, we must make changes in our own lives and priorities. Most importantly, we must learn both to jealously protect our kids' time and freedom and to carve out more time to spend together. Reducing television's hold on your family's attention and time is the first step. The second is to find meaningful ways to fill the gap created by television's absence.

It does not take the genius of a child development expert to determine what kids really like to do with their time. Simply observe the things they naturally gravitate towards and incorporate these things more fully into their lives. If you are still stumped, there are a great number of books available to help you with ideas. Beginning on page 229, Appendix D gives a full listing; some of the most well-known works include *365 TV-Free Activities You Can Do With Your Child* by Steve and Ruth Bennett and *What to Do After You Turn Off the TV* by Francis Moore Lappe.

Though the list of potential alternative activities is as long as the imagination is wide, certain ones deserve priority. For children, there are three pursuits in particular that should never be compromised for the temporal charm of television: play and imagination, reading, and participation in a strong family life. These are the simple building blocks of a bright, secure, and fulfilling childhood.

Play and Imagination

It seems somehow odd to stress the importance of play. Like eating and breathing, it should need no reminder. Play is, after all, the essence of childhood, a simple act that yields a bounty of happy effects. It propels children toward discovery, leads them into marvelous imaginary worlds, and provides the stuff of wild laughter.

Though it should be one of the central acts of a child's life, for many kids the act of playing has lost much of its original joy. In *For the Love of Children,* authors Edward Ford and Steven Englund discuss the demise of true play in our culture:

> As a society we have lost touch with spontaneity, joy, lightness, improvisation, and humor as the springs and sources of culture, and in their place, we have only seriousness, regimentation, system, growth, profit, material. In place of true play we have developed any number of inadequate surrogates—what the Romans used to call "bread and circuses." Indeed we are fairly strangling in our leisure machines; we straightjacket ourselves and our children with organized sports and competition. We bedizen the landscape with gaudy amusement parks, luxurious campsites, the plush inessentials of a Hilton hotel, and massive stadiums and arenas where we stage our own variety of gladiatorial contests; yet we are like starving men who don't know how to eat surrounded by banquets. We are a nation of leisure, a people cowed and cajoled into making fun the strenuously sought-after goal of our lives; yet we know so little about true play.[4]

Simple play seems to be a relic from a simpler age. Who now has time for it? In between soccer practice and scout meetings, swimming lessons and summer camp, Sega Genesis and *Sesame Street*, kids have few moments to simply set their minds, bodies, and imaginations free. Ever bombarded by flashing electronic stimulation and hyperorganized activities, kids everywhere seem to be forgetting *how* to play. Too often the natural joy of an exploring toddler turns into the boredom and weariness of a school-aged child; the thought of a wide-open Saturday may baffle the child who has long discarded the simple charm of imaginative play. And so children find any number of pale substitutes to fill their time. Watching TV becomes "playing." Using Nintendo becomes "playing." Joining a team (complete with nagging, competitive, overbearing parents) becomes "playing." As parents, we often contribute to play's demise by believing that it must be a major scheduled event ("Okay, kids, plan on having fun between 6:30 and 8:30 next Friday night!"). Thus promised, we load the children in the car for an expensive night of mediocre pizza, garish dancing bears, and loud token-activated games; at the end of the evening the kids are usually overstimulated, overstuffed, and missing at least one brand new shoe. Parents, for their part, have nightmares of dancing bears for weeks on end.

None of these activities, of course, represents the true spirit of play. They are artificial and limiting, and too often they cost a great deal of money. Though the preceding pursuits may seem to bring enjoyment, we are cheating our kids if this is all we encourage in the way of play.

Happily, play is a far simpler prospect than we make it out to be. To begin, it needn't cost any money. In limiting television viewing, our first thought might be to buy out an entire aisle of toys and games at Toys "R" Us to keep our kids occupied. This would be a serious mistake. Not only would it unduly stress our credit cards, but it would also insult our children's own powers of imagination and resourcefulness. As we've earlier stated, kids have an amazing knack for making the ordinary extraordinary. Our babies and toddlers provide daily examples of this very point. As soon as they become mobile, they move away from brimming toy chests and crawl straight into the kitchen. Their treasure is found in cabinets holding pots and pans, Tupperware, and unopened boxes of Jell-O. Older children can similarly entertain themselves with very little in the way of formal toys. An empty cardboard box becomes a pirate ship, an old blanket turns into the salty sea, and scattered gym shoes are transformed into slippery fish, sharks, and whales. Ahoy, matey! The resourcefulness of child's play is a joy to behold.

In addition to being virtually free of cost, play is also free of agendas and outward purposes and plans. During a conversation with her then 4-year-old nephew Brett, this book's second author asked what he was up to. His honest and simple reply has endured for years: "Oh, I'm just walking around, looking at things." Early on Brett learned the art of independent and aimless playing. As a result, he has become a first-rate discoverer, often stretching a simple 5-minute walk to the park into an hour-long examination of bugs in sidewalk cracks. The aimless, unpredictable quality of play can also be seen with groups of children playing together. A game of tickle-monster evolves into tag which leads to hide-and-seek which unfolds into making dandelion chains; the string of incarnations seems endless, halted only by the call to supper or to bed.

Encouraging Play. As parents, there is plenty we can do to encourage play. First, give your kids the time and freedom to play. Be sure to leave room in each day for unstructured play—without the television or video games. Your kids may or may not appreciate your initial efforts, for the prospect of filling time with original play may truly intimidate kids who are used to being passively entertained by television. If this is the case, gently head them in a few general directions. Soon enough they'll be scheming and dreaming all on their own. Also, encourage a balance between having your kids play with other kids (siblings or friends) and having them play by themselves. Both are important. Playing with others teaches essential social skills and is the glue of most young friendships. Playing alone, on the other hand, leads to self-discovery and reflection. Though most kids can strike a balance for themselves, exceptionally extroverted or introverted children may need occasional nudges in one direction or the other.

It is important also to provide a place to play, one that gives children the freedom to move about and drip paint without fear of reproach. To be sure, play is not always the neatest or calmest of activities. A spare play room, the backyard, or a cleared out area in the basement is the most desirable spot—kids can be loud and messy without causing too many headaches. If these options are impractical or unavailable, try to learn to live with a bit of a mess. To that end, you may want to rethink your need for displaying the fancy crystal and fragile, generations-old antiques. A home that fosters creative play should not be a keep-your-hands-at-your-sides gallery of breakables and stainables, for kids by nature do break things and stain things.

Similarly, save the stylish Gap Kids clothes for school and special occasions; old, faded hand-me-downs will do just fine.

In addition to carving out the time and space for play, parents should also provide the tools for play. Again, these need not be formal toys. Leave a chest of old clothes available for play-acting and dress-up. Save appliance-sized boxes, paper towel rolls, plastic bottles, and any other throw-away item that might find a new life. Teach them indoor and outdoor games, or better yet, have them make up their own. Provide them with malleable, textured materials like clay, water, Play-Doh, and sand—kids love to squeeze, pound, shape, and build. As for the question of toys, there is room, certainly, for them in a child's life. Be selective, however. A few well-chosen, long-lasting toys (Brio, Legos, simple baby dolls, for example) are usually preferable to a hoard of flimsy, trendy ones that break into millions of pieces and then fall victim either to the vacuum cleaner or a passing fad.

Finally, besides giving the time, space, and tools for play, create a family environment that celebrates play. To that end, stop being so serious! Encourage everyone to tell jokes, ask riddles, and relate funny stories (realizing that around age 8 or 9 bathroom humor becomes uproariously funny). Make up songs and stories. Have family game nights. Create goofy contests. Wrestle and chase one another outside. Tickle each other. It is in these simple acts that a playful and imaginative approach to life takes shape.

Reading

Jacqueline Kennedy Onassis, widely celebrated for her love of her children, once said this about children and books: "There are many little ways to enlarge [your child's] world. Love of books is the best of all." There is nothing like a book to carry the mind (young or old) to a far-off place or to teach it a brand new way of looking at things. Moreover, the lessons and appeal of good literature are timeless. Unlike the fleeting, flavor-of-the-minute pace of television, books endure through the ages. For many us, the beloved characters we met in our childhood—Curious George, Charlotte and Wilbur, Peter Rabbit, Nancy Drew, Frog and Toad, Madeline, and many others—remain warmly rooted in memory.

One of the most pleasurable aspects of reading is that the reader so thoroughly interacts with the unseen author and his or her words. In the reading process, single letters form into words that string into meaningful sentences, paragraphs, and pages. Whole thoughts and ideas emerge, and an image soon evolves in the reader's eye. This is the great thrill of reading—merging the author's words, either simple or elaborate, with one's own imagination. Perhaps this is why film adaptations of favorite books are often such a disappointment, for they rarely approximate the rich images that readers long ago created in their minds.

Books also differ from television and film in that they invite reflection and control. In their book *The House of Make-Believe*, Dorothy and Jerome Singer explain:

> We can control our reading in many ways: by rereading a sentence, pausing to reflect, pondering a difficult word, stopping to consult a dictionary, flipping back the pages in the book to an earlier section or even peeking ahead if we want to, skipping over sentences we don't enjoy or understand or savoring sentences that have particular beauty or meaning for us. We control the pace when we read. We can go quickly or slowly. We can read with intent or we can skim. We can finish a book and then start all over again—immediately, if we so choose.[5]

We should add that reading has the added benefit of never being interrupted by a commercial break.

Solid reading skills, we know, form the foundation of a successful academic career. But dwelling on arguments of academic merit has its own dangers. For far worse than parents who rarely read to their children are those who make it a compulsion, turning what should be a natural delight into forced academic preparation. This is antithetical to the spirit of reading! More than a ticket to the honor roll, reading is a tonic for the soul. On the other hand, there are many children who are never encouraged to read for any reason, academic or otherwise. In the highly recommended *The New Read-Aloud Handbook*, writer Jim Trelease notes that "The child who is unaware of the riches of literature certainly can have no desire for them."[6] Conversely, the child who glimpses the magic between two hard covers will hunger for more. This is an appetite we should heartily feed.

Encouraging Reading. To foster a love of reading in your children, it's crucial to make reading a high priority in the life of your family. First, take *time* to read. Make it fun and make it frequent. If your kids are too young to read for themselves, read aloud to them. Even newborns seem to appreciate being read to, perhaps finding comfort in a rhythmic, familiar voice. For children who have learned to talk, stop occasionally while reading to ask "What if . . . " questions and to solicit predictions. Though some kids will not tolerate any deviation from a favorite book, pictures and words in a book can be terrific springboards to discussions as well as sparks for entirely new made-up stories. You'll never know where a story may go when the gears of a child's imagination start clicking. Finally, when your children reach reading age, take time to allow them to read to *you* (preferably before bedtime, when their words won't be punctuated by sleepy yawns). In addition to improving fluency, the act of reading aloud brings to children a great sense of achievement and pride.

To encourage reading for the whole family, regularly plan reading nights in your home—no TV, just everyone's favorite books and magazines. It should not be a somber, silent affair, however—no one would much look forward to it. Make popcorn, sprawl on the furniture and floor, and allow plenty of time and freedom for questions and discussion. Such evenings will probably be the most satisfying of your week.

It is also easy to weave reading into everyday activities. Have your kids read recipes out loud to you. Teach them to read a map, then have them navigate you through town. If you have the patience, have them read directions out loud as you assemble a toy or a simple household apparatus. Start younger kids in the habit of reading newspapers by asking them to check sports scores for you. Meanwhile, encourage your teenagers to read newspapers and news magazine articles, taking time to ask their opinions. Be on the lookout, and each day will bring new opportunities to practice the skills of reading.

Finally, establish bedtime reading rituals. Some of the most important moments between parent and child occur in the quiet peace of the night. While it is often very natural to read books in bed to younger kids, don't forget about your older ones. Many kids, no matter what their ages, still enjoy those intimate moments of being read to. If your kids absolutely are past that stage, perhaps you could take time each night to talk about what they read on their own that day. You might be surprised at how well this fosters communication. Older kids, especially teenagers, are often reluctant to discuss personal matters with their parents. When a neutral, nonthreatening issue like a book is the focus of a discussion, kids may feel more freedom to reveal themselves by identifying with a particular character or situation. As Trelease writes, literature, "more than television, more than film, more than art or overhead projectors . . . brings us closest to the human heart."[7]

Besides taking the time to read, you can emphasize reading by *having books readily available.* Fill your home with books. Stack them everywhere: in the kitchen, in the car, in all bedrooms, and, yes, in the bathroom. Keep them readily available for empty moments like lining up for a turn in the shower or while waiting for the cookies to finish baking.

The easiest and most economical way to build these wobbly stacks is to borrow books from your local public library. For all their long-entrenched images of stuffiness and their intimidating codes of silence, libraries are places of wonder and magic. Teach your children at young ages how to make their way through a library's aisles, rows, and stacks. Show them where books for their reading levels are located, allowing them to choose personally the ones that will join the stacks at home. When they are old enough, teach them how to use the catalogue system, now typically on computer systems. Be sure also to take advantage of children's story hours and reading clubs.

Though libraries are great resources and testing grounds, consider buying books when possible. There is an old saying "Wear the old coat and buy the new book." In our case it might be said that instead of buying each new toy advertised on TV, invest in quality literature. Unlike toys that break and lose their pieces, the bones and spirit of a good story stay with us forever.

The most obvious tactic is to head to a nearby bookstore, family in tow. Bookstores big and small are making a comeback these days, and many of the larger bookstore chains like Borders Books and Barnes & Noble create a truly memorable experience for book buyers of all ages. Stuffed chairs encourage slow browsing and espresso bars lure customers to sit down and enjoy their new finds. Just visiting such a store can be an occasion in itself. Many of these stores seem to try to outdo each other with dazzling customer service, especially in area of children's books. Some seem more like well-endowed public libraries than retail chains, offering children's activities such as story hours, mask-making, and African dance lessons. Try also to seek out children's bookstores. Their shelves are crammed with bright books for kids of all ages and every conceivable interest. Moreover, you'll be hard pressed to find a sales staff so interested in the developing mind and imagination of your child.

Buying new books, we know, is not in everyone's budget. If that is the case, scour garage sales and flea markets for great deals on reading material. Used bookstores are another good source. In most cities and towns they are plentiful, often located in little noticed strip malls and dilapidated old buildings. Don't let appearances throw you off, for used bookstores, with their musty smells and hazy light, are treasure houses for inexpensive books. Besides coming home with a bargain, there is the added mystery in imagining who held the book before you.

Wherever you ultimately find your books, encourage a balance between old and new literature. Children's literature is ever expanding, having been especially invigorated by tales from foreign lands and cultures. Discovering new titles can be great fun, but be sure to revisit the classics of children's literature. Books like *Stuart Little, Charlotte's Web, Make Way for Ducklings, Old Yeller, Where the Red Fern Grows, Sounder, Little Women, A Wrinkle in Time,* and the collections of writers like C. S. Lewis and Laura Ingalls Wilder remain on bookshelves because of the enduring joy that they bring. Finally, if there are books new or old that your child particularly loves, set them aside when he or she outgrows them. Find a box for the attic and pack them safely away for the future. Pull them out again when that child has grown up and hand them over as gifts, for there are few treasures as great as the literature once loved as a child.

Family Life

When the TV is turned off, family life can come alive. Without television occupying center stage, family members who once just shared bathrooms and breakfast cereal begin to share thoughts, ideas, tears, and laughter.

The initial act of turning off the television is a most important start in developing a strong and memorable family life for your kids. But again, it is just a start and not always a comfortable one at that. Reducing TV will leave a noticeable gap in your family's life. Hours that once were spent in silent communion with the television set suddenly stretch wide open. Like an empty lull in a conversation, the unstructured time can put an uncomfortable pall over the family. Yet this lull, this gap, is *the key* to forging a family life that is stronger than ever.

It would be something of an overpromise to say that turning off the television on Thursday will create a family who sits around the fireplace, hugging and telling wonderful stories on Friday. Taken alone, the act of turning off the television is usually insufficient to create an environment of family intimacy. Families must also find ways to spend time together. Find ways to talk together. Find ways to discover together. And find ways to laugh together. The process soon becomes self-sustaining: A family who learns to spend time together will soon turn into a family who discovers together, and a family who talks together will surely become a family who laughs together. In the end, you'll become a family who truly *lives* together.

Encouraging Family Life. As with the notion of play, our first instinct may be to complicate what is really a very simple process. Instead of grabbing a crammed datebook to pencil in quality time with your family, start by making the most of time that is already available. Everyday routines like driving to school or getting ready for bed offer enormous opportunities for family togetherness and fun. The trick is to recognize those times and act on them. For example, there is no experience in the life of the family that better provides an environment for talking, sharing, laughing, and joking than sitting down together for a meal each evening. Unfortunately, the dinnertime ritual for many families seems to have gone the way of 8-track tapes—outdated and obsolete. With zigzagging, crisscrossing schedules of work, team practices, after-school activities, meetings, and other demands, it would take a professional planner to carve out time for a joint supper in many households. And even when a group dinner is possible, kids often scramble from their seats at the earliest possible moment, either to catch the start of a favorite television show or to escape dull adult conversation and the rigorous demands of sitting still.

Yet taking time to eat together can be the very best part of a family's day. Gathered around the table, family members can share the funny, crazy, or just plain horrible aspects of their day. As one of the few "gathering points" left in the modern world, the dinner ritual encourages us to remain in each other's lives. After dashing off in different directions throughout the day, suppertime finally gives everyone a chance to come together for some unified respite and a small (sometimes very small) amount of civility. Moreover, food, especially homemade food, is one of life's great balms; few things in this world match the familiar comfort of buttery mashed potatoes or warm apple pie.

Besides offering refuge, unity, and comfort, the dinner table also fulfills a very practical human need: eating. And because everyone needs to eat, why not take advantage of this need by turning dinnertime into a bona fide household event? For starters, include your kids in meal preparation. Not only does this lift the burden from just one person (usually Mom), but it also teaches kids how to maneuver around in a kitchen, a skill that typically doesn't surface until they strike out on their own. Most importantly, cooking can be great creative fun, and introducing your children early to its pleasures gives them one more enjoyable alternative to television. So put on some lively music and get busy. Be warned, though: If you want your kitchen to still resemble a kitchen when the meal is over, it's best to find easy, non-disaster-provoking things for your kids to do, like washing vegetables and setting the table. They will have the rest of their lives to chop tomatoes, run blenders, and scorch the bottoms of cookware.

Meanwhile, never let guilt get in the way of a good meal. Every night need not be a culinary triumph—for kids at least, peanut butter and jelly sandwiches and macaroni and cheese are far more thrilling (and recognizable) than the latest concoctions from *Bon Appétit*. Even if it's skinny burgers from a fast food joint, dinner can be special. Your kids certainly will be elated—home cooked meals never come in a box with a toy! In the end, whether you are a gourmet cook or a kitchen flop is really beside the point. The important thing is that you take time to provide a regular arena for family togetherness.

One of the best parts of eating together is the natural consequence of talking together. But while we might hope for meaningful discussion during dinner, most family meals are not marked by great and inspiring dialogue. More likely the kids are busy spilling their milk, feeding beans to the dog, and showing each other the chewed up meatloaf in their mouths. Still, there is no better time of the day to try for quality conversation, so give it your best shot.

First, be interested in their world. It is not surprising that many kids entertain themselves and each other with food tricks when the conversation revolves around gas tax hikes and gossip from the latest school board meeting. Actively include them in conversation by finding a subject that will interest them and by keeping it at a level they can understand. Most discussions should revolve around *their* lives—school, sports, activities of the day. To keep the conversation flowing, be sure to ask questions that require more verbal response than the usual "Fine," "Nothin'," "I dunno," or the universal silent shoulder shrug. Get away from perfunctory questioning ("How was school today, dear?") and show a true interest in your child by asking more open-ended questions like

1. What was the *best* thing that happened to you today?
2. What's something *new* that you learned today?
3. What was the *hardest* thing you did today?

4. What helped you choose *that particular topic* for a report?
5. Which do you like better—social studies or science? Why?

Despite their sometimes tough façades, kids yearn to be known, especially by their parents. Genuine, thoughtful questioning will go a long way toward making your kids feel both special and understood.

Occasionally, especially with school-aged children, it's also fun to discuss recent news events. Again, remember to keep it at their level. For example, if there is a great local furor over a proposed landfill in town, ask your children what *they* think should be done with people's garbage. Here is a prime opportunity to see a child's imagination take flight. Their answers to life's most vexing questions result in creative, sometimes common sensical, and often hilarious proposals. Moreover, such generalized, theoretical discussions can often be whittled down to suggestions and brainstorming on related issues in the family's own life. In the case of our preceding landfill discussion, the conversation may lead to thinking up innovative ways to recycle ("Use the blank side of a sheet of used paper for coloring and doodling") and how to cut down on the family's own trash ("Buy ice cream in a cone, not in a cup!").

Dinnertime is also often a great time to discuss prickly moral issues, again in a general, easygoing sense. Thomas Lickona, a well-known authority on moral development and author of *Raising Good Children,* offers a marvelous suggestion for families with older grade school children or teenagers.[8] In his family, dinnertime frequently includes a visit from Dear Abby. Her column (and others like it) is a source of real-life moral dilemmas that are, as Lickona writes, "both challenging to the mind and easy on the stomach." One of the family members reads the letter out loud, but not the advice. As a family they hash out dilemmas like the 16-year-old girl who had an accident with the family car through her own fault: Should her father carry out his threat to take away her driving privileges for a whole year if this ever happened? Or should a boy tell his teacher he saw a classmate defacing school property? Only *after* they all say what advice they'd give and why do they read Abby's advice aloud. Lickona adds that it's important to be selective in choosing the letters—a great deal of today's advice column material is unsuitable for youngsters.

While the dinner table provides a natural arena for lively discussion, grab every other opportunity to talk and spend quality time with your children. Often the most meaningful exchanges come right out of the blue. One mother we know spent an entire afternoon chatting with her teenage daughter (a feat in itself) about her own life as a teenager as they cleaned out old mementos in the attic. Free of the pressure and overly serious expectations that often mark planned birds and bees-type discussions, ordinary activities like making dinner and raking leaves often provide an easy atmosphere in which to talk and share. One father finds that the best time for talking to his preteen kids is while driving in the car. Because their time in the car is limited (meaning the conversation can't go on forever) and Dad has to keep his eyes on the road (meaning no judgmental staring), his kids feel comfortable discussing issues both trivial and touchy. And bedtime, as we've said earlier, is often the perfect time for quiet sharing. Finally, the simple act of turning off the television allows for conversations that might otherwise have been lost; without the persistent drone of the TV set, family voices finally can be heard.

In addition to maximizing time together and communication, maximize your family's opportunities to celebrate things big and small. So often we develop highly elaborate rituals for the holidays and birthdays that we forget to celebrate the little things. The "little things," though, are what often bring the most color to life.

Without television using up your hours together, your family will find unlimited occasions and events to celebrate. One family we know celebrates the beginning of each season with the same event each year (in the spring everyone works for a day in the garden, capped by a family backyard picnic; in the summer they throw a neighborhood barbecue; in the fall they go for a hayride; and in the winter they go sledding and invite friends back to their house for hot cocoa). In another family, every time the kids learn to do something new, like going off the diving board or riding their bike without training wheels, their mom bakes a "blooming cake" for the whole gang, specially decorated for the occasion. Not only is this a yummy treat, but it reinforces the family's commitment to be out in the world living life, not sitting inside watching people on TV living theirs.

As with the previous examples, try to think of small celebrations that encourage alternatives to television. Plan a special night out for improved grades at school. Throw a back-to-school party. Display your kids' best artwork and other creations around the house. Make banners and signs supporting and applauding your kids for achievements and efforts big (making the gymnastics team) and a bit less big, though no less important (trying out for the gymnastics team); as a consequence, you will probably raise children who not only keep on trying, but, more importantly, find joy in trying. This for a parent is no small success.

In addition to celebrating specific events and occasions, try to weave an unexpected celebratory spirit into everyday experiences. Do the unexpected every once in a while. Tape "Good Morning" notes to the bathroom mirror. Spread out a sheet for protection and eat dinner on the floor of the living room or family room. Pick your kids up from school and go somewhere special as a surprise. Put a small ad in the paper telling your kids you love them. Cook favorite breakfast foods like waffles and pancakes for dinner. Though these may seem like small, inconsequential acts, they form the stuff of lasting childhood memories. In her fine book *Prime-Time Parenting,* author Kay Kuzma relates how one brief, unexpected act long remained in one child's memory:

> I once read an unforgettable account about a father and his seven-year-old son. On an August night, the father bundled up the sleeping child and carried him out into the darkness. As the boy's sleep-filled eyes began to focus on his surroundings, the father shouted "Look!" And there in the sky the little boy saw a star leap from its place and fall toward the ground. Then, incredibly, another star fell, and another and another. That was all. But the boy never forgot that night when his father did the unexpected, and he determined that he would do the same some August evening when his boy was seven.[9]

Celebrations and acts of grace — big or small, planned or unexpected — go a long way toward creating a memorable home environment. And always they will bring to children more satisfaction than the transient gratification of television. In comparison to the thrill of truly living and celebrating life, the flat world of television will seem mighty dull indeed.

101 Fun and Simple Things To Do With Your Family

It's not always easy to think of fun, interesting things to do with your children. Nor is it always easy to find time. But when you have a moment, an afternoon, or even an entire day to spend with your kids, here are some simple, inexpensive, and memorable ways both to spend time with your kids and to encourage their own independent play.

Anytime Fun

1. Have a story hour each evening. Break a long story into short segments, say 10 or 15 minutes a night. Encourage your older kids to read to the younger ones.
2. Gaze at the stars and identify constellations. Over the seasons kids can chart their movement in the sky.
3. Play favorite board games like Candyland, Monopoly, or Risk.
4. Visit garage sales together to find quality second-hand books and toys.
5. On Friday or Saturday nights, involve the entire family in making an ethnic dinner.
6. Designate a homework hour each evening during the school year. While kids do homework, parents should do something similarly quiet, like reading or paying bills.
7. Fill an old box or chest with old clothes for dress-up.
8. Listen to "Rabbit Ears Radio" on Public Radio International. Each week (check your local listings) famous actors tell favorite folk tales, tall tales, and other classic children's stories.
9. Make papier-mâché sculpture.
10. Make your own play-dough.
11. Build a fort or tree house. If there's not much yard space, build an indoor fort out of seat cushions, cardboard boxes, and blankets.
12. Tell your kids about their early childhood. Look at their baby books.
13. Tell your kids about your own childhood. Look at *your* baby book.
14. Encourage older siblings to teach younger siblings things like tying their shoes and making their beds.
15. Make a family tree.
16. Make a family scrapbook filled with favorite memories.
17. Play Go Fish, Hearts, Spit, and other fun card games.
18. While you're at it, build a house of cards.
19. Have a family slumber party. Roll out the sleeping bags and take turns telling stories by flashlight.
20. Make art out of recyclable trash.
21. Make a kite together, then go fly it.
22. Let older kids help with easy household repairs (handing you the right tool, holding things in place).

23. Subscribe to children's magazines like *Ranger Rick, My Big Backyard, Highlights,* and *Sports Illustrated for Kids.* Ask your kids about their favorite pictures and articles.
24. Give children responsibility for taking care of pets—feeding, grooming, and taking them for walks.
25. Sing songs together.
26. Provide preschool children who no longer need naps with at least an hour each day of unstructured quiet time in their rooms.
27. Skip using the dishwasher every once in a while and enlist your children to help dry dishes. It's a great time for conversation.
28. Create a durable art supply box, filled with crayons, markers, glue, and scrap paper. Put it in an easy-to-reach spot so the kids can help themselves.
29. Read Shel Silverstein poetry together.
30. Do a jigsaw puzzle together.
31. Encourage your kids to play a musical instrument. Try to first borrow or buy used instruments until your kids find ones they enjoy playing. Play or sing along with them!
32. Arrange for your child to have a pen pal from another state or better yet from across the seas.
33. Buy beads and create jewelry. Braid friendship bracelets.
34. Look at family photos.
35. Buy sidewalk chalk for your kids. Let them become street corner artists!
36. Have your kids make a small time capsule and bury it in the backyard.
37. Play catch.
38. Lie on the grass and watch the clouds float by.

Fun for the Seasons

39. Help your kids plant their own garden.
40. Go to a professional baseball game.
41. Organize a neighborhood Olympics, with fun, goofy events for "athletes" of all ages.
42. Spend a hot summer afternoon at the public library.
43. Go swimming.
44. Have a watermelon seed spitting contest.
45. Cool off by running through the water sprinkler.
46. Hunt for lightning bugs and creepy, crawly creatures of the night.

47. Have a water balloon contest.
48. Help your kids set up a lemonade stand.
49. Eat dinner outside in the yard.
50. Rake leaves together.
51. Go to a pumpkin patch to find a Halloween pumpkin.
52. Together plan and host a holiday party.
53. Make homemade Christmas or Hanukkah gifts.
54. Let the kids stay up late for a family New Year's Eve celebration.
55. Go sledding and ice skating.
56. Make a snowman and snow angels.

Teach Your Children Well

57. Teach your kids how to fill out a score card for a baseball game.
58. Teach your kids the names of the flowers, plants, and trees in your yard or neighborhood.
59. Teach your children to play checkers and chess.
60. Teach older kids first aid basics.
61. Teach younger kids their phone number and address. Sometimes it helps to put the information in song or chant form.
62. Teach your children how to swim or sign them up for lessons at a local pool.
63. Teach older children how to use a camera.
64. Teach your children to say "Hello" in other languages (Spanish: "Hola"; French: "Bonjour"; Italian: "Bongiorno"; German: "Guten Tag").
65. Teach your kids what to do in case of fire. Teach them the emergency number 9-1-1.
66. Teach your kids how to sew.
67. Teach your children to skip stones at a nearby pond or lake.
68. Teach your kids to cook and bake.
69. Teach your kids the old games you used to play like Kick-the-Can, Running Bases, Jacks, Blindman's Bluff, and Sardines.
70. Teach your kids how to read a map.

Family Trips Near and Far

71. Take a child to work with you.

72. Have kids help plan a family vacation. Give them maps to chart the travel and let them have a voice in planning activities.
73. Plan a visit to the country. Try to arrange seeing a farm, complete with mooing cows, neighing horses, and clucking chickens.
74. Go to a roller skating rink.
75. Go to the zoo. Be sure to stop by the petting zoo if one is available.
76. Go to family hour at your local YMCA.
77. Go to a puppet show.
78. Go bowling.
79. Explore a nearby city.
80. Visit a children's museum. Most have terrific hands-on exhibits that thrill kids and adults alike.
81. Take your kids to see a local dance troupe.
82. Go square dancing.
83. Go to a local children's theater production. It could spark some thespian aspirations in your own kids!
84. Go on a nature walk and collect neat leaves and rocks. When home, make leaf rubbings with crayons and wax paper.
85. Regularly visit (from a safe distance) a construction site to see a building in its various stages of construction.
86. Attend children's story hour at the library.
87. Go camping (even if it's in your own backyard).
88. Head out for an ice cream cone.
89. Go to an art museum. Ask the kids to choose their favorite painting or sculpture.
90. Go fishing.
91. Go for a long bike ride. When possible, ride bikes instead of driving the car.
92. Go on a picnic to a nearby park.
93. Go to the airport and watch the planes take off and land.

Thinking of Others

94. Have kids make and decorate home-made birthday cards for family and friends
95. Visit an elderly neighbor. Bring homemade cookies.
96. Have kids help organize clothes and household items to give to charity.
97. Have kids write a letter or draw a picture to mail to out-of-town relatives.

98. Volunteer as a family to help clean up a littered lot. Make sure everyone wears gloves and takes safety precautions.
99. Once a year have your children pick a few toys from their collection to give to charity. Go as a family to the collection drop-off.
100. Spend a Saturday morning helping to distribute food at a food pantry.
101. Pay regular visits to a nursing home—it will bring untold joy to the residents.

Summary

Despite its faults and limitations, television is not a one-eyed monster that must be forever banished from your home. On the contrary, used wisely it can be a fun, compelling source of entertainment and information. The trick is to use television to your family's advantage by keeping the viewing experience active (ask lots of questions) and special (view less frequently). In making the important decision to cut back on television, parents must then decide how to fill the family's time. Though there are a great number of possibilities, three essential childhood pursuits deserve special time and attention: play, reading, and spending time together as a family. Unlike the fleeting charm of a TV show, the benefits of these pursuits will last a lifetime.

In the end, we can't promise that limiting the role of the electronic media in the lives of your children will produce stunning, earth-shattering results. On its own, the act won't mend broken relationships, keep storms at bay, guarantee As on the report card, or prevent children from fighting, pouting, or crying. What it will do, however, is give your kids more of a chance to just be kids. And this, today, is no small feat.

Appendices

Appendix A
    Sample Log of Activities   221
    Log of Activities   223

Appendix B
    Sample Contract   225
    Contract   226

Appendix C
    Contacting Networks   227

Appendix D
    Suggested Reading   229

Appendix A

Sample Log of Activities

Name: __Cara__

Day of the week: __Tuesday, May 13__

Time	Activity
7:00-8:00 a.m	Woke up, shower, Breakfast, Watched "Scooby Doo" 'til School Bus came
8:00-9:00 a.m.	School Bus at 8:10 a.m.
9:00-10:00 a.m.	School
10:00-11:00 a.m.	⎫
11:00-12:00 p.m.	⎬
12:00-1:00 p.m.	⎬
1:00-2:00 p.m.	⎬
2:00-3:00 p.m.	↓
3:00-4:00 p.m.	Brownies meeting til 4:15 pm
4:00-5:00 p.m.	Math and language arts homework til 5 pm
5:00-6:00 p.m.	Watched "The Flintstones" (2 episodes)

Time	Activity
6:00-7:00 p.m.	Dinner til 6:30; Watched "Tiny Toons" til 7 pm
7:00-8:00 p.m.	Watched "Home Improvement" w/ family til 7:30 pm, then "hung out" for ½ hour or so
8:00-9:00 p.m.	Played "Super Mario" video games w/ Jason
9:00-10:00 p.m.	Started getting ready for bed; bed at 9:20 pm
10:00-11:00 p.m.	Sleep
11:00-12:00 a.m.	↓ til 6:50 am

Totals:

Hours Spent Watching TV: 2 ½

Hours Spent Playing Video Games: 1

Hours Spent on the Computer: 0

Log of Activities

Name:_____

Day of the week:_____

Time	
7:00-8:00 a.m	
8:00-9:00 a.m.	
9:00-10:00 a.m.	
10:00-11:00 a.m.	
11:00-12:00 p.m.	
12:00-1:00 p.m.	
1:00-2:00 p.m.	
2:00-3:00 p.m.	
3:00-4:00 p.m.	
4:00-5:00 p.m.	
5:00-6:00 p.m.	

6:00-7:00 p.m.	
7:00-8:00 p.m.	
8:00-9:00 p.m.	
9:00-10:00 p.m.	
10:00-11:00 p.m.	
11:00-12:00 a.m.	

Totals:

Hours Spent Watching TV: _____

Hours Spent Playing Video Games: _____

Hours Spent on the Computer: _____

Appendix B

Sample Contract

A TV contract for: __Cara__

One ticket earns one-half hour of television watching or video game playing.

I can earn a ticket for doing the following things:

- ½ hour of reading
- ½ hour of coloring or drawing
- 1 hour of playing outside
- 1 hour of swimming lessons
- ½ hour of helping build the tree house
- ½ hour of cooking or baking with Mom or Dad
- Writing a letter to Grandparents, Cousins, and Friends

If I have __5__ unspent tickets at the end of the week, then I can:

__Go on a special trip to the water park__!

Signature: __Cara__   Date: __May 26__

Contract

A TV contract for:_____

*One ticket earns one-half hour of television
watching or video game playing.*

I can earn a ticket for doing the following things:

_____

_____

_____

_____

_____

_____

_____

If I have _____ unspent tickets at the end of the week, then I can:

_____!

_____   _____
Signature   Date

Appendix C
Contacting Networks*

Jaime Tarses, President
ABC Entertainment
2040 Avenue of the Stars
Century City, CA 90067

Leslie Moonves, President
CBS Entertainment
7800 Beverly Boulevard
Los Angeles, CA 90036

Peter Roth, President
Fox Entertainment Group
10201 West Pico Boulevard
Los Angeles, CA 90035

Warren Littlefield, President
NBC Entertainment
3000 Alameda Avenue
Burbank, CA 91523

Evan S. Duggan, President/CEO
PBS
1320 Braddock Place
Alexandria, VA 22314

---

*It's helpful to include the name of the network president in your letters. Do check, however, that the individuals listed above are still corporate presidents when you write. The job security for entertainment executives is sometimes short lived.

Lucille Salhany, President/CEO
UPN
11800 Wilshire Boulevard
Los Angeles, CA 90025

Jaime Kellner, CEO
WB Network
4000 Warner Boulevard, Building 34R
Burbank, CA 91522

Appendix D
Suggested Reading

Family Fun

Arp, Claudia and Linda Dillow. *The Big Book of Family Fun: Year-Round Creative Activities.* Nashville: Thomas Nelson, 1994.

Bennett, Steve and Ruth Bennett. *365 Outdoor Activities You Can Do With Your Child.* Holbrook, MA: Bob Adams, 1993.

Bennett, Steve and Ruth Bennett. *365 TV-Free Activities You Can Do With Your Child.* Holbrook, MA: Bob Adams, 1991.

Free Stuff for Kids: Hundreds of Free and Up-to-a-Dollar Things Kids Can Send for by Mail. New York: Meadowbrook Press, 1994.

Hart, Avery and Paul Mantell. *Kids & Weekends: Creative Ways to Make Special Days.* Charlotte, VT: Williamson, 1992.

Hickman, Danielle and Valerie Teurlay. *101 Great Ways to Keep Your Child Entertained While You Get Something Else Done: Creative and Stimulating Activities for Your Toddler or Preschooler.* New York: St. Martin's Press, 1992.

Katz, Adrienne. *What to Do With the Kids on a Rainy Day.* New York: St. Martin's Press, 1989.

Lappe, Francis Moore. *What to Do After You Turn Off the TV.* New York: Ballantine Books, 1986.

MacGregor, Cynthia. *Free* Family Fun *(and Super-Cheap).* New York: Berkley Books, 1994.

The Official Freebies for Families: Something for Next-to-Nothing for Everyone. Los Angeles: Lowell House, 1994.

Shedd, Warner. *The Kids' Wildlife Book: Exploring Animal Worlds Through Indoor/Outdoor Experiences.* Charlotte, VT: Williamson, 1994.

Vecchione, Glen. *World's Best Outdoor Games.* New York: Sterling, 1993.

Encouraging the Mind and Imagination

Burnie, David. *How Nature Works: 100 Ways Parents and Kids Can Share the Secrets of Nature.* Pleasantville, NY: Reader's Digest Association, 1991.
Children's Television Workshop. *Parents' Guide to Raising Kids Who Love to Learn.* New York: Prentice Hall Press, 1989.
Friedes, Harriet. *The Preschool Resource Guide: Educating and Entertaining Children Aged Two Through Five.* New York: Insight Books, 1993.
Haas, Carolyn Buhai. *Big Book of Fun: Creative Learning Activities for Home and School, Ages 4-12.* Chicago: Chicago Review Press, 1987.
Haas, Carolyn Buhai and Anita Cross Friedman. *My Own Fun: Creative Learning Activities for Home and School, Ages 7-12.* Chicago: Chicago Review Press, 1990.
Harlan, Jean Durgin With Carolyn Good Quattrocchi. *Science as It Happens! Family Activities With Children Ages 4 to 8.* New York: Henry Holt, 1994.
Hauser, Jill Frankel. *Growing Up Reading: Learning to Read Through Creative Play.* Charlotte, VT: Williamson, 1993.
Klavan, Ellen. *Taming the Homework Monster: How to Make Homework a Positive Learning Experience for Your Child.* New York: Poseidon Press, 1992.
Leonhardt, Mary. *Keeping Kids Reading: How to Raise Avid Readers in the Video Age.* New York: Random House, 1996.
Leonhardt, Mary. *Parents Who Love Reading, Kids Who Don't: How It Happens and What You Can Do About It.* New York: Crown, 1993.
Richards, Roy. *101 Science Surprises: Exciting Experiments With Everyday Materials.* New York: Sterling, 1992.
Roberts, Allene. *The Curiosity Club: Kids' Nature Activity Book.* New York: John Wiley & Sons, 1992.
Sonna, Linda Agler. *The Homework Solution: Getting Kids to Do Their Homework.* Charlotte, VT: Williamson, 1990.
Trelease, Jim. *The New Read-Aloud Handbook.* New York: Penguin Books, 1989.
Tuttle, Cheryl and Penny Paquette. *Thinking Games With Your Child: Easy Ways to Develop Creative and Critical Thinking Skills.* Los Angeles: Lowell House, 1991.

Arts and Crafts

Hamilton, Leslie. *Child's Play, 6-12: 160 Instant Activities, Crafts, and Science Projects for Grade Schoolers.* New York: Crown, 1991.

Hamilton, Leslie. *Child's Play: 200 Instant Crafts and Activities for Preschoolers.* New York: Crown Trade Paperbacks, 1989.

Johnson, Mia. *Teach Your Child to Draw: Bringing Out Your Child's Talents and Appreciation for Art.* Los Angeles: Lowell House, 1990.

Kohl, Mary Ann F. *Scribble Cookies and Other Independent Creative Art Experiences for Children.* Bellingham, WA: Bright Ring Publications, 1985.

Mason, Kate. *My First Friendship Bracelets: A Complete Easy to Follow Guide for Beginners.* Watermill Press, 1994.

McGraw, Sheila. *Papier Mâché for Kids.* Buffalo, NY: Firefly Books, 1992.

Solga, Kim. *Make Gifts!* Cincinnati, OH: North Light Books, 1991.

Terzian, Alexandra M. *The Kids' Multicultural Art Book: Art & Craft Experiences from Around the World.* Charlotte, VT: Williamson, 1993.

Walker, Lester. *Carpentry for Children: Simple Step-by-Step Plans for Great Do-It-Yourself Projects.* Woodstock, NY: The Overlook Press, 1982.

Warner, Sally. *Encouraging the Artist in Your Child (Even if You Can't Draw): 101 Failure-Proof, Home-Tested Projects for Kids Age 2-10.* New York: St. Martin's Press, 1989.

Cooking

Green, Caroline. *My Cook Book.* Racine, WI: Western Publishing, 1993.

Katzen, Molly and Ann Henderson. *Pretend Soup and Other Real Recipes: A Cookbook for Preschoolers & Up.* Berkeley, CA: Tricycle Press, 1994.

Kenda, Margaret and Phyllis S. Williams. *Cooking Wizardry for Kids: Learn About Food . . . While Making Good Things to Eat!* Hauppauge, NY: Barron's, 1990.

Kid's Cooking: A Very Slightly Messy Manual. Palo Alto, CA: Klutz Press, 1987.

Parham, Vanessa Roberts. *The African-American Child's Heritage Cookbook.* South Pasadena, CA: Sandcastle Publishing, 1993.

Scobey, Jean. *Fannie Farmer Junior Cookbook.* Boston: Little, Brown, 1993.

Wilkes, Angela. *The Children's Step-by-Step Cookbook: Photographic Cooking Lessons for Young Chefs.* London: Dorling Kindersley, 1994.

Williamson, Sarah and Zachary Williamson. *Kids Cook! Food for the Whole Family.* Charlotte, VT: Williamson, 1992.

Parenting and Children

Brazelton, T. Berry. *Touchpoints: Your Child's Emotional and Behavioral Development.* Reading, MA: Addison-Wesley, 1992.

Elkind, David. *The Hurried Child: Growing Up Too Fast Too Soon* (rev. ed.). Reading, MA: Addison-Wesley, 1988.

Ford, Edward E. and Steven Englund. *For the Love of Children: A Realistic Approach to Raising Your Child.* Garden City, NY: Anchor Press, 1977.

Gore, Tipper. *Raising PG Kids in an X-Rated Society.* New York: Bantam Books, 1988.

Kaye, Kenneth. *Family Rules: Raising Responsible Children (Without Slapping, Yelling, or Nagging).* New York: St. Martin's Paperbacks, 1991.

Lickona, Thomas. *Raising Good Children: From Birth Through the Teenage Years.* New York: Bantam Books, 1985.

Newman, Susan. *Little Things Long Remembered: Making Your Children Feel Special Every Day.* New York: Crown, 1993.

Pipher, Mary. *The Shelter of Each Other: Rebuilding Our Families.* New York: G. P. Putnam's Sons, 1996.

Pipher, Mary. *Reviving Ophelia: Saving the Selves of Adolescent Girls.* New York: Ballantine Books, 1994.

Postman, Neil. *The Disappearance of Childhood.* New York: Delacorte Press, 1982.

Rogers, Fred and Barry Head. *Mister Rogers Talks to Parents.* New York: Berkley Books, 1983.

Singer, Dorothy G. and Jerome L. Singer. *The House of Make-Believe: Play and the Developing Imagination.* Cambridge, MA: Harvard University Press, 1990.

Taffel, Ron With Melinda Blau. *Parenting by Heart.* Reading, MA: Addison-Wesley, 1991.

Weston, Denise Chapman and Mark S. Weston. *Playful Parenting: Turning the Dilemma of Discipline into Fun and Games.* New York: G. P. Putnam's Sons, 1993.

Winn, Marie. *Children Without Childhood.* New York: Penguin Books, 1985.

The Use and Abuse of Television

Biggar, Bill. *Danger Zones: What Parents Should Know About the Internet.* Kansas City: Andrews & McMeel, 1996.

Chen, Milton. *The Smart Parent's Guide to Kids' TV.* San Francisco: KQED Books, 1994.

De Franco, Ellen. *TV On/Off: Better Family Use of Television.* Santa Monica, CA: Goodyear, 1980.

Kaye, Evelyn. *The ACT Guide to Children's Television: How to Treat TV With TLC.* Boston: Beacon Press, 1979.

Kelley, Michael R. *A Parent's Guide to Television: Making the Most of It.* New York: John Wiley & Sons, 1983.

Mander, Jerry. *Four Arguments for the Elimination of Television.* New York: William Morrow, 1978.

McKeehan, Julie. *Safe Surfing: A Family Tour Through the Net.* Orlando, FL: Academic Press, 1996.

Minow, Newton N. and Craig L. LaMay. *Abandoned in the Wasteland: Children, Television, and the First Amendment.* New York: Hill and Wang, 1995.

Postman, Neil. *Amusing Ourselves to Death: Public Discourse in the Age of Show Business.* New York: Viking, 1985.

Schultze, Quentin, Roy M. Anker, James D. Bratt, William D. Romanowski, John W. Worst, and Lambert Zuidervaart. *Dancing in the Dark: Youth, Popular Culture, and the Electronic Media.* Grand Rapids, MI: William B. Eerdmans, 1991.

Singer, Dorothy G., Jerome L. Singer, and Diana M. Zuckerman. *Teaching Television: How to Use TV to Your Child's Advantage.* New York: The Dial Press, 1981.

Winn, Marie. *Unplugging the Plug-In Drug: Help Your Child Break the TV Habit.* New York: Penguin Books, 1987.

Winn, Marie. *The Plug-In Drug: Television, Children, and the Family* (rev. ed.). New York: Penguin Books, 1985.

End Notes

Introduction

1. Lucinda Franks, "Little Big People," *New York Times Magazine*, 10 October 1993, p. 31.
2. Neil Postman, *The Disappearance of Childhood* (New York: Delacorte Press, 1982), p. 97.

Chapter 1: Myths and Messages of Television

1. Aletha C. Huston, Edward Donnerstein, Halford Fairchild, Norma D. Feshbach, Phyllis A. Katz, John P. Murray, Eli A. Rubenstein, Brian L. Wilcox, and Diana Zuckerman, *Big World, Small Screen: The Role of Television in American Society* (Lincoln: University of Nebraska Press, 1992).
2. George Gerbner, Larry Gross, Michael Morgan, and Nancy Signorielli, "The 'Mainstreaming' of America: Violence Profile No. 11," *Journal of Communication* 30, no. 3 (1980): 11.
3. *Ibid.*
4. Huston, Donnerstein, Fairchild, Feshbach, Katz, Murray, Rubenstein, Wilcox, and Zuckerman, *Big World, Small Screen: The Role of Television in American Society.*
5. Lawrie Mifflin, "Study Says Networks Have Cut Violence," *The New York Times*, 16 October 1996, pp. C11, C16.
6. Kathleen Maguire and Ann L. Pastore, eds., *Bureau of Justice Statistics: Sourcebook of Criminal Justice Statistics – 1994*, Washington, DC: U. S. Government Printing Office, 1995; Federal Bureau of Investigation, *Uniform Crime Reports for the United States: 1994*, Washington DC: U. S. Government Printing Office, 1995.
7. Albert Bandura, "What TV Violence Can Do to Your Child," *Look*, 27 October 1963, pp. 46-52.

8. Albert Bandura, "Influence of Models' Reinforcement Contingencies on the Acquisition of Imitative Responses," *Journal of Personality and Social Psychology* 1 (1965): 589-595.
9. Albert Bandura, Dorothea Ross, and Sheila A. Ross, "Imitation of Film-Mediated Aggressive Models," *Journal of Abnormal and Social Psychology* 66 (1963): 3-11.
10. *Television and Growing Up: The Impact of Televised Violence – Report to the Surgeon General* (Washington DC: U. S. Government Printing Office, 1972).
11. David Pearl, Lorraine Bouthilet, and Joyce B. Lazar, eds., *Television and Behavior: Ten Years of Scientific Progress and Implications for the Eighties, Vol. 1: Summary Report* (Washington DC: U. S. Government Printing Office, 1982a), p. 37.
12. T. H. A. Van der Voort, *Television Violence: A Child's Eye View* (Amsterdam: North-Holland, 1986).
13. Leonard D. Eron, "Prescription for Reduction of Aggression," *American Psychologist* 35 (1980): 244-252.
14. George Comstock, "New Emphases in Research on the Effects of Television and Film Violence," in *Children and the Faces of Television: Teaching, Violence, Selling*, eds. Edward L. Palmer and Aimée Dorr (New York: Academic Press, 1980): 129-148.
15. Don Oldenburg, "Primal Screen: Kids—TV Violence & Real Life Behavior," *Washington Post*, 7 April 1992, p. E5.
16. Joyce N. Sprafkin and L. Theresa Silverman, "Update: Physically Intimate and Sexual Behavior on Prime-Time Television, 1978-1979," *Journal of Communication* 31, no. 1 (1981): 34-40.
17. Diana Workman, "What You See Is What You Think: More and More, Prime-Time Television Uses Sex to Draw Viewers," *Media & Values* 46 (1989): 2-5.
18. Dennis T. Lowry and David E. Towles, "Primetime Portrayals of Sex, Contraception, and Venereal Diseases," *Journalism Quarterly* 66 (1989): 347-352.
19. Barry S. Sapolsky and Joseph O. Tabarlet, "Sex in Primetime Television: 1979 Versus 1989," *Journal of Broadcasting and Electronic Media* 35 (1991): 505-516.
20. Barry L. Sherman and Joseph R. Dominick, "Violence and Sex in Music Videos: TV and Rock 'n' Roll," *Journal of Communication* 36, no. 1 (1986): 79-93.
21. Joyce N. Sprafkin, L. Theresa Silverman, and Eli A. Rubenstein, "Reactions to Sex on Television: An Exploratory Study," *Public Opinion Quarterly* 44 (1980): 303-315.

22. Louis Harris and Associates, *American Teens Speak: Sex, Myths, TV, and Birth Control* (New York: Planned Parenthood Federation of America, 1986).
23. Lowry and Towles, "Primetime Portrayals of Sex, Contraception, and Venereal Diseases."
24. Planned Parenthood Federation of America, *Sexual Material on American Network Television During the 1987-1988 Season* (New York: Author, 1988).
25. George Gerbner, "Women and Minorities on Television: A Study in Casting and Fate," *The Amplifier* (Summer 1994), pp. 5-6, 8.
26. G. Mendelson and M. Young, *Network Children's Programming: A Content Analysis of Black and Minority Treatment in Children's Television* (Newtonville, MA: Action for Children's Television, 1972).
27. Huston, Donnerstein, Fairchild, Feshbach, Katz, Murray, Rubenstein, Wilcox, and Zuckerman, *Big World, Small Screen: The Role of Television in American Society*.
28. Cited in Gordon L. Berry and Claudia Mitchell-Kernan, eds., *Television and the Socialization of the Minority Child* (New York: Academic Press, 1982).
29. Cited in Robert M. Liebert, Joyce N. Sprafkin, and Emily S. Davidson, *The Early Window: Effects of Television on Children and Youth*, 2nd ed. (New York: Pergamon Press, 1982).
30. Nancy Signorielli, "Children and Adolescents on Television: A Consistent Pattern of Devaluation," *Journal of Early Adolescence* 7 (1987): 255-268.
31. George Gerbner, "Women and Minorities on Television: A Study in Casting and Fate."
32. Jerome Weeks, "Young Boys' Network: Where Are the Girls in Children's Entertainment?" *Dallas Life Magazine*, 22 November 1992, p. 20.
33. F. Earle Barcus, *Images of Life on Children's Television: Sex Roles, Minorities, and Families* (New York: Praeger, 1983).
34. Mary Pipher, *Reviving Ophelia: Saving the Selves of Adolescent Girls* (New York: Ballantine Books, 1994), p. 42.
35. Signorielli, "Children and Adolescents on Television: A Consistent Pattern of Devaluation."
36. Barcus, *Images of Life on Children's Television: Sex Roles, Minorities, and Families*.
37. Staff, "Women on TV: Work Is In," *Psychology Today*, October 1985, p. 12.
38. T. S. Williams, *The Impact of Television: A Natural Experiment in Three Communities* (New York: Academic Press, 1986).

39. Alexis S. Tan, "TV Beauty Ads and Role Expectations of Adolescent Female Viewers," *Journalism Quarterly* 56 (1979): 283-288.
40. Jennifer Mangan, "Fine Tuning: Diversity and Realistic Roles Sought for Girls on Television," *Chicago Tribune*, 26 May 1996, pp. 1, 6.
41. George Gerbner, Larry Gross, Nancy Signorielli, and Michael Morgan, "Aging With Television: Images on Televised Drama and Conceptions of Social Reality," *Journal of Communication* 30, no. 1 (1980): 37-47.
42. Signorielli, "Children and Adolescents on Television: A Consistent Pattern of Devaluation."
43. George Comstock, Steven Chaffee, Natan Katzman, Maxwell McCombs, and Donald Roberts, *Television and Human Behavior* (New York: Columbia University Press, 1978).
44. Cited in Peggy Charren and Martin W. Sandler, *Changing Channels: Living (Sensibly) With Television* (Reading, MA: Addison-Wesley, 1983), p. 55.
45. Gerbner, "Women and Minorities on Television: A Study in Casting and Fate."
46. Cy Schneider, *Children's Television: The Art, the Business, and How It Works* (Lincolnwood, IL: NTC Business Books, 1987), p. 5.
47. Hal Himmelstein, *Television Myth and the American Mind* (New York: Praeger, 1984).
48. Scott Ward and Daniel B. Wackman, "Children's Purchase Influence Attempts and Parental Yielding," *Journal of Marketing Research* 9 (1972): 316-319.
49. James U. McNeal, *Kids as Customers: A Handbook of Marketing to Children* (New York: Lexington Books, 1992).
50. *Ibid.*
51. Stephen Kline, *Out of the Garden: Toys, TV, and Children's Culture in the Age of Marketing* (London: Verso, 1993), p. 182h.
52. Renate L. Welch, Aletha Huston-Stein, John C. Wright, and Robert Plehal, "Subtle Sex Role Cues in Children's Commercials," *Journal of Communication* 29, no. 3 (1979): 202-209.
53. Ellen Seiter, *Sold Separately: Children and Parents in Consumer Culture* (New Brunswick, NJ: Rutgers University Press, 1993), p.131.
54. *Ibid.*, p. 88.
55. Bob Garfield, "Nintendo Aims to 'Be Heard' by Exploiting Kids' Distress," *Advertising Age*, 25 July 1994, p. 3.
56. Allison James, "Confections, Concoctions, and Conceptions," *Journal of the Anthropological Society of Oxford* 10 (1982): 92.
57. William Melody, *Children and Television: The Economics of Exploitation* (New Haven, CT: Yale University Press, 1973).

58. *Ibid.*
59. Newton Minow, Speech as Chairman of the Federal Communications Commission to National Association of Broadcasters, Washington, DC, May 9, 1961.
60. Ed Bark, "Family Hour Fade-Out," *Dallas Morning News*, 22 August 1995, p.1C
61. *Ibid.*, p. 10C.
62. *Ibid.*, p. 10C.
63. James Kaplan, "Superheroes or Zeroes?" *TV Guide*, 29 October 1994, p. 36.
64. Lawrie Mifflin, "Pied Piper of Cable Beguiles Rivals' Children," *New York Times*, 29 October 1996, p. C13.
65. Edward L. Palmer, *Television and America's Children: A Crisis of Neglect* (New York: Oxford University Press, 1988), p. 93.

Chapter 2: A Child's View of Television

1. Aimée Dorr, *Children and Television: A Special Medium for a Special Audience* (Beverly Hills: Sage, 1986).
2. *Ibid.*, p. 13.
3. Marie Winn, *The Plug-In Drug: Television, Children, and the Family* (New York: Penguin Books, 1985), p. 4.
4. Jerry Mander, *Four Arguments for the Elimination of Television* (New York: Morrow, 1978), p. 204.
5. Jerome Singer, "The Power and Limitations of Television: A Cognitive-Affective Analysis," in *The Entertainment Functions of Television*, ed. Percy H. Tannenbaum (Hillsdale, NJ: Lawrence Erlbaum, 1980), p. 46.
6. Wilbur Schramm, Jack Lyle, and Edwin B. Parker, *Television in the Lives of Our Children* (Stanford, CA: Stanford University Press, 1961), p. 1.
7. Daniel R. Anderson and Elizabeth P. Lorch, "Looking at Television: Action or Reaction?" in *Children's Understanding of Television: Research on Attention and Comprehension*, eds. Jennings Bryant and Daniel R. Anderson (New York: Academic Press, 1983), p. 9.
8. Cedric Cullingford, *Children and Television* (Hampshire, England: Gower, 1984), p. 25.
9. Aletha C. Huston and John C. Wright, "Children's Processing of Television: The Informative Functions of Formal Features," in *Children's Understanding of Television: Research on Attention and Comprehension*, eds. Jennings Bryant and Daniel R. Anderson (New York: Academic Press, 1983), p. 46.

10. George Comstock (With Haejung Paik), *Television and the American Child* (San Diego: Academic Press, 1990).
11. Mariann P. Winick and Charles Winick, *The Television Experience: What Children See* (Beverly Hills: Sage, 1979).
12. Jerome L. Singer and Dorothy G. Singer, "Implications of Childhood Television Viewing," in *Children's Understanding of Television: Research on Attention and Comprehension*, eds. Jennings Bryant and Daniel R. Anderson (New York: Academic Press, 1983): 265-295.
13. Dorr, *Children and Television: A Special Medium for a Special Audience*, p. 14.
14. Comstock (With Paik), *Television and the American Child*.
15. Anderson and Lorch, "Looking at Television: Action or Reaction?" p. 6.
16. Jerome L. Singer, Diana M. Zuckerman, and Dorothy G. Singer, "Helping Elementary School Children Learn About TV," *Journal of Communication* 30, no. 3 (1980): 84-93.
17. Dorr, *Children and Television: A Special Medium for a Special Audience*, p. 53.
18. Andrew F. Newcomb and W. Andrew Collins, "Children's Comprehension of Family Role Portrayals in Televised Dramas: Effects of Socioeconomic Status, Ethnicity, and Age," *Developmental Psychology* 15 (1979): 417-423.
19. Dorr, *Children and Television: A Special Medium for a Special Audience*, p. 43.
20. Comstock (With Paik), *Television and the American Child*, p. 198.
21. Scott Ward, Daniel B. Wackman, and Ellen Wartella, *Consumer Socialization: An Information Processing Approach to Consumer Learning* (Beverly Hills: Sage, 1977).
22. Comstock (With Paik), *Television and the American Child*, p. 198.
23. Cy Schneider, *Children's Television: The Art, the Business, and How It Works* (Lincolnwood, IL: NTC Business Books, 1987), p. 94.
24. R. P. Ross, Toni Campbell, John C. Wright, Aletha C. Huston, Mabel L. Rice, and Peter Turk, "When Celebrities Talk, Children Listen: An Experimental Analysis of Children's Responses to TV Ads With Celebrity Endorsement," *Journal of Applied Developmental Psychology* 5 (1984): 185-202.
25. *Ibid.*, p. 187.
26. Edward L. Palmer and Cynthia N. McDowell, "Children's Understanding of Nutritional Information Presented in Breakfast Cereal Commercials," *Journal of Broadcasting and Electronic Media* 25 (1981): 295-301.

27. Diane E. Liebert, Joyce N. Sprafkin, Robert M. Liebert, and Eli A. Rubenstein, "Effects of Television Commercial Disclaimers on the Product Expectations of Children," *Journal of Communication* 27, no. 1 (1977): 118-124.
28. Ward, Wackman, and Wartella, *Consumer Socialization: An Information Processing Approach to Consumer Learning*.
29. John Greenwald, "Will Teens Buy It?" *Time*, 30 May 1994, p. 51.
30. Patricia Marks Greenfield, *Mind and Media: The Effects of Television, Video Games, and Computers* (Cambridge, MA: Harvard University Press, 1984).
31. *Ibid.*, p. 100.
32. Philip Elmer-Dewitt, "The Amazing Video Game Boom," *Time*, 27 September 1993, p. 71.
33. Claude M. J. Braun and Josette Giroux, "Arcade Video Games: Proxemics, Cognitive and Content Analyses," *Journal of Leisure Research* 21 (1989): 101.
34. Philip Elmer-Dewitt, "On a Screen Near You: Cyberporn," *Time*, 3 July 1995, pp. 38-45.
35. Pamela Tuchscherer, *TV Interactive Toys: The New High-Tech Threat to Children* (Bend, OR: Pinnaroo, 1988), p. 1.

Chapter 3: The Charm and Cost of Television

1. John P. Murray, *Television and Youth: Twenty-Five Years of Research and Controversy* (Boys Town, NE: Boys Town Center for the Study of Youth Development, 1980).
2. O. E. Dunlop, Jr., "Act 1, Scene 1, Telecast to Homes Begin on April 30 — World's Fair Will Be the Stage," *New York Times*, 19 March 1939, p. 12.
3. Margaret S. Andreasen, "Evolution in the Family's Use of Television: Normative Data From the Industry and the Academe," in *Television and the American Family*, ed. Jennings Bryant (Hillsdale, NJ: Lawrence Erlbaum, 1990): 3-55.
4. Louis Kronenberger, "Uncivilized and Uncivilizing," *TV Guide*, 26 February, 1966, pp. 15-16.
5. Thomas R. Lindolf and Milton J. Shatzer, "VCR Usage and the American Family," in *Television and the American Family*, ed. Jennings Bryant (Hillsdale, NJ: Lawrence Erlbaum, 1990): 89-109.
6. George Comstock (With Haejung Paik), *Television and the American Child* (San Diego: Academic Press, 1990).

7. J. G. Webster, J. C. Pearson, and D. B. Webster, "Children's Television Viewing as Affected by Contextual Variables in the Home," *Communications Research Reports* 3 (1986): 1-8.
8. Cecilia von Feilitzen, "The Functions Served By the Media," in *Children and Television,* ed. Ray Brown (Beverly Hills: Sage, 1976): 90-115.
9. Wilbur Schramm, Jack Lyle, and Edwin B. Parker, *Television in the Lives of Our Children* (Stanford, CA: Stanford University Press, 1961), p. 58.
10. Joseph R. Dominick, "Videogames, Television Violence, and Aggression in Teenagers," *Journal of Communication* 34, no. 2 (1984): 136-147.
11. Abigail Foerstner, "Being There: Stepping into the Make-Believe World of Virtual Reality," *Chicago Tribune Magazine*, 19 April 1992, p. 19.
12. Schramm, Lyle, and Parker, *Television in the Lives of Our Children*, pp. 79-82.
13. George Comstock, Steven Chaffee, Natan Katzman, Maxwell McCombs, and Donald Roberts, *Television and Human Behavior* (New York: Columbia University Press, 1978).
14. California Assessment Program, *Student Achievement in California Schools. 1979-1980 Annual Report: Television and Student Achievement* (Sacramento, CA: California State Department of Education, 1980).
15. California Assessment Program, *Survey of Sixth Grade School Achievement and Television Viewing Habits* (Sacramento, CA: California State Department of Education, 1982).
16. Sydney G. Burton, James M. Calonico, and Dennis R. McSeveney, "Effects of Preschool Television Watching on First-Grade Children," *Journal of Communication* 29, no. 3 (1979): 164-170.
17. Gary W. Selnow and Erwin P. Bettinghaus, "Television Exposure and Language Level," *Journal of Broadcasting and Electronic Media* 26 (1982): 469-479.
18. Michael Morgan and Larry Gross, "Television Viewing, IQ, and Academic Achievement," *Journal of Broadcasting and Electronic Media* 24 (1980): 117-133.
19. R. S. Corteen and T. M. Williams, "Television and Reading Skills," in *The Impact of Television*, ed. T. M. Williams (Orlando, FL: Academic Press, 1986).
20. M. Doerken, *Classroom Combat: Teaching and Television* (Englewood Cliffs, NJ: Educational Technology Productions, 1983).
21. Bruce Watkins, "Children's Representations of Television and Real-Life Stories," *Communication Research* 15 (1988): 159-184.
22. Lawrie Mifflin, "Study Links Higher Test Scores, TV," *Dallas Morning News*, 31 May 1996, p. 32A.
23. Comstock (With Paik), *Television and the American Child*, p. 128.

24. Cedric Cullingford, *Children and Television* (Hampshire, England: Gower, 1984), p. 176.
25. David Elkind, *The Hurried Child: Growing Up Too Fast Too Soon*, rev. ed. (Reading, MA: Addison-Wesley, 1988), pp. 78-79.
26. Dale Kunkel, "Children's Television Advertising in the Multichannel Environment," *Journal of Communication* 42, no. 3 (1992): 134-152.
27. Quoted in Charles K. Atkin, "Effects of Television Advertising on Children," in *Children and the Faces of Television: Teaching, Violence, Selling*, eds. Edward L. Palmer and Aimée Dorr (New York: Academic Press, 1981), p. 276.
28. William H. Dietz, "You Are What You Eat: What You Eat Is What You Are," *Journal of Adolescent Health Care* 11 (1990): 76-81.
29. Nathan D. Wong, Thomas K. Hei, Paul Y. Qaqunduh, Dennis M. Davidson, Stanley L. Bassin, and Kurt V. Gold, "Television Viewing and Pediatric Hypercholesterolemia," *Pediatrics* 90 (Part 1, July 1992): 75-79.
30. Robert W. Kubey and Mihaly Csikszentmihalyi, *Television and the Quality of Life: How Viewing Shapes Everyday Experiences* (Hillsdale, NJ: Lawrence Erlbaum, 1990).
31. Jeffrey Greenfield, *Television: The First Fifty Years* (New York: Crescent Books, 1981), p. 72.
32. Michael Morgan, "Television and Adolescents' Sex Role Stereotypes," *Journal of Early Adolescence* 7 (1987): 269-282.
33. Quoted in Atkin, "Effects of Television Advertising on Children," p. 288.
34. Dorothy G. Singer and Jerome L. Singer, "Television Viewing and Aggressive Behavior in Preschool Children: A Field Study," *Annals of the New York Academy of Science* 347 (1980a): 289.
35. Jerome L. Singer, Dorothy G. Singer, and Wanda S. Rapaczyniski, "Family Patterns and Television Viewing as Predictors of Children's Beliefs and Aggression," *Journal of Communication* 34, no. 2 (1984): 73-89.
36. Quoted in John P. Murray, "On TV Violence," *American Psychological Association, Division of Child, Youth and Family Services Newsletter* 11, no. 3 (Summer 1988), p. 12.
37. Ronald S. Drabman and Margaret H. Thomas, "Does Media Violence Increase Toleration of Real-Life Aggression?" *Developmental Psychology* 10 (1974): 418-421.
38. Burton, Calonico, and McSeveney, "Effects of Preschool Television Watching on First-Grade Children."
39. David Bjorklund and Barbara Bjorklund, "A Clearer View of Television," *Parents' Magazine*, November 1989, p. 219.

40. Edward E. Ford and Steven Englund, *For the Love of Children: A Realistic Approach to Raising Your Child* (Garden City, NY: Anchor Press, 1977), p. 10.
41. Christine Titchi, *Electronic Hearth* (New York: Oxford University Press, 1991).
42. Marie Winn, *The Plug-In Drug: Television, Children, and the Family* (New York: Penguin Books, 1985), p. 4.
43. Ann Melvin, " 'Family Hour' Died When TV Arrived, "*Dallas Morning News*, 17 February 1996, p. 29A.
44. Gene H. Brody, Zolinda Stoneman, and Alice K. Sanders, "Effects of Television Viewing on Family Interactions: An Observational Study," *Family Relations* 29 (1980): 216-220.
45. Paul C. Rosenblatt and Michael R. Cunningham, "Television Watching and Family Tensions," *Journal of Marriage and the Family* 38 (1976): 105-111.
46. Quoted in Atkin, "Effects of Television Advertising on Children," p. 298.
47. Robert T. Bower, *The Changing Television Audience in America* (New York: Columbia University Press, 1985).
48. Nathan Cobb, "New Screens, Old Battles," *Dallas Morning News*, 28 February 1995, p. 4C.
49. Quentin J. Schultze, Roy M. Anker, James D. Bratt, William D. Romanowski, John W. Worst, and Lambert Zuidervaart, *Dancing in the Dark: Youth, Popular Culture, and the Electronic Media* (Grand Rapids, MI: William B. Eerdmans, 1991), p. 58.
50. Dorothy G. Singer and Jerome L. Singer, *The House of Make-Believe: Play and the Developing Imagination* (Cambridge, MA: Harvard University Press, 1990), p. 177. In turn, D. L. Singer and J. L. Singer referred to Marlise Simons, "The Amazon's Savvy Indians," *New York Times Magazine*, 26 February 1989, p. 37.
51. Bob Greene, "American Mass Entertainment and the Backyard Fence," *Dallas Morning News*, 11 July 1993, p. 7J.

Chapter 4: A Parent's Role

1. Amitai Etzioni, *The Spirit of Community: Rights, Responsibilities, and the Communitarian Agenda* (New York: Crown, 1993), p. 55.
2. Anna Quindlen, "TV Guide," *New York Times*, 28 October 1993, p. A27.
3. Jerome L. Singer, Diana M. Zuckerman, and Dorothy G. Singer, "Helping Elementary School Children Learn About TV," *Journal of Communication* 30, no. 3 (1980): 84-93.

4. Newton N. Minow and Craig L. LaMay, *Abandoned in the Wasteland: Children, Television, and the First Amendment* (New York: Hill and Wang, 1995), p. 6.
5. Gus Venditto, "Safe Computing: Seven Programs That Filter Internet Access," *Internet World*, September 1996, pp. 49-58.
6. Frank Rich, "The PG-Files," *New York Times*, 18 December 1996, p. A27.
7. Leonard A. Jason, "Self-Monitoring in Reducing Excessive Television Viewing," *Psychological Reports* 53 (1983): 1280.
8. George Comstock (With Haejung Paik), *Television and the American Child* (San Diego: Academic Press, 1990).

Chapter 5: Options for Change

1. Jim Trelease, *The New Read-Aloud Handbook*, 2nd ed. (New York: Penguin Books, 1989), p. 129.
2. *Ibid.*, p. 130.
3. Gregory Sarlo, Leonard A. Jason, and Cheryl Lonak, "Parents' Strategies for Limiting Television Watching," *Psychological Reports* 63 (1988): 435-438.
4. Susan Quattrochi-Tubin and Leonard A. Jason, "Enhancing Social Interactions and Activity Among the Elderly Through Stimulus Control," *Journal of Applied Behavior Analysis* 13 (1980): 159-163.
5. Barbara Hall Palar, "Real-Family Solutions for Tuning Out," *Better Homes and Gardens*, February 1996, pp. 48, 50.
6. "Family Network: Reader's Solutions," *Better Homes and Gardens*, June 1994, p. 18.
7. Palar, "Real-Family Solutions for Tuning Out," pp. 48, 50.
8. Leonard A. Jason and Michele M. Klitch, "Use of Feedback in Reducing Television Watching," *Psychological Reports* 51 (1980): 812-814.
9. Marie Winn, *Unplugging the Plug-In Drug* (New York: Penguin Books, 1987). Most of the ideas and information in this section can be directly attributed to Winn. For more detailed information on holding a No-TV Week, we encourage you to obtain a copy of her book.
10. *Ibid.*, pp. 40-46.
11. *Ibid.*, pp. 126-127.
12. *Ibid.*, pp. 30-31.
13. "The Great TV Experiment," *The Oprah Winfrey Show*, 1 March 1993, p. 45 of transcript.
14. Jessica Seigal, "A Key to Weaning Kids from TV," *Chicago Tribune*, 9 August 1991, section 5, pp. 1, 5.
15. Addie Jurs, *Becoming Unglued* (Claredon Hills, IL: Addie Jurs, 1990).

16. Leonard A. Jason, Sharon Z. Johnson, and Addie J. Jurs, "Reducing Children's Television Viewing With an Inexpensive Lock," *Child & Family Behavior Therapy* 15 (1992): 45-54.
17. Leonard A. Jason and Sharon Z. Johnson, "Evaluation of a Device Aimed at Reducing Children's Television Viewing," Letter to the Editor in *Child and Family Behavior Therapy* 18 (1996): 59-61.
18. "The Great TV Experiment," *The Oprah Winfrey Show*, 1 March, 1993, p. 50 of transcript.
19. Dawn Sinclair, "TV Allowance Lets Kids Pay as They Play," *Chicago Tribune*, 17 September 1993, section 7, pp. 73, 78.
20. Leonard A. Jason and Sharon Z. Johnson, "Reducing Excessive Television Viewing While Increasing Physical Activity," *Child & Family Behavior Therapy* 17 (1995): 35-45.
21. Bob Greene, "Addicts Kicking Habit of Their TV Fix-ations," *Chicago Tribune*, 11 February 1981, section 3, p. 1.
22. Leonard A. Jason and Patty Rooney-Rebeck, "Reducing Excessive Television Viewing," *Child & Family Behavior Therapy* 6 (1984): 61-69.
23. Leonard A. Jason, "Using a Token-Actuated Timer to Reduce Television Viewing," *Journal of Applied Behavior Analysis* 18 (1985): 269-272.
24. Leonard A. Jason, "Reducing Excessive Television Viewing Among Seven Children in One Family," *The Behavior Therapist* 7 (1984): 2-4.
25. David A. Wolfe, Maria G. Mendes, and David Factor, "A Parent-Administered Program to Reduce Children's Television Viewing," *Journal of Applied Behavior Analysis* 17 (1984): 267-272.
26. Michael W. McCanna, *The Effects of a Television Watching Reduction Program on Television Viewing and Alternative Activities* (unpublished PhD dissertation, DePaul University, 1987).
27. Leonard A. Jason, "Reducing Children's Excessive Television Viewing and Assessing Secondary Changes," *Journal of Clinical Child Psychology* 16 (1987): 249.

Chapter 6: Family Life (With and Without Television)

1. "Should Your Kids Watch the TV News?" *TV Guide*, 12 March 1994, p. 25.
2. Ibid., p. 26.
3. Ibid., p. 25.
4. Edward E. Ford and Steven Englund, *For the Love of Children: A Realistic Approach to Raising Your Child* (Garden City, NY: 1977), p. 114.

5. Dorothy G. Singer and Jerome L. Singer, *The House of Make-Believe: Play and the Developing Imagination* (Cambridge, MA: Harvard University Press, 1990), p. 186.
6. Jim Trelease, *The New Read-Aloud Handbook*, 2nd ed. (New York: Penguin Books, 1989), p. 12.
7. *Ibid.*, p. 13.
8. Thomas Lickona, *Raising Good Children: Helping Your Child Through the Stages of Moral Development* (Toronto: Bantam Books, 1983), pp. 261-262.
9. Kay Kuzma, *Prime-Time Parenting* (New York: Rawson, Wade, 1980), p. 158.

Indices

Subject Index	251
Author Index	257
Index of Television Programs	261

Subject Index

A

Abandoned in the Wasteland (Minow and LaMay), 129
ABC Television Network, 9, 28, 33, 50, 51, 53, 54, 132
Action for Children's Television (ACT), 9, 48, 52, 131
Active viewing theory, 66-67, 75
Adult co-viewing, 64, 78-79, 195-199
Advertising, 40-49, 79-84
  comprehension of, children's, 79-84
  content, 42-43, 81
  critical viewing of, 197
  criticism of, 48-49, 80-81, 83
  effects on children, 44, 109-110, 118
  of food products, 109-110
  influence on household purchases, 43-44
  licensed merchandising, 82-83
  psychological manipulation, 47-48
  stereotyping found in, 45-47
Advocate groups, 9, 131, 134
Alternative activities, 200-218
  family life, 208-213
  "101 Fun and Simple Things to Do," 213-218

Alternative activities (Continued)
  play and imagination, 201-204
  reading, 204-208

B

Bandura, Albert, 12-13, 65
Beavis and Butt-head, 11, 73, 127
Behavior modification, 179-186

C

Cable television, 7-8, 20, 55-57, 190
Cartoon Network, The, 55-56
CBS Television Network, 9, 26, 50, 53, 54, 131
Children and Television (Cullingford), 67
Children and Television (Dorr), 63
Children's programming, 49-59
  cable, 55-57
  network, 50-55
  public television, 57-59
Children's Television (Schneider), 81
Children's Television Act of 1990, 52-53, 56, 130
Comprehension of television, children's, 69-84
  advertising, 79-84
  formal features, and use of, 71-72, 74

251

Comprehension of television, children's (Continued)
   general limitations to, 62-64
   by preschool-aged children, 70-73
   schemas, and use of, 74-75
   by school-aged children, 73-76
Computers and computer technology, xvi, 84-91, 97 (see also Internet)
   advantages of, 85-87, 101-102
   computer games (see video and computer games)
   disadvantages to, 87-91, 102-104, 115
   economic barriers to, 88
   healthy use of, 199-200
   impact on families, 118-119
   limiting use of, xvi, 193
   virtual reality, 103-104
Contacting networks and sponsors, 131, 190-191, 227-228
Content rules, 158-159, 188-192, 198-199
Critical viewing of television, 194-199

D

Dancing in the Dark (Schultze et al.), 120
"Dear Abby," 211
Disappearance of Childhood, The (Postman), xiii
Disney Channel, The, 55-56, 190

E

Earn TV, 175-178
Excessive viewing, children's, 93-122
   children's attraction to television, 98-104
   and effect of advertising, 109-110, 118
   and effect of violent content, 113

Excessive viewing, children's, (Continued)
   impact on cognitive and academic achievement, 105-109
   impact on community life, 119-122
   impact on family life, 116-119
   impact on health, 109-111
   impact on social and emotional development, 111-116

F

Family Channel, the, 55, 190
"Family hour," decline of, 53-54, 56
Family life
   contemporary stresses on, x, 125-126
   how to strengthen, 208-213
   television's effect on, 116-119
Federal Communications Commission (FCC), 10, 52, 56, 130, 133 (see also Government regulation of television)
For the Love of Children (Ford and Englund), 115-116, 201
Four Arguments for the Elimination of Television (Mander), 65
Fox Broadcasting Company, 9, 53, 54

G

Government regulation of television, 9-10, 14-15, 52, 130, 132-135 (see also Federal Communications Commission [FCC])

H

HBO (Home Box Office), 190
Heavy viewing (see Excessive viewing, children's)

House of Make-Believe, The (D. G. Singer and J. L. Singer), 205
Hurried Child, The (Elkind), 109

I

Internet (*see also* Computers and computer technology)
  advantages of 101-102
  disadvantages to, 102-104, 115, 118-119
  encouraging healthy family use of, 199-200
  impact on families, 118-119
  parental/content controls, 131-132
  and sexual content, 90

L

Letter-writing campaigns, 131, 190-191, 227-228
Limiting television (*see also* Reducing and managing television)
  government efforts, 9-10, 14-15, 52, 130, 132-135
  industry efforts, 9, 132-135
  parental responsibilities, 126-130

M

Mighty Morphin Power Rangers, 11-12
Minow, Newton, 52, 129
Mortal Kombat, 8, 131
Mr. Rogers' Neighborhood, 72
MTV, 22, 119

N

National Institute of Mental Health (NIMH), 14-15
NBC Television Network, 9, 50, 53, 54

New Read-Aloud Handbook, The (Trelease), 205
News, television, 191-192, 194, 197
Nickelodeon, 33, 55-56, 155, 190

O

Oprah Winfrey Show, The, 165-166, 173

P

Parenting
  difficulties of, *x*, 125-126, 128
  responsibilities toward television, 126-130
  trends in, *xi-xii*
Passive viewing theory, 65-66
Piaget, Jean
  cognitive development theory, 70
Play and imagination
  decline of, 113-114, 201-203
  how to encourage, 202-204
  TV-interactive toys, 90-91, 114
Plug-In Drug, The (Winn), 65
Prime-Time Parenting (Kuzma), 213
Public television, 57-59

R

Raising Good Children (Lickona), 211
Reading
  how to encourage, 205-208
  impact of television on, 107
  importance of, 204-205
Record-keeping, 136-140, 160, 180, 221-224
Reducing and managing television (*see also* Limiting television)
  behavior modification, 179-186
  content rules, 158-159, 188-192, 198-199

Reducing and managing television (Continued)
de-emphasizing television, 150-153
electronic devices and tools, 166-178
general guidelines for, 141-145
"No-TV Week," 159-166
record-keeping, 136-140, 160, 180, 221-224
resistance to, children's, 141-142, 147-149, 160
spouses, reluctant, 142-143, 152
TV rules, 154-166
Reviving Ophelia (Pipher), 30-31
Rules, TV, 154-166

S

Sesame Street, 30, 57-58, 72, 78, 99-100, 107, 108, 134
Sexual content on television, 18-24
effects on children, 22-24
and violent content, 22
Sold Separately (Seiter), 45
Stereotyping on television, 25-40, 45-47
in advertising, 45-47
age, 33-35
critical viewing of, 196
effects on children, 29, 32
of families, 36-37
gender, 29-33
of health issues, 39-40
of minorities, 26-29
of work, 38-39
SuperVision, 170-173
Surgeon General's report, the, 14-15
Switch, The, 167-170

T

Telecommunications Act of 1996, 10, 133

Television
children's attraction to, 98-104
children's comprehension of, 69-84 (*see also* Comprehension of television, children's)
critical viewing of, 194-199
government regulation of, 9-10, 14-15, 52, 130, 132-135
industry regulation of, 9, 132-135
multiple sets in households, 98, 118
news, 191-192, 194, 197
parental responsibility toward, 126-130
popularity of, *xii*, 95-96, 98-99
reduction strategies (*see* Reducing and managing television)
violence (*see* Violence, television)
365 TV-Free Activities You Can Do With Your Child (S. Bennett and R. Bennett), 201
TimeSlot, 174-175
TV Allowance, 173-174
TV Guide, 54, 96, 191-192
TV-Interactive Toys (Tuchscherer), 90-91

U

Unplugging the Plug-In Drug (Winn), 160-166
UPN/United Paramount Network, 27

V

V-chip, 9-10, 132-135
VCRs
active orientation of, 85
advantages over television, 189
limiting use of, 193
popularity of, 97

Video and computer games, 84-85, 101
 "addiction" to, 88-89
 advantages of, 85-87
 companionship provided by, 102-104
 disadvantages to, 87-91
 early versions of, 96-97
 gender bias, 87-88
 healthy use of, 199-200
 and increased cognitive and sensorimotor skills, 86-87
 limiting use of, *xvi*, 155, 168, 189-190, 193
 ratings of, 131
 violent content, 8-9, 90-91
Viewing habits and patterns
 adult co-viewing, benefits of, 64, 78-79, 195-199
 differences within families, 68-69
 heavy/excessive viewing, definition of, 94 (*see also* Excessive viewing, children's)
 hours children spend viewing television, 93-94
 improving viewing habits, approaches to, 192-200

Viewing habits and patterns (Continued)
 influences on, 138-139
 multiple sets in household, 98, 118
 passive versus active viewing, 64-69, 75
Violence, television, 5-18, 113
 content, 5-8, 11-12
 critical viewing of, 195-196
 effects on children, 11, 12-17, 113
 government response to, 9-10, 14-15, 130, 132-135
 public response to, 9, 134
 and sexual content, 22
 "Violence Index," 6
Violence, video and computer games, 8-9, 90-91
Virtual reality, 103-104

W

WB/Warner Brothers Network, 27, 53, 54
What to Do After You Turn Off the TV (Lappe), 201
Winn, Marie, 65, 116, 160-165

Author Index

A

Anderson, Daniel R., 67, 75
Andreasen, Margaret S., 95
Anker, Roy M., 120
Atkin, Charles K., 109-110, 112, 118

B

Bandura, Albert, 12-13
Barcus, F. Earle, 30, 31
Bark, Ed, 53-54
Bassin, Stanley L., 110
Bennett, Ruth, 201
Bennett, Steve, 201
Berry, Gordon L., 28
Better Homes and Gardens, 156
Bettinghaus, Erwin P., 107
Bjorklund, Barbara, 115
Bjorklund, David, 115
Bouthilet, Lorraine, 15
Bower, Robert T., 118
Bratt, James D., 120
Braun, Claude M. J., 88-89
Brody, Gene H., 117
Burton, Sydney G., 106, 114

C

California Assessment Program, 106
Calonico, James M., 106, 114
Campbell, Toni, 80-81
Chaffee, Steven, 35, 106
Charren, Peggy, 36
Cobb, Nathan, 118-119
Collins, W. Andrew, 77
Comstock, George, 16, 35, 71-72, 73, 80-81, 98, 106, 108, 138-139
Corteen, R. S., 107
Csikszentmihalyi, Mihaly, 111
Cullingford, Cedric, 67-68, 108
Cunningham, Michael R., 117-118

D

Davidson, Dennis M., 110
Davidson, Emily S., 29
Dietz, William H., 110
Doerken, M., 107
Dominick, Joseph R., 22, 102-103
Donnerstein, Edward, 5, 6, 16, 27
Dorr, Aimée, 63, 72-73, 76, 77-78
Drabman, Ronald S., 113
Dunlop, Jr., O. E., 95

E

Elkind, David, 109
Elmer-Dewitt, Philip, 87-88, 90
Englund, Steven, 115-116, 201
Eron, Leonard D., 16
Etzioni, Amitai, 126

F

Factor, David, 185
Fairchild, Halford, 5, 6, 27
Feshbach, Norma D., 5, 6, 27
Foerstner, Abigail, 103-104
Ford, Edward E., 115-116, 201
Franks, Lucinda, *xi-xii*

G

Garfield, Bob, 47
Gerbner, George, 6, 26-27, 29-30, 33-34, 39
Giroux, Josette, 88-89
Gold, Kurt V., 110
Graves, Sherryl, 29
Greene, Bob, 121-122, 179
Greenfield, Jeffrey, 36, 112
Greenfield, Patricia Marks, 86
Greenwald, John, 84
Gross, Larry, 6, 33-34, 107

H

Hei, Thomas K., 110
Himmelstein, Hal, 43
Huston, Aletha C., 5, 6, 27, 52, 71, 108

J

James, Allison, 47
Jason, Leonard A., 138, 149, 152, 158-159, 169-170, 171-173, 177-178, 184, 185
Johnson, Sharon Z., 169-170, 171-173, 177-178
Jurs, Addie, 168-170

K

Kaplan, James, 54
Katz, Phyllis A., 5, 6, 27
Katzman, Natan, 35, 106
Kline, Stephen, 45
Klitch, Michele, 158-159
Kronenberger, Louis, 96
Kubey, Robert W., 111
Kunkel, Dale, 109
Kuzma, Kay, 213

L

LaMay, Craig L., 129
Lappe, F. M., 201
Lazar, Joyce B., 15
Lickona, Thomas, 211
Liebert, Diane E., 84
Liebert, Robert M., 29, 84
Lindolf, Thomas, R., 97
Lonak, Cheryl, 149
Lorch, Elizabeth P., 67, 75
Louis Harris and Associates, 24
Lowry, Dennis T., 19, 24
Lyle, Jack, 66, 100, 106

M

Maguire, Kathleen, 10
Mander, Jerry, 65
Mangan, Jennifer, 33
McCanna, Michael, 185
McCombs, Maxwell, 35, 106
McDowell, Cynthia N., 83
McNeal, James U., 43-44
McSeveney, Dennis R., 106, 114
Medved, Michael, 53-54
Melody, William, 50-51
Melvin, Ann, 116-117
Mendelson, G., 27
Mendes, Maria G., 185
Mifflin, Lawrie, 6, 56, 108

Minow, Newton N., 52, 129
Mitchell-Kernan, Claudia, 28
Morgan, Michael, 6, 33-34, 107, 112
Murray, John P., 5, 6, 27, 94, 113

N

Newcomb, Andrew F., 77

O

Oldenburg, Don, 16
Oprah Winfrey Show, The, 165-166, 173

P

Paik, Haejung, 71-72, 73, 80-81, 98, 108, 138-139
Palar, Barbara Hall, 155, 157
Palmer, Edward L., 58, 83
Parker, Edwin B., 66, 100, 106
Pastore, Ann L., 10
Pearl, David, 15
Pearson, J. C., 98
Pipher, Mary, 30-31
Planned Parenthood Federation of America, 24
Plehal, Robert, 45
Postman, Neil, *xiii*
Psychology Today, 32

Q

Qaqunduh, Paul Y., 110
Quattrochi-Tubin, Susan, 152
Quindlen, Anna, 127

R

Rapaczyniski, Wanda S., 113
Rice, Mabel L., 80-81

Rich, Frank, 135
Roberts, Donald, 35, 106
Romanowski, William D., 120
Rooney-Rebeck, Patty, 184
Rosenblatt, Paul C., 117-118
Ross, R. P., 80-81
Rubenstein, Eli A., 5, 6, 23, 27, 84

S

Sanders, Alice K., 117
Sandler, Martin W., 36
Sapolsky, Barry S., 19
Sarlo, Gregory, 149
Schneider, Cy, 41, 81
Schramm, Wilbur, 66, 100, 106
Schultze, Quentin J., 120
Seigal, Jessica, 168
Seiter, Ellen, 45, 46
Selnow, Gary W., 107
Shatzer, Milton J., 97
Sherman, Barry L., 22
Signorielli, Nancy, 6, 29, 31, 33-34, 35
Silverman, L. Theresa, 18, 23
Simons, Marlise, 120
Sinclair, Dawn, 174
Singer, Dorothy G., 72, 75, 113, 120, 128, 205
Singer, Jerome L., 65, 72, 75, 113, 120, 128, 205
Sprafkin, Joyce N., 18, 23, 29, 84
Stoneman, Zolinda, 117

T

Tabarlet, Joseph O., 19
Tan, Alexis S., 32
Thomas, Margaret H., 113
Titchi, Christine, 116
Towles, David E., 19, 24
Trelease, Jim, 147, 148-149, 205, 206
Tuchscherer, Pamela, 90-91

Turk, Peter, 80-81
TV Guide, 191-192, 194

V

Van der Voort, T. H. A., 16
Venditto, Gus, 131
von Feilitzen, Cecilia, 99

W

Wackman, Daniel B., 43, 80, 84
Ward, Scott, 43, 80, 84
Wartella, Ellen, 80, 84
Watkins, Bruce, 107
Webster, D. B., 98
Webster, J. G., 98
Weeks, Jerome, 30
Welch, Renate L., 45
Wilcox, Brian L., 5, 6, 27

Williams, T. M., 107
Williams, T. S., 32
Winick, Charles, 72
Winick, Mariann P., 72
Winn, Marie, 65, 116, 160-166
Wolfe, David A., 185
Wong, Nathan D., 110
Workman, Diana, 19
Worst, John W., 120
Wright, John C., 45, 71, 108

Y

Young, M., 27

Z

Zuckerman, Diana, 5, 6, 27, 75, 128
Zuidervaart, Lambert, 120

Index of Television Programs

A

A Different World, 27
ABC After School Specials, 54
All in the Family, 26
All-American Girl, 28
Allegra's Window, 33, 55
Amos 'n' Andy, 26
Avonlea, 56

B

Barbie, 83
Baretta, 11
Barney & Friends, 57
Baywatch, 20
Beakman's World, 54, 100
Beavis and Butt-head, 11, 73, 127
Beverly Hills 90210, 21, 34
Big Bag, 56
Bill Nye the Science Guy, 54
Blossom, 34, 37
Blue's Clues, 56
Bobby's World, 54
Boy Meets World, 34
Brady Bunch, The, 31, 36
Brand Spanking New Doug, 54
Brooklyn Bridge, 54, 131

C

California Dreams, 34
Captain Kangaroo, 51, 53
Care Bears, The, 83
C-Bear and Jamal, 78
CBS Morning News, 53
CBS School Break Specials, 54
Charlie's Angels, 18
Christy, 54
Clarissa Explains It All, 33, 55
Cops, 5
Cosby, 36
Cosby Show, The, 27, 53
Cro, 54
Cybill, 33

D

Dallas, 35
Dave's World, 33
Diff'rent Strokes, 27
Ding Dong School, 51
Disneyland, 51
Doctor Quinn, Medicine Woman, 100
Donahue, 59
Dynasty, 35

E

Ed Sullivan Show, The, 18
Electric Company, The, 58
Ellen, 33
ER, 37
Eureeka's Castle, 55

F

Family Matters, 34, 101
Family Ties, 53
Flintstones, The, 59, 82, 120
Frasier, 101
Fresh Prince of Bel-Air, The, 27, 34, 101
Friends, 6
Full House, 34, 37, 53

G

G.I. Joe, 83
Ghostwriter, 58
Golden Girls, The, 33
Grace Under Fire, 33, 36, 37
Gullah Gullah Island, 55, 78
Gulliver's Travels, 54

H

Hard Copy, 134
High Incident, 6
Home Improvement, 33, 36, 54
Homicide: Life on the Street, 6, 28, 134
Howdy Doody, 50, 51
Hudson Street, 53

I

I Love Lucy, 26
I'll Fly Away, 54

In Living Color, 27
In the Heat of the Night, 33
In the House, 27
Inside Edition, 134

J

Jetsons, The, 59

K

Katie and Orbie, 58
Kojak, 11
Kukla, Fran, and Ollie, 50, 51

L

LA Law, 38
Lamb Chop's Play-Along, 57, 130
Late Show with David Letterman, 19
Law and Order, 192
Leave It to Beaver, 31, 36
Life Goes On, 54
Little House on the Prairie, 54
Lou Grant, 38
Love, American Style, 18
Love Boat, The, 38

M

Mad About You, 33, 36
Madeline, 55
Magic School Bus, The, 58
Married . . . With Children, 36, 195
Martin, 27
Marvel Action Hour, 54
Mary Tyler Moore Show, The, 31, 75
M*A*S*H, 108
Matlock, 33
Me and the Boys, 37, 53
Melrose Place, 30
Mickey Mouse Club, The, 51

Mighty Morphin Power Rangers, 11-12, 21, 40, 83, 114
Moesha, 27
Mr. Rogers' Neighborhood, 57, 58, 72, 100
Muppets, The, 31
Murder, She Wrote, 33
Murphy Brown, 33, 37, 38
My Little Pony Tales, 83
My So-Called Life, 34-35, 54

N

Name Your Adventure, 54
Nanny, The, 34, 37
Nash Bridges, 6
New York Undercover, 6
News for Kids, 101
Nick News, 101
Northern Exposure, 29
NYPD Blue, 6, 20, 132, 190

O

O Pioneer, 54
Oprah Winfrey Show, The, 165-166, 173

P

Parent 'Hood, The, 27
Party of Five, 21, 34, 54
Piano Lesson, The, 54
Profiler, 6
Puzzle Place, The, 58, 78

R

Reading Rainbow, 57, 58, 134
Reboot, 54
Rhoda, 31
Roc, 38

Roots, 27, 54
Roseanne, 19, 36, 53
Rugrats, 55

S

Sarah Plain and Tall, 54
Saved by the Bell, 34
Secret World of Alex Mack, The, 33, 56
Seinfeld, 6, 19, 101
Sesame Street, 30, 57-58, 72, 78, 99-100, 107, 108, 134
Shining Time Station, 100
Simpsons, The, 158
Sister, Sister, 34
Skeletal Warriors, 54
Soap, 19
Star Trek, 101, 103
Starsky and Hutch, 11
Step by Step, 34, 37
Steven Spielburg Presents Animaniacs, 54
Strawberry Shortcake, 83

T

Teenage Mutant Ninja Turtles, 82
thirtysomething, 77
Three Stooges, The, 134
Three's Company, 18
TV Nation, 192

W

Walker, Texas Ranger, 5, 6
Waltons, The, 54
What's Happenin', 27
Where in the World is Carmen Sandiego?, 57, 58
WILDC.A.T.S., 54
Wings, 53

Wishbone, 58, 100
Wonder Years, The, 34, 54

X

X-Files, The, 6, 103
X-Men, 54

TO THE OWNER OF THIS BOOK

We hope that you have enjoyed *Remote Control*. We would like to know as much about your experiences with this book as possible. Only through your comments and those of others can we learn how to improve it for future readers.

1. What I like most about this book is

2. What I like least about this book is

3. My specific suggestions for improving the book are

4. Would you recommend this book to your friends? If not, why?

5. Additional Comments:

Please Mail To:

Leonard A. Jason, PhD
Department of Psychology
DePaul University
2219 North Kenmore Avenue
Chicago, IL 60614-3504
email: ljason@wppost.depaul.edu